RED
TEAM

RED
TEAM

HOW TO SUCCEED BY
THINKING LIKE THE ENEMY

MICAH ZENKO

A COUNCIL ON FOREIGN RELATIONS BOOK

BASIC BOOKS
A Member of the Perseus Books Group
New York

Published by Basic Books,
A Member of the Perseus Books Group

Books published by Basic Books are available at special discounts for
bulk purchases in the United States by corporations, institutions, and
other organizations. For more information, please contact the Special
Markets Department at the Perseus Books Group, 2300 Chestnut
Street, Suite 200, Philadelphia, PA 19103, or call (800) 810-4145,
ext. 5000, or e-mail special.markets@perseusbooks.com.

A Council on Foreign Relations Book

Designed by Pauline Brown

Library of Congress Cataloging-in-Publication Data
Zenko, Micah.
  Red team : how to succeed by thinking like the enemy / Micah
Zenko.
    pages   cm
  Includes bibliographical references and index.
  ISBN 978-0-465-04894-6 (hardback)—ISBN 978-0-465-07395-5
(ebook) 1. Success in business. 2. Risk management. 3. Private
security services. 4. Competition. I. Title.
HF5386.Z46 2015
658.4'01—dc23
                                                        2015015268

10 9 8 7 6 5 4 3 2 1

CONTENTS

INTRODUCTION

Within the Roman Catholic Church, the formal title was the *Promotor Fidei*, or Promoter of the Faith. More commonly, the position became known within the Church and the laity as the *Advocatus Diaboli*, or Devil's Advocate. Today, the term applies to anyone who is a skeptic, or takes an unpopular or contrary position for the sake of argument alone. A professor who provokes discussion by countering students' assumptions, a trial attorney attempting to predict opposing counsel's arguments, or simply a crank—all might be branded devil's advocates according to the more flexible understanding of the term. Within the Catholic Church, however, the role of the Devil's Advocate emerged as a clearly defined position with a specific responsibility: to challenge the purported virtues and miracles of nominees for sainthood.

During its first thousand years, the Church's saint-making process had been relatively haphazard and decentralized.[1] Local Christian communities could assign sainthood based on *vox populi*, or popular sentiment, and they avidly awarded the title to those who had died as a martyr, to some who had greatly professed their faith, or even to those who had done little more than live a particularly pious life. The result was an explosion of locally proclaimed saints.

In an effort to add rigor to the process in the fifth century, bishops began to require written *vitae*—documentation of the life, virtues, and miracles of candidates—in order for someone to be considered for sainthood. However, those *vitae* were largely based on local gossip and hearsay, with little examination and verification of testimonies. As late as the ninth century, the canonization process, as one scholar described it, was "still essentially, as it had been in the second century, the spontaneous act of the local community."[2] Vatican officials perceived that allowing sainthood to be determined by the whims of *vox populi* was becoming a threat to the central authority of the Church.

By the thirteenth century, popes sought to exert greater direct control over the canonization process in an effort to consolidate power within the Vatican and protect the sanctity and legitimacy of sainthood. In 1234, Pope Gregory IX—best known for establishing the Inquisition to confront alleged heretics—decreed that the papacy had "absolute jurisdiction" over all aspects of the canonization process. Under subsequent reforms, the framework, standards, and procedures of determining sainthood were formalized and centralized within the Sacred Congregation of Rites, the Vatican's committee of cardinals that oversaw and vetted all papal canonizations. In the process, the Devil's Advocate was born.

The Church authorities introduced the position of the *Advocatus Diaboli* to serve as an independent investigator and designated dissenter. It would be his job to provide point-by-point objections to all evidence presented on behalf of the candidate, and to detail all the unfavorable evidence in a written summary. Throughout a canonization process that could last decades, corroborating details and objections alike were presented to the sacred Congregation, and ultimately to the pope, before final approval could be granted.[3] Thus, Pope Gregory IX made clear to everyone the need for the position of Devil's Advocate, a knowledgeable insider who was empowered to step outside of the Church and objectively assess each candidate for sainthood.

For centuries, these reforms kept the process in check. In 1781, Scottish physician and author John Moore published an account of an abbreviated canonization debate that he witnessed as a tourist in the Vatican:

> The business is carried on in the manner of a lawsuit. The Devil is supposed to have an interest in preventing men from being made Saints. That all justice may be done, and that Satan may have his due, an advocate is employed to plead against the pretensions of the Saint Expectant, and the person thus employed is denominated by the people, the Devil's Advocate. He calls in question the miracles

said to have been wrought by the Saint and his bones, and raises as many objections to the proofs brought of the purity of his life and conversation as he can. It is the business of the Advocate on the other side, to obviate and refute these cavils.[4]

Over time, the Devil's Advocate was transformed from a formal ecclesiastical position into a commonplace figure of speech used to describe an argumentative person, and soon enough, the Vatican's most senior official decided that the position had outlived its usefulness. In 1983, in an effort to streamline the canonization process, Pope John Paul II issued an Apostolic Constitution reducing the number of miracles required from four to two, and eliminating the office of the Devil's Advocate. The reforms were intended to foster a more cooperative spirit by making the process simpler, faster, and far less adversarial. Subsequently, Pope John Paul II produced more beatifications (1,338) and canonizations (482) in some twenty years than all of his 263 predecessors combined over almost two thousand years.[5] With fewer requirements and the removal of an independent and dissenting voice, the Vatican was transformed into what was dubbed the "saint factory."[6] In becoming far more commonplace, saints were increasingly less venerated, and, in the words of one critic, "inflation produced a devaluation."[7] By eradicating this centuries-old institutional check on saint-making, the integrity associated with the process and outcome was negated as well. Yet, even though the Vatican eventually abandoned the position, the enduring value of its thirteenth-century innovation should not be forgotten.

The office of the Devil's Advocate was the first established and routine use of "red teaming." However, red teaming was not formally referred to as such by the US military until the Cold War, and it was only standardized in the 2000s. As it is known today, red teaming is a structured process that seeks to better understand the interests, intentions, and capabilities of an institution—or a potential competitor—through simulations, vulnerability probes, and alternative analyses. Though red teaming has subsequently been adopted in a wide range of fields and tailored to various needs, it remains woefully underexplored and severely underutilized by corporate boardrooms, military commands, cyber-security firms, and countless other institutions that find themselves facing threats, complex decisions, and strategic surprises. By employing a red team, institutions can get a fresh and alternative perspective on how they do things. It can help them reveal and test unstated assumptions, identify blind spots, and potentially improve their performance.

Al Kibar: "Gotta Be Secret, Gotta Be Sure"

Red teaming is not only about using a devil's advocate to scrutinize and challenge day-to-day operations. For institutions facing a significant decision, red teaming may also be a one-time effort. We can see how a properly administrated red team can help ensure that a crucial decision is the right one by studying the following example found in recent national security decision making.

In April 2007, Israeli national security officials surprised their American counterparts by informing them about a large building under construction at Al Kibar in a valley in the eastern desert of Syria. In one-on-one briefings, the Israeli officials provided dozens of internal and external color photographs dating back to before 2003. The evidence strongly suggested that the building was a nuclear reactor, remarkably similar to the gas-cooled, graphite-moderated reactor in Yongbyon, North Korea. Israeli Prime Minister Ehud Olmert then delivered his request to President George W. Bush: "George, I'm asking you to bomb the compound."[8]

Senior Bush administration officials were deeply troubled. North Korea had conducted its first nuclear weapons test the previous October using plutonium produced in the Yongbyon reactor. The Israeli briefings reinforced the US intelligence community (IC) assessments of "sustained nuclear cooperation" between North Korea and Syria. Though the IC had been monitoring the construction of a facility that they had described as "enigmatic" since 2005, the new Israeli photographs cast the compound in Al Kibar under a harsh new light. Immediately, a Central Intelligence Agency (CIA)-led task force reevaluated all of the available intelligence related to Al Kibar and North Korea's nuclear cooperation with Syria. Given the flawed intelligence assessment that resulted in the incorrect conclusion in 2002 about Iraq possessing weapons of mass destruction (WMD), nobody wanted to be wrong again. As Bush told his intelligence chiefs: "Gotta be secret, and gotta be sure."[9]

The CIA task force reaffirmed the Israeli officials' claims, but Bush administration officials took extraordinary measures to increase their confidence level. To ensure that they could be nearly certain in their assessment of Al Kibar, they employed devil's advocate techniques markedly similar to those invented by the Vatican centuries earlier. National Security Advisor Stephen Hadley told IC officials to assemble some of their best analysts to review the data to see if the facility could be anything other than a reactor.[10] The CIA director, General Michael Hayden, was similarly concerned given that "we had a poor record of assessing the WMD programs of countries bordering the Euphrates River." He noted, "You increase your certainty by widening the circle, but we still had to keep the circle small to keep it a secret." To do this, the IC employed two red teams that were totally independent from the task force and had not yet been "read in" on the intelligence regarding Al Kibar.[11]

Bush's intelligence chiefs so thoroughly bought into the concept of red teaming that they issued the two groups opposing goals: one would be commissioned to prove "yes" and the other to prove "no." The "yes" red team assessment came from a private sector analyst who held a top-secret security clearance and was well known for his proficiency in monitoring nuclear weapons programs. The analyst was not told where the facility was located, but was provided with the Israeli and American internal and overhead imagery of it. The obvious efforts to camouflage the reactor vessel and the spent fuel pools within a building that had nearly an identical footprint to that of the Yongbyon reactor, and the trenches and pipes leading to a nearby water source (the Euphrates) were among several telltale giveaways. Within a few days, the analyst informed the IC officials, "That's a North Korean reactor."[12]

Hayden's "no" red team was composed of senior analysts from the CIA's Weapons Intelligence, Nonproliferation, and Arms Control

Center (WINPAC). This team received the same access to all the available data and intelligence as its counterpart, but was explicitly instructed to reach a hypothesis that the facility in Syria *was not* a nuclear reactor. "Prove to me that it is something else," the CIA director told them. Over the course of the following week, the WINPAC group considered whether Al Kibar could contain a chemical weapons production or storage site, or something related to missile or rocket programs. Anything was plausible—they even investigated the possibility that it might be some sort of secretive non-weapons-related vanity project of Syrian President Bashar al-Assad. They also explored whether al-Assad had directed that a mock-up of a reactor be built, simply because he *wanted* it to be bombed for some reason. Another senior CIA official recalled that they had particular difficulty finding an alternative explanation for the internal photographs of the facility, which not only closely resembled Yongbyon but also even contained what appeared to be North Korean workers.[13] "The alternative hypothesis that they came up with, for which the most evidence unquestionably and markedly lined up behind, was that it was a fake nuclear reactor," Hayden recalled.[14]

At the weekly Tuesday afternoon meeting in Hadley's office, a handful of senior officials met to discuss what to do about the purported Syrian reactor. The results of the red-teaming exercises gave officials a high degree of confidence that they had their facts straight. They took comfort in the additional levels of scrutiny that had been applied to the initial intelligence estimates. "It gave us more confidence about the instinct and conclusion of the intelligence community regarding whether it was a reactor. Every other alternative explanation was not plausible," according to Hadley.[15] Secretary of Defense Robert Gates, who attended all of these meetings, also recalled, "Everybody agreed that we could not find an alternative to this being a nuclear reactor."[16]

However, even though the Al Kibar compound was all but confirmed to be a nuclear reactor, this did not mean that the United States should accede to Prime Minister Olmert's request to destroy it. While Hayden could comfortably declare, "That's a reactor. I have high confidence," the red teams had notably found no evidence of a facility required to separate spent reactor fuel into bomb-grade plutonium or of weaponization work, which further led him to state, "On [the question whether] it is part of a nuclear weapons program, I have low confidence."[17] Bush subsequently told Olmert that the United States would not participate in a military attack: "I cannot justify an attack on a sovereign nation unless my intelligence agencies stand up and say it's a weapons program."[18]

The two independent intelligence assessments provided Bush administration officials with far greater confidence about what was being constructed in the Syrian desert. They informed Bush's decision-making calculus, even though his primary concern remained the risks to US interests in the Middle East if he authorized another preemptive attack on a Muslim country. With bombing now off the table, the CIA developed options to covertly sabotage the reactor before it went critical; however, CIA Deputy Director Stephen Kappes told the White House that sabotage had a low likelihood of success.[19] Therefore, Bush chose to pursue diplomatic channels by going public with the intelligence to the United Nations Security Council and International Atomic Energy Agency, in order to pressure Syria to verifiably dismantle the reactor. Before this could happen, four Israeli fighter jets destroyed the suspected reactor at Al Kibar on September 6, 2007, without any resistance from Syria's air defenses or overt support from the United States.

In this case, the findings of the two devil's advocates, based on their independent analysis of available intelligence, greatly enhanced the credibility of the intelligence estimates regarding the existence of a nuclear reactor, and enabled Bush to make up his mind on the basis of more complete and vetted information. Ultimately, the president decided to refrain from launching strikes. This was a classic example of red teaming in action—having outsiders test the validity of the intelligence and consider the possibility of alternate hypotheses.

Why Organizations Fail, But Can't Know It

This is a book about how to improve the performance of an institution by enabling it to see the world in a new and different way. Institutions—whether they are military units, government agencies, or small businesses—operate according to some combination of long-range strategies, near-term plans, day-to-day operations, and to-do lists. Decision-makers and their employees do not simply show up at their jobs each morning anew and decide then and there how to work and what to work on. The existing guidance, practices, and culture of an institution are essential to its functioning effectively. Yet, the dilemma for any institution operating in a competitive environment characterized by incomplete information and rapid change is how to determine when its standard processes and strategies are resulting in a suboptimal outcome, or, more seriously, leading to a potential catastrophe. Even worse, if the methods an institution uses to process corrective information are themselves flawed, they can become the ultimate cause of failure.

This inherent problem leads to the central theme of this book: you cannot grade your own homework. Think back to a high school class where you struggled every day to grasp the subject. Now, imagine that the teacher empowered you to grade your own homework. At first this would seem like a great boon—a guaranteed 100 percent every time! No matter how poorly you actually performed, you could decide your own grade for each assignment. In correcting those assignments you would develop a range of rationalizations as to why you really deserved an A, in spite of inferior results: "this wasn't covered in class," "the teacher did a lousy job," "I was really tired," or maybe "just this one last time." Now, imagine your shock when, after a semester of self-grading, the teacher hands out the final exam and announces that this time she will be the one holding the red pen. This would expose all the things that you should have learned or maybe thought you understood, but never really did. Grading your own homework might feel good in the short term, but it completely clouds one's self-awareness, and can eventually lead to a failing grade.

The warning that "you cannot grade your own homework" has relevance far beyond the classroom. Consider the mistaken self-evaluation strategy that was employed by the CIA in its post-9/11 detention and interrogation program. Internal assessments of its operations' necessity and effectiveness—including the use of "enhanced interrogation techniques" (i.e., torture) against suspected terrorists—were conducted by the same CIA personnel that had been assigned to develop and manage the program, and also by outside contractors who had obvious financial interests in continuing or expanding it. In June 2013, an internal CIA review found that its personnel regularly made "assessments on an ad hoc basis" to determine if "various enhanced techniques were effective based upon their own 'before and after' observations" of changes in a detainee's demeanor.[20] Unsurprisingly, the CIA personnel and outside contractors judged with confidence that the program they worked in was both highly effective and needed.

Despite requests by National Security Advisor Condoleezza Rice and the Senate Select Committee on Intelligence in the mid-2000s to commission what was the equivalent of a red team alternative analysis of these programs, none was ever ordered by senior CIA officials. As the Agency acknowledged: "The sole external analysis of the CIA interrogation program relied on two reviewers; one admitted to lacking the requisite expertise to review the program, and the other noted that he did not have the requisite information to accurately assess the program."[21] An informed and empowered red team, comprised of knowledgeable experts holding the requisite security clearances, would have offered a more realistic evaluation of the use of torture and provided recommendations for how to revise or terminate the detention and interrogation program.

An astonishing number of senior leaders are systemically incapable of identifying their organization's most glaring and dangerous shortcomings. This is not a function of stupidity, but rather stems from two routine pressures that constrain everybody's thinking and behavior. The first is comprised of cognitive biases, such as mirror imaging, anchoring, and confirmation bias. These unconscious motivations on decision-making under uncertain conditions make it inherently difficult to evaluate one's own judgments and actions. As David Dunning, a professor of psychology at Cornell University, has shown in countless environments, people who are highly incompetent in terms of their skills or knowledge are also terrible judges of their own performance. For example, people who perform the worst on pop quizzes also have the widest variance between how they thought they performed and the actual score that they earned.[22]

The second related pressure stems from organizational biases—whereby employees become captured by the institutional culture that they experience daily and adopt the personal preferences of their bosses and workplaces more generally. Over a century ago, the brilliant economist and sociologist Thorstein Veblen illustrated how our minds become shaped and narrowed by our daily occupations:

> What men can do easily is what they do habitually, and this decides what they can think and know easily. They feel at home in the range of ideas which is familiar through their everyday line of action. A habitual line of action constitutes a habitual line of thought, and gives the point of view from which facts and events are apprehended and reduced to a body of knowledge. What is consistent with the habitual course of action is consistent with the habitual line of thought, and gives the definitive ground of knowledge as well as the conventional standard of complacency or approval in any community.[23]

Though we would now refer to this derisively as "going native" or "clientism"—whereby people become incapable of perceiving a subject critically after years of continuous study—any honest employee or staffer should recognize this all-pervasive phenomenon that results in organizational biases. This is particularly prominent in jobs that require deep immersion in narrow fields of technical or classified knowledge, and those that are characterized by rigid hierarchical authority—the military is a clear example. Taken together, these common human and organizational pressures generally prevent institutions from hearing bad news, without which corrective steps will not be taken to address existing or emerging problems.

When discussing their own leadership and management styles, bosses usually acknowledge the need to encourage, appreciate, and thoughtfully listen to dissenting views from their employees. No reputable boss would proclaim, "I make it a point to discourage my staff from speaking up, and I maintain a culture that prevents dissenting viewpoints from ever getting aired." If anything, most bosses even say that they are pro-dissent. This sentiment can be found throughout the *New York Times*'s "Corner Office" series of conversations with corporate, university, and nonprofit leaders, published weekly in the newspaper's business section. In these interviews, the featured leader is asked about their management techniques, and regularly claims to continually foster internal protest from more junior staffers. As Bob Pittman, chief executive of Clear Channel Communications, remarked in one of these conversations: "I want us to listen to these dissenters because they may intend to tell you why we can't do something, but if you listen hard, what they're really telling you is what you must do to get something done."[24] To hear American leaders describe their organizations, it seems they are run more like cooperative anarchist collectives than hierarchical institutions.

The trouble is that Pittman's approach wrongly assumes that the people who work for these leaders have the skills to identify emerging problems (highly unlikely), that they will tell their bosses about these problems (potentially career damaging), and that they will face no negative consequences for bringing such issues to their leaders' attention (rare, since it disrupts the conventional wisdom). Think about what you perceive as obvious and readily apparent shortcomings in your own job. Would you risk your reputation or career by raising them with your boss, even if asked to do so? Now, assume that there are unseen disasters on the horizon. How likely is it that you could identify and then warn your boss about them given such constraints? Harvard Business School professor Amy Edmondson researches why employees in a range of settings believe it is unsafe to admit to and report on failures that they observe in their workplaces. "We have a deep, hardwiring that we have inherited that leads us to be worried about impression-making in hierarchies," she says, adding that "no one ever got fired for silence."[25] Just as institutions cannot be counted upon to grade their own homework, they also do not reliably self-generate dissenting viewpoints that are presented to senior leaders.

One prominent, recent example of this phenomenon can be seen in the independent investigation into General Motors's (GM's) decision to wait a decade before recalling its Chevrolet Cobalt compact car that had a faulty ignition switch. This defect caused the ignition to inadvertently shut the engine off while driving—likely due to a heavy keychain or a shift in its weight—subsequently cutting off power to the power steering and brakes, airbags, and antilock brakes. The results included at least 119 deaths and 243 major injuries, costs to the company of up to $600 million in victim compensation, and the firings of fifteen members of senior management.[26]

Employees interviewed as part of the investigation "provided examples where culture, atmosphere, and the response of supervisors may have discouraged individuals from raising safety concerns."[27] GM employees received formal training in how to describe safety issues in written documents so that their warnings would appear less vivid and alarmist. Thus, the suggested replacement for "safety" was "has potential safety implications," and "defect" became "does not perform to design." In an apparent attempt at humor, employees were also told not to use phrases like "Kevorkianesque," "tomblike," and "rolling sarcophagus." The reason for insisting upon the watered-down language was to deny ammunition to any plaintiff's legal team that might sue GM over safety issues. However, it also served to undersell the seriousness of the safety and security problems that the company's employees witnessed. The investigation concluded: "Whether general 'cultural' issues are to blame is difficult to ascertain, but the story of the Cobalt is one in which GM personnel failed to raise significant issues to key decision-makers."[28] It's not that the GM employees who refrained from speaking up were unaware of the extent of the ignition switch problems, nor were they evil people. Rather, they were simply behaving as they believed they should, based upon the tone and formal guidance established by higher management. Instead of employing red teaming to identify and rectify the problems at the heart of their organization, GM made the problem worse by attempting to avoid the issues by diminishing and outright ignoring them. The result was a near catastrophe for GM, and was truly catastrophic for the victims and their families.

How Red Teams Function

In recent years, red teaming has grown increasingly important as a means of forestalling disasters like that suffered by GM. More and more institutions are using the three core red-teaming techniques of simulations, vulnerability probes, and alternative analyses. These tactics are employed by red teams that vary widely in composition and activities: from in-house contrarians (like the Vatican's defunct Devil's Advocate), to externally hired "tiger teams" that attempt to break into secure buildings or computer networks, and management consultants tasked with scrubbing a company's strategy. Red teams can also be temporary, such as when a company's staff uses "liberating structures"—brainstorming techniques used to generate innovation and break conventional thought processes—to stimulate divergent thinking that would not have occurred otherwise.

Ultimately, whether comprised of outside consultants or everyday employees, red teams help institutions in competitive environments visualize themselves outside of daily routines, evaluate plans, identify institutional and strategic vulnerabilities and weaknesses, and potentially improve performance via three techniques: simulations, vulnerability probes, and alternative analyses.

Simulations

Prior to scheduled events or anticipated scenarios, institutions develop, test, and refine their strategies by modeling how they could play out in the foreseen situation. The simulations capture each of the actors' motivations and capabilities, and the likely interactions between them. In this scenario, red teams can consist of consultants that model litigation outcomes to help law firms decide how they should settle cases; football scout teams that emulate the next opponent the starting team will face to show their tendencies in various in-game situations; or business war-gamers who independently consider future outcomes that can then inform strategic decision-making. The US military also routinely models what are believed to be the emerging international security trends to help develop the concepts and force structure for future defense planning. Two examples are the annual North Atlantic Treaty Organization (NATO) Unified Vision war-game exercises that test collaboration and information sharing in simulated combat settings, and the US Army's Unified Quest program that aims to determine how the Army will fight in future operating environments. The military also conducts war games for possible large-scale interventions and discrete military operations. For example, the May 2011 US Navy SEAL raid in Pakistan that killed Osama bin Laden was "red teamed to death," according to Secretary of Defense Leon Panetta.[29] The SEAL team ran through real-life simulations to test every "what if?" contingency that might arise. Even when one of the SEALs' two transportation helicopters crash-landed in bin Laden's compound, the mission went off without a hitch because they had planned and trained for that exact contingency.

Vulnerability probes

Computer networks, facilities, and people require protection from their potential adversaries. Red teams can assume the role of "surrogate adversaries" to test the reliability of a targeted institution's defensive systems and procedures to identify any weaknesses. Vulnerability probes should be independent and unannounced, based on an updated evaluation of likely adversaries' capabilities and motivations, and conducted in a manner realistic as to how they would attempt to breach or damage the targeted institution or system. They can be external hires, such as "white-hat" (or ethical) hackers contracted by firms to assume the role of "black-hat" (or malicious) hackers and attempt to compromise that firm's computer systems—the findings of which are then shared with the firm. Or they can be Government Accountability Office undercover investigators who examine the defenses of government agencies, such as those that smuggled radioactive material across the southern and northern US borders in 2006, bomb components into nineteen unidentified airports in 2007, and bomb components into ten federal buildings—out of ten attempts—in 2009. There are also internal probes by undercover counterintelligence agents within firms or government agencies that uncover insider threats by bribing or coercing employees to gauge their honesty and dependability.

Alternative analyses

Traditional analyses characterize the current environment within which an institution exists, analyze specific topics, and generate forecasts. These analyses are conducted to support senior leaders who face critical decisions, and to help institutions refine their everyday plans and operations. However, analysts can be held back by normal cognitive biases, or by the patterns of thinking commonly accepted within their organizations. These biases often include mirror imaging, in which analysts instinctively assume that their adversary would think in the same way that the analyst would under similar circumstances; anchoring, when analysts rely too heavily on initial information or impressions that make significant shifts in their judgments unlikely; or confirmation bias, in which analysts favor those findings that support their personal theories or beliefs. The objective of alternative analysis is to hedge against these natural human and organizational constraints by using liberating structures or structured analytic techniques, or by employing a wholly different team not already immersed in an issue to challenge assumptions or present alternative hypotheses and outcomes.[30]

Alternative analysis by its nature involves different people, processes, or products than those involved in traditional analysis. Over time, individuals conducting traditional analysis can become heavily influenced by the institutional culture they experience and the personal preferences of their bosses. As a result, even longtime analysts are susceptible to adopting the assumptions and biases of the institutions and subjects they are supposed to be objectively studying. When properly developed and applied, the approaches and frameworks used in alternative analysis limit cognitive biases and allow for unconventional thinking.

One prominent, publicly available example is the small CIA Red Cell. Separate from mainline authoritative analytical units within the

Agency, the Red Cell conducts alternative assessments of IC products, or alerts policymakers to unexpected or unorthodox issues.[31] A 2010 Red Cell memo that ran completely counter to conventional thinking on the sources of terrorism was aptly titled, "What if Foreigners See the United States as an 'Exporter of Terrorism'?" This type of bracing, counterintuitive approach can compel policymakers to challenge assumptions that they had previously been unaware of, and conceive of an issue from a fresh perspective.

How Red Teams Succeed or Fail

Though red teams are unique, like any other management tool their impact can range from priceless to worthless. This predominantly depends on the willingness and receptiveness of an institution's leaders. When red teaming is faithfully conducted, correctly interpreted, and judiciously acted upon, it can reveal important shortcomings in an institution's methods or strategies. Yet it is just as possible for red teams to be flawed in design or execution, or, as some practitioners say, "prostituted."

Corporations often convene managers to purportedly conduct a red team analysis before launching a new product or entering an unexplored market. In essence, such exercises can be intended to provide internal validation for the decisions already made by senior management. The Nuclear Regulatory Commission (NRC), which regulates commercial nuclear power plants, is tasked with conducting force-on-force performance testing—in which inspectors simulate a plausible, fictional adversary and conduct a surprise commando-style attack to probe the facility's defensive vulnerabilities. After the 9/11 terrorist attacks, the NRC was found to be conducting fraudulent testing of simulated terrorist attacks, which included giving up-to-twelve months advance notice of a mock attack so that the nuclear facility could increase the number of its security guards in preparation. US generals and admirals have increasingly adopted their own personal Commander's Initiatives Groups (CIG), which are groups of staffers who are supposed to provide critical thinking of strategies unfettered from the daily activities required of a military commander's staff. In practice, many of the CIGs become "captured" by the daily demands of the office, and find themselves writing speeches, preparing congressional testimony, and presenting memos that they know their bosses want to hear.

Finally, red teams can be scrupulous in their execution and simply find themselves ignored by decision-makers. In 2010, the US Department of Health and Human Services (HHS) hired McKinsey & Company to serve as "an independent team charged with 'pressure testing' existing trajectory of federal marketplaces" of the Patient Protection and Affordable Care Act, or ObamaCare.[32] The McKinsey red team reviewed HHS's strategy and privately warned the White House six months before the October 2013 ObamaCare rollout of likely glitches in the HealthCare.gov website and that "insufficient time and scope of end-to-end testing" had been devoted during preparation for the launch. McKinsey also briefed members of the HealthCare.gov development team—though apparently not its key leaders—about many of the management and technical glitches that would eventually plague the federal healthcare website. Though McKinsey had diligently uncovered shortcomings that HHS had not found on its own, the red team's findings and warnings were disregarded. Ultimately, the ObamaCare rollout was a needless political disaster for the White House and President Barack Obama's approval ratings.[33]

The inherent tension for red teams is how to operate successfully within an institution—obtaining the information and access needed, and having their results listened to—while maintaining the requisite independence to honestly question and rigorously challenge that same institution. This requires the red team to be intimately aware of the personalities and culture that surround it, without becoming constrained by the commonly accepted range of perspectives. The best red teams exist somewhere in an undefined sweet spot between institutional capture and institutional irrelevance. Global health expert Gregory Pirio compared the most proficient red teamers to the *ronin* samurai in feudal Japan who, because they had no master, were "free to tell the shogun that he was an idiot." As Pirio further explained, slipping into twenty-first century consultant-speak, "Since the ronin were de-institutionalized, they didn't know how to shape their messages to meet the mimetic environments."[34] What distinguishes the lone *ronin* speaking truth to a ruler from the red teams assessed throughout this book is that the latter has a more formal routine and relationship with an institution and its decision-makers. However, both embody one of the most important aspects of an effective red team—functioning either at the very edges of, or outside of, the institution it is analyzing.

Into the World of Red Teaming

Red teaming is an inherently social phenomenon that can only be understood by speaking to its practitioners and observing how they apply their techniques in the real world. In an effort to convey the best practices and essence of red teaming, this book tells the stories of red teamers at work, often in their own words. These anecdotes have been compiled through interviews with more than two hundred prominent red teamers and their colleagues in a wide variety of fields—from twenty-something-year-old white-hat hackers to senior vice presidents, from former CIA directors to retired four-star generals. A few of them cannot be identified by name because they are not authorized by their employers, or are simply secretive by nature, but all were willing to share their thoughts and experiences because of their belief in the need to expand the practice of red teaming. Beyond conversations, it was essential to witness red teaming in action: the "A-ha! moment" generated by a consultant forcing corporate staffers to assume the role of competing firms, or the zombie-like trance of a hacker intently scanning source code for vulnerabilities. Finally, this exploration would have been incomplete without taking courses at the Fuld Gilad Herring Academy of Competitive Intelligence, where business war-gaming is taught, and the University of Foreign Military and Cultural Studies (UFMCS) (i.e., Red Team University), where red team techniques are taught to military officers (and me, the rare civilian) in a refurbished former military prison at Fort Leavenworth, Kansas. Since its transformation in 2004, detailed in chapter 2, UFMCS has become the preeminent hub for the study and instruction of red teaming.

This book focuses on the kind of red teaming that occurs in the context of a relatively competitive environment. This includes potential military conflicts between two or more enemies; marketplace settings where firms contend for market share or returns on investment with direct competitors; legal and regulatory regimes that firms "game" to reduce costs and burdens; threatening environments where individuals, facilities, and critical infrastructure face a heightened risk of attack from potential adversaries; or environments of uncertainty where individuals, firms, or intelligence agencies require alternative analyses to limit or mitigate the consequences of strategic surprises. In short, this book deals with competitive environments in which there are obvious gains from success, and costs for poor performance.

The seventeen case studies described and analyzed were selected with the objective of presenting readers with the greatest variety of red teaming. For government secrecy, proprietary, or reputational reasons, most institutions that employ red teams strive to keep them well hidden, sometimes even misrepresenting their structure and impact for outside audiences. Based upon several years of digging, sifting, and interviews, the mini-cases presented in chapters 2 through 6 emerged as those that were the most rich in information and granular detail, being bolstered with insider accounts that are essential to understanding how red teams are actually formed and operate. The cases also have different compositions, methods of operation, and outcomes—some fail, some succeed, while others have inconclusive or yet-to-be-determined results. Some are diagnostic in nature, while others are intended to elicit new and unconventional thinking. Finally, they include both historical and contemporary examples that demonstrate several commonly recurring barriers to improved institutional performance, and how the six specific red team best practices detailed in chapter 1 evolved.

Though red teams exist in multiple challenging environments, no single work has yet assessed and evaluated how they are utilized across various fields, nor has one identified best practices that are similarly applicable across those fields. One reason for the lack of comparative analytical research on red teaming is that the US government and military rarely provide money to federally funded research organizations—such as the RAND Corporation—to draw upon nonmilitary fields. Conversely, the private sector does not publish its own red-teaming processes or results, since this is closely held proprietary information that is often guarded by nondisclosure agreements with clients. Meanwhile, news accounts of "red teams"—often mentioned in quotes—usually lack the proper context and perspective needed to understand how they are used beyond the single issue covered in an article. This book fills the knowledge gap by providing a typology of techniques, a survey of its uses by way of practitioners and their experiences, and practical guidance that any institution's leader needs to know about how to utilize red teams. Most of the examples are drawn from the military and national security worlds—communities that have few insights into one another's red-teaming efforts—but they have profound applications for the private sector as well.

This exploration into red teaming begins with chapter 1's presentation of the six red-teaming best practices leaders could use to mitigate the cognitive and organizational biases that harm performance. Identified through interviews with more than two hundred red teamers and their colleagues, the six best practices are: 1) The boss must buy in. Without providing "top cover" support and approval for dissenting views, red teams will be under-resourced, marginalized, or wholly ignored. 2) Outside and objective, while inside and aware. Effective red teams have to be designed with the correct structure relative to the targeted institution they assess, scope of the activities they pursue, and sensitivity with which they operate and present their findings and recommendations. 3) Fearless skeptics with finesse. Red teamers are weird—get over it. They tend to be loners, mavericks, and arrogant, which is exactly why they think and act differently—the most vital skill of a red teamer. 4) Have a big bag of tricks. Red teams must not become predictable. If they use the same methods over and over, they become victims of institutional capture, and their findings become predictable and are then ignored. Red teaming changes everyone. Even those merely exposed to the results will rethink the issue under examination, and, more generally, think differently in their day-to-day routines. 5) Be willing to hear bad news and act on it. If institutions will not learn, then red-teaming results will not matter. Institutions unwilling to absorb and integrate red team findings should not bother going through the process. 6) Red team just enough, but no more. Red teaming can be a stressful and demoralizing activity if done too often, which in turn can be irreparably disruptive to an institution's strategies and plans. However, if red teaming is done too infrequently, the institution soon becomes hidebound and complacent.

Chapter 2 covers the most prominent recent red-teaming units and events that have been developed and employed by the US military, concluding with a look at how red teaming has spread abroad. These include the Red Team University initiative at Fort Leavenworth where more than 2,700 officers and government employees have received formal training in red team approaches and methodologies since 2005; a 2012 example in which two Red Team University instructors were called upon to facilitate a moderated discussion and an analysis of an important military concept document to identify assumptions, possible failures, and alternatives; the halting and still incomplete attempts to develop and integrate formal red team units within US Marine Corps command staffs since it was made a top priority by former Marine Corps Commandant General James Amos; and the notorious summer 2002 Millennium Challenge concept-development exercise in which Pentagon leaders' hopes for a rapid transformation in how the military would fight future wars were dashed by a devious retired three-star Marine lieutenant general. This is the first evaluation of Millennium Challenge based upon the military's own declassified after-action report and interviews with all of the key officials involved. This chapter will also describe the more limited uses of red teams outside of the United States, including in the Israel Defense Forces, the United Kingdom's Ministry of Defence, and NATO's Allied Command Transformation.

Chapter 3 examines how the spies and analysts of the US intelligence community (IC) have applied red-teaming techniques in recent years.

The featured events and units include the 1976 Team B competitive intelligence analysis by non-IC experts of the CIA's National Intelligence Estimate of Soviet Union strategic nuclear weapons capabilities and intentions; the August 1998 absence of an independent alternative analysis of the CIA's estimate that the Al Shifa pharmaceutical factory in Khartoum, Sudan, was producing VX nerve gas and was tied to Osama bin Laden; the first-ever inside look at the CIA's Red Cell, which was created the day after the September 11, 2001, terrorist attacks to serve as an alternative-analysis unit semi-independent of all other mainline analytical offices; and the three 2011 red team probability estimates conducted to assess whether bin Laden was living in a compound in Abbottabad, Pakistan.

Chapter 4 looks into the activities of several US government homeland security agencies, which conduct vulnerability probes and simulations of defenses and critical infrastructure to test and (ostensibly) improve security systems. Features include the tragic story of the pre-9/11 Federal Aviation Administration (FAA) red team, which found systematic failures in commercial airline security but was ignored by FAA officials in Washington who did little to address the shortcomings or mandate the airline industry to do so; the mid-2000s red team simulation of the threat to New York City airports posed by terrorists armed with Man-Portable Air Defense Systems (MANPADS); another unprecedented look inside the New York Police Department's (NYPD's) tabletop exercises, authorized and led by the NYPD commissioner, which review and evaluate New York City's preparations for responding to catastrophic terrorism scenarios; and, finally, the Information Design Assurance Red Team (IDART), a small unit based within the Sandia National Laboratories in Albuquerque, New Mexico, which has served as the elite US government adversarial hacking unit, breaking into software, computer networks, and defended facilities in order to improve their security since 1996.

Chapter 5 investigates the application of red teaming in the ultimate competitive environment—the private sector. Featured is the role of outside consultants who run business war games for corporations in order to simulate and evaluate the wisdom of a strategic decision; an immersion into the rapidly expanding field of "white-hat" hackers who conduct lawful and commissioned penetration tests of their clients' computer networks and software programs; a successful and shocking white-hat hack that demonstrates how a small group was able to obtain root access on a Verizon femtocell (i.e., a miniature cell-phone tower that looks like a wireless router) in order to steal all of the voice and data from any phone that unknowingly associate itself with the femtocell; and, finally, a firsthand account of the relative ease with which one can obtain unauthorized access into supposedly secure buildings, and an exploration of red team physical penetration testers who easily, and often amusingly, break into supposedly secure buildings over and over.

Chapter 6 presents some of red teaming's realistic outcomes, misimpressions, and misuses that decision-makers should be conscious of when considering the use of red teams. This includes cases highlighted previously, and additional examples of how and why it is too often underappreciated, underutilized, or misapplied. The five worst practices revealed include: 1) Flawed ad hoc approaches, by which leaders appoint one person to provide a dissenting view to unrealistically prevent groupthink; 2) Mistaking the findings of a red team for policy, usually placing them in the wrong context or oversubscribing to their findings; 3) Empowering red teams to direct the decision-making process; 4) Freelance red teaming that fails to consider the institution's structure, processes, and culture; and 5) Distrust of the red team practitioners by leaders and managers who are unable or unwilling to listen to their findings. This chapter will also look at the tendency of government or business officials to misuse a red team's findings. It concludes with a series of recommendations for government red teams and a brief look at the future of the process.

While not yet a commonly used phrase, red teaming is a concept that people intuitively and readily grasp once presented with real-world examples. By the time you finish reading this book, you will have been exposed to both a new and largely unknown process, and a fascinating cast of characters who do it for a living. In addition, leaders and managers should become unpleasantly conscious of how unaware they are about the shortcomings and vulnerabilities of the companies or organizations they run. Moreover, they should also understand why red teaming matters and how it can best be utilized to improve their institutions.

Just as the Vatican abolished the Devil's Advocate role in its saint-making process, leaders could choose to silence challenging voices. If nothing else, this book will convince you that such an approach is unlikely to triumph in the long run. As enticing as the prospect of unruffled consensus in the workplace may be, when leaders dissuade dissent and divergent thinking, they create an environment that may allow disasters to materialize. Red teaming is the method for making it more likely that those disasters will be foreseen and thereby prevented.

ONE

BEST PRACTICES IN RED TEAMING

When you hear "best practices," run for your lives. The *Titanic* was built with best practices. It was faithfully operated in accordance with best practices.

— Retired US Army Colonel Gregory Fontenot, Director of the University of
Foreign Military and Cultural Studies (Red Team University), 2011[1]

As Gregory Fontenot's above observation makes clear, the very concept of "best practices" is one that true red teamers might find alien to their profession. By definition, red teaming exists outside of institutional strategy, standard operating procedures, and structure. By nature its practitioners are contrarian thinkers, deeply skeptical of any outsider who would impose a rigid classification on what they do. Over the course of the more than two hundred interviews conducted for this book with those who red team for a living, as a side job, or as just a component of their work, some visibly winced just hearing the term "best practices," and resisted the notion that their tradecraft could be distilled or summarized into a how-to manual. Indeed, there is no single blueprint that applies to all settings. One might conclude that the overarching best practice is to be flexible in the approaches or techniques applied. As subsequent chapters will demonstrate, there are often severe costs and

1

consequences for institutions in competitive environments that do not employ any best practices by disregarding a red team's findings and recommendations, as well as powerful benefits for those that listen.

Best practices are never a one-size-fits-all set of instructions, but rather are a set of pragmatic principles to guide and inform a red team and the organization that it targets—or, the "targeted institution." If they adhere to best practices, red teamers are much more likely to mitigate the cognitive and organizational biases that routinely hamper institutional performance. The alternative to relying upon such informed guidelines is to arbitrarily "red team" based upon intuition and whatever information one stumbles across. There are clear perils to red teaming in such a haphazard manner. As retired US Marine colonel and current red team instructor and facilitator Mark Monroe asks: "Would you go into surgery with somebody who had no medical training or experience?"

Research demonstrates that the following six principles—drawn from the red teamers' firsthand experiences detailed in upcoming chapters—are, in fact, the real best practices because they have been repeatedly effective. While delving into the four fields that are assessed in the chapters to come, the reader should keep the following six principles in mind.

1. The Boss Must Buy In

Despite the widespread perception that performance is improved when hierarchy is flattened, almost all institutions still have a small team in charge, or, more likely, a singular boss at the top of an organizational chart. Hierarchy and a clear chain of command can be essential to resolving collective-action problems and establishing responsibility and accountability for decision-making. An effective boss will instill and reinforce the ethics, values, and expected behaviors for the staffs and employees throughout an institution. And the boss's buy-in is absolutely crucial to getting things done.

Unsurprisingly, the best practice that was most often raised by red teamers and those exposed to their results was the need for a boss to be willing to endorse and support the red team and its results. Whether the boss is a military commander, a government agency official, a chief information officer, or a senior vice president, someone in charge must value red teaming, and, just as importantly, signal their support to all of the employees for whom the findings are relevant. This "top cover," in military parlance, is highly critical. It comes in many forms and with differing intensities, but everyone is well aware of its presence or absence. As Paul Van Riper, the retired Marine lieutenant general and widely acknowledged red-teaming guru, declared: "Unless the commanders themselves want it, support it, resource it, institutionalize it, and respond to it, it won't matter."[2]

This buy-in must manifest itself in several ways.

First, bosses must recognize that there is a vulnerability within their organization that red teaming can help uncover and address. Organizations tend to be poor judges of their own performance, and are often blind to shortcomings and pitfalls. Indeed, in many instances, a readily apparent failure or disaster must have already occurred—resulting in meaningful human, financial, or reputational costs—before a boss will willingly listen to appeals for red teaming. For example, it was not until after the bombing of Pan Am Flight 103 over Lockerbie, Scotland, in which 270 people died, that the administrator of the Federal Aviation Administration (FAA) institutionalized a small red team to conduct realistic threat and vulnerability assessments. (Even after these assessments, the FAA clearly disregarded what the exercises had revealed. As demonstrated in chapter 4, the troubling security lapses that this red team consistently reported even went unheeded prior to the terrorist attacks of 9/11.)

Alternatively, when senior managers are about to make a consequential decision for which they will be held directly accountable, they might seek out a simulation or alternative analysis to provide cover in case of failure. Ben Gilad, who has run simplified but rigorous business war games for Fortune 500 companies for more than thirty years, has learned that presidents or vice presidents actively seek him out when they are about to roll out a new product or enter a new market. Gilad notes that these bosses "might go out (be fired) or up (get promoted), but they know that it is a major decision," and commissioning him to run a war game serves as both a "pressure test" evaluation of that decision and a potential "cover your ass" warranty.[3]

The need for buy-in not only applies to the highest node on the hierarchy. Bosses need to be aware of the likelihood that when this requirement to red team is just perfunctorily imposed on a manager by a more senior leader, the junior person will be less likely to value it, utilize it willingly, or listen to and implement the findings. As detailed in chapter 2, beginning in 2010, Marine Corps Commandant General James Amos ordered that all Marine Expeditionary Forces (MEF) and deploying Marine Expeditionary Brigades (MEB) incorporate a red-teaming element within their command staffs. According to military personnel and civilians who served on MEF and MEB red teams, they were often underutilized or ignored by the commanding general, or, more frequently, by their senior staffs during their initial years. The Marine commanders had not been properly instructed in how to employ their red teams, and were not made fully aware of the potential added value. In the private sector, a corporate board could similarly mandate that the chief executive officer or senior vice president subject a company's business strategy to a simulation that is conducted by an outside consultant. A senior vice president from a multinational energy corporation, who was directed to commission such a simulation, noted that his unit decided to "sleepwalk our way through the thing," and produced a pro forma after-action report that they could simply tout as evidence to the board of having done it.[4] It is clear from these examples that, for red teaming to be of the greatest value, not only the most senior leaders, but also leaders throughout the targeted institution's hierarchy, should lend the effort their support.

Second, bosses must be willing to commit the resources, personnel, and time to support either an in-house or outside red team hired to scrutinize their institution. Red teaming is rarely an activity essential to an organization's core mission. As a result, it can face funding barriers, and all too often gets cut when its need is not immediately apparent. For example, a typical penetration test of a medium-sized company's computer networks costs between $1,500 and $10,000 per day, while an elaborate business war game costs $500,000 or more. For employees who participate in or facilitate the red team, the amount of lost work hours can be substantial. This can lead senior managers to treat the red team as a "dumping ground" for marginal employees, or those whom they are not sure what to do with—many Army and Marine Corps red teamers have reported experiencing this phenomenon. Even when the boss recognizes the need for red teaming, several acknowledged that it is "nice to have, but not a must have." When they hold this opinion and express it publicly, it can dramatically reduce the viability of a red team's effectiveness.

Third, the boss must allow the red teamers to be completely truthful about their findings. They cannot be punished for pointing out that the strategies or processes that the boss personally developed and authorized are deeply flawed, or that the conventional wisdom among the targeted institution's employees is misleading or riddled with inherent contradictions. If the boss punishes or conspicuously ignores people for speaking up, nobody will speak up again.

In many real-world instances, bosses have adopted a number of techniques to publicly embrace and empower their red teams, ensuring that a red team's dissenting and contradictory viewpoints will be heard. They can attend the red team event to demonstrate their support, just as New York Police Department (NYPD) Commissioner Ray Kelly and his successor William Bratton made it a point to participate in every single tabletop exercise, described in chapter 4, that was conducted with senior commanders during his tenure. Red teams can also be rewarded for their work—for example, the CIA Red Cell has received the National Intelligence Meritorious Unit Citation on multiple occasions—or a proficient red teamer can conspicuously be promoted to a more senior position. Former Iraq and Afghanistan commander General David Petraeus found that in order to encourage dissenting viewpoints within a command, "you have to create a culture that preserves and protects the iconoclasts."[5]

Fourth, of course, it is up to the boss to decide whether the red team's findings are assimilated or ignored. This judgment is based on whether the boss believes the targeted institution can live with the risks or challenges presented by the red team, or should commit the resources—in terms of money, personnel, and opportunity costs—to undertake the necessary changes. Ideally, the same boss who commissions the red team should also have the authority to authorize the implementation of its findings, or to strongly recommend that a more senior boss endorses them. Without first securing the bosses' buy-in, and having that buy-in signaled to all relevant employees, the next five best practices will likely be ignored or irrelevant.

2. Outside and Objective, While Inside and Aware

Red teams are most effective when they are properly positioned in—and out of—the targeted institution. They have to balance several competing principles: being semi-independent and objective while remaining sensitive to the organization's operating environment and its available resources. In addition, red teams must avoid becoming institutionally captured, while also making a sustained contribution to that institution's core mission. Jami Miscik, who was appointed deputy director of intelligence for the CIA shortly after its Red Cell was first created in September 2001, said that for an ideal red team, "They cannot be a separate back-office group that studies their navels, and isn't engaged with the rest of the building."[6]

Three notions should guide the positioning and identity of a successful red team: The *structure* of the red team relative to the targeted institution (the where), the *scope* of the activities that it pursues (the why), and the *sensitivity* with which it operates and provides its findings and recommendations (the how). Getting these three factors correct is difficult yet critical. One of the most common causes for red team failure is a misunderstanding among leaders and employees within an institution as to what exactly the red team is intended to do. Indeed, a consistent problem found in the cases detailed in later chapters is an inability to identify why the red team was created in the first place, what its initial guidance was from senior leadership, what criteria, if any, determined who would serve on the red team, and what were the expectations for how the targeted institution would utilize its findings.

Structure involves properly situating the red team—either temporarily or permanently—on the targeted institution's organizational chart. Ideally, the red team should be semi-independent from the hierarchy on a dotted line leading directly to the highest boss to whom it answers. At times, the red team's relationship to an institution must be apparent to everybody, such as when a business war game is conducted for a pharmaceutical giant to forecast how its competitors will react to one of its drugs going off-patent. At other times, the red team should report only to the boss or the directly affected personnel. For example, Petraeus was a particularly strong proponent of employing temporary red teams to conduct alternative analyses of ongoing military operations while commanding US and multinational forces in Iraq and Afghanistan. He would seek out a general officer on leave, a think tank analyst, or someone else outside of his command structure to do a "directed telescope" review of an important issue or an upcoming decision. "Nobody else knew that they were doing this, and they reported directly back to me."[7] In 2008, then-Colonel H. R. McMaster of the US Army led several reviews for Petraeus regarding Iraq—including an independent three-month "council of colonels" assessment of the campaign plan, which determined that sectarian violence was worsening and US actions were directly exacerbating this.[8]

Getting the structure correct is also necessary to ensure that the red team is granted access to the people and information needed to perform its duties. When the red team is placed—either physically or metaphorically—in a back office, the employees within the targeted institution will be less likely to cooperate with or listen to them. An Army colonel who commanded a Brigade Combat Team in Kandahar Province, Afghanistan, made it a point to place his small red team directly in the middle of his headquarters—both to make sure they were given access to whomever they needed to talk to, and to signal that "they were my guys."[9] For outside red teams, this degree of access is dependent on how tightly scoped the engagement with the targeted institution is from the outset.

Correctly framing the scope of activities that the red team will undertake is just as crucial as its structure, though this is often underappreciated. Before starting its work, the red team must have an explicit and mutual understanding with the targeted institution about exactly who or what is to be red teamed, for how long, with what degree of flexibility, and to what ultimate end. External red teams prevent "scope creep" through questionnaires and conversations with the relevant staff of the targeted institution to specify start and end dates, acceptable methods of operation, and the service or product to be delivered. Ken Sawka of the business war gaming firm Fuld & Company believes "scoping is essential because it helps us understand what structured analytical techniques we will use, and what the client can reasonably accomplish with the outcome."[10] In-house red teams, especially in the military, have often been forced to figure out what is and will be expected of them through a time-wasting iterative trial-and-error process.

If the red team does not scope the engagement correctly, it is essentially operating blindly. Scope includes being relevant and realistic to the mission of the institution while also challenging any conventional processes and principles that constrain the institution's employees. Ideally, this scoping guidance should be written down and circulated to the relevant employees and staffs, and referred to during the engagement if disagreements arise. If a red team and a targeted institution cannot agree upon a basic understanding of what will be accomplished beforehand, then the engagement should not be initiated.

The scope should also ensure that the red team engagement is conducted at the appropriate level of detail and intensity. While serving as a US Navy SEAL, Steve Elson helped to design and conduct vulnerability probes of highly sensitive and purportedly secure government sites, including Navy nuclear facilities and the presidential retreat in Camp David, Maryland. The perimeter securities of new Navy installations were among the targets that would be routinely subjected to vulnerability probes. He recalled that initially "we were always way too good for what the base security could handle." While breaking into the facility made the SEALs temporarily feel good, it was too easy and thus ultimately pointless. Elson determined: "If you just steamroll them, they won't learn anything, they would just roll up into a little ball and wait to die."[11] Rather than overwhelm the base's security on day one, the SEAL red teams learned that they were better off gradually increasing the intensity and sophistication of their probes, so security personnel could better integrate the lessons and recommendations that emerged from the previous test.

The sensitivity with which a red team operates requires that it do its homework to gain a solid understanding of the targeted institution. This includes learning what previous concerns or shortcomings first led it to engage a red team, what legal regimen or regulatory structures it operates under, what level of resources it can plausibly commit to implement the red team's findings, and what its timelines are. The latter concern is particularly important for red teaming of a strategy or product that has been many months in development. If the red team simply shows up near the end of the development process—as was the case for the 2012 Chairman of the Joint Chief's Capstone Concept for Joint Operations red team (discussed in chapter 2)—its findings risk being disregarded for having arrived too late to be incorporated. In summary, the ability to empathize with the leaders and affected employees within the targeted institution, and synchronize the red team engagement with their needs, goes a long way toward being heard.

How the red team conducts the simulation, vulnerability probe, or alternative analysis, and then presents its findings to the targeted institution, is also of vast importance. Of course, the red team cannot cheat. For example, the US Government Accountability Office's Office of Special Investigation (OSI) conducts "black box" vulnerability probes of government processes, facilities, or borders—just about anything that receives federal funds—under the direction of the comptroller general of the United States. These types of probes are carried out only with publicly available information, in order to emulate what a relatively motivated and competent adversary who lacked an insider accomplice would be able to learn. The OSI's director, Wayne McElrath, noted that "using insider info would be cheating the whole purpose of an investigation."[12] One private-sector leader in the physical penetration testing field cautions against hiring testers who "acted more like Ocean's Eleven [during an engagement], than the crook that some firm should actually be worried about."[13]

Beyond fundamental issues of structure and scope, there are all manner of additional calibrations that a red team will need to balance. The red team's engagement should not be done in a "gotcha" manner to embarrass or humiliate an office or individual. Nor should it keep the targeted institution unnecessarily in the dark. To avoid this scenario, the CIA's Red Cell, for example, will often give the relevant office a heads-up about the conclusions of their alternative analysis, and when the findings will be published for everyone else to see. The Red Cell does not request nor does it receive permission from the office, but rather requests this as a professional courtesy, and to make collaboration with that office more likely and fruitful in the future. Or, as Lieutenant Colonel Brendan Mulvaney, who directed the Marine Corps Commandant's Red Team in its first three years, described the interaction between an independent red team and a planning staff: "You don't want to be the seagull who comes in and craps on the plan, and then flies away."[14]

Furthermore, red team efforts should not result in inadvertent disruption or damage. Vulnerability probes should not inadvertently lead to "fratricide"—events that materially harm the security system being tested. There are many examples—including one involving a Fortune 10 company where a penetration test accidentally knocked the company off-line for twenty minutes—where a red team exercise proved too expansive or disruptive. Carefully calibrating the scope and power of a red team penetration test is especially important to evaluate the supervisory control and data acquisition (SCADA) systems for critical infrastructure facilities, where one wrong move could cause massive economic disruption or even death. Such instances of friendly fire can damage the red team's relationship with the targeted institution and diminish the impact of its findings.

Rather than making people look bad, or temporarily worsening their situation, the goal is to educate and improve the targeted institution as a whole. The effectiveness of a red team and the applicability of its findings are greater if the red team is aware of the values and language of the targeted institution. But, most importantly, the remediation must be clear, reasonable, and implementable. Security professional Charles Henderson of the information security company Trustwave Holdings oversees vulnerability probes of cyber and physical security systems for a range of corporate and government clients. He says that it is essential for all red teamers to keep in mind that "our job isn't to break into a computer network or building, it's to improve the security of the client." Henderson added, "If we haven't done that, then we have failed."[15] Indeed, improving the targeted institution should always be the ultimate objective of all red teams.

3. Fearless Skeptics with Finesse

Just as perfecting the red team's placement in relation to the targeted institution is important, so is staffing the red team with the right people. If a red team is assembled thoughtlessly, bringing in whoever might be available at the time regardless of their skillset or personality type, it will almost certainly fail. A red team needs to be thinking or doing something differently from everyone else within the targeted institution. Therefore, its members should be somewhat outside of the norm.

The best red teamers tend to be self-described "oddballs" and "weirdoes," as well as critical and divergent thinkers inherently skeptical of authority and conventional wisdom. Lieutenant Colonel Daniel Geisenhof, who is a red team instructor at Marine Corps University, characterized his own team by saying, "In many ways, we are in the land of misfit toys."[16] Through experience, the instructors best appreciate how necessary this dissimilarity is when forming red teams.

Most people like to believe that they are nonconformists capable of divergent and creative thinking. Polling shows that people overwhelmingly claim to highly value creativity. Though most people acknowledge the prevalence of conventional wisdom, they also like to believe that they think outside the box themselves. Yet, in reality, few are capable of this without training and practice. People are strongly shaped and constrained by their own personal biases, experiences, and everyday environments. No matter how open-minded people may think they are, studies show that most people exhibit a strong "existence bias"—the natural tendency for humans to believe that something is morally good simply because it exists. They cannot help but assume that the way things are at the moment must be innately correct, which results in overvaluing existing precedents and status quos, and making judgments based on mere existence rather than reason or principle.[17] Red teamers escape such biases and environmental constraints, either because they are composed of inherently distinct personality types, received the right training, or are directed and empowered to exist semi-independently from the targeted institution.

Three variables are most directly correlated with being a good red teamer. First is the possession of the right combination of personality and character traits. Successful red teamers tend to be quick on their feet, adaptive, self-motivated, and fearless in pursuing what they believe to be true, yet also innately curious and willing to listen to and learn from others. Rodney Faraon, who participated in red teaming as a CIA analyst and as a consultant in the private sector, notes that "the best red teamers are like method actors" in that they identify and internalize the motives and values of an adversary so that they can become that adversary.[18] Because they generally do not self-censor, red teamers who are not attentive to their audience may be dismissed as "pessimists" or labeled as "crotchety." As Marissa Michel, who was an analyst in the Analytic Methods Application Branch, a small red team unit in the National Counterterrorism Center, described it: "There is a difference with being crotchety, versus being an open thinker. You can have great ideas, but if you are crotchety nobody will pay attention to you."[19]

An additional element in the mix of traits necessary to successful red teaming is that team members tend not to be "climbers," Unlike those who are willing to do or say whatever is needed to advance their careers, they should prioritize speaking their mind over being a team player, or they have accepted that they have hit a ceiling above which they will not be promoted. For instance, in the military, there is often no more divergent thinker or honest voice than "terminal colonel" who is no longer looking for promotion to general officer. In the world of white-hat hacking, teenagers who are still trying to show off will probably try things that their older counterparts would not consider. In short, proficient red teamers come in a variety of forms with differing motivations, but they are inevitably different from most everybody else.

The second variable that correlates to successful red teaming has to do with experience. There is a reliable, recognizable set of educational and professional experiences that lend themselves to the skills required for red teaming: being widely read (especially in history), having held multiple postings in a profession, and demonstrating the ability to brief and write exceptionally well. A common refrain enunciated by red teamers across a number of fields was that, to adequately convey and emphasize their points, effective practitioners of the art of red teaming have to be able to tell a story. Humans are hardwired to respond more strongly to stories than they ever would to a memo, Excel spreadsheet, or PowerPoint presentation. Red teamers also generally have an expertise or specialty in some subject area, but are still able to see the big picture and ask difficult questions. In the past, they have likely been exposed to large systemic failures, which helps them envision future failures. It is no coincidence that the US military's decision to support red-teaming efforts was led by former officers who had seen firsthand in Afghanistan and Iraq the wasted efforts and lives lost pursuing a strategy that did not take into account its adversaries' perspectives and interests.

The third and final attribute that accompanies successful red teaming is that its practitioners must possess tacit interpersonal communication skills that enable them to work well with each other. Several directors of red team units use the phrase: "You must be able to play well in the sandbox with others." Retired Air Force Colonel James Baker directed the Chairman of the Joint Chiefs' Chairman's Action Group (CAG) from 2007 to 2011, which, among its other duties, conducts alternative analyses for the military's most senior uniformed official. Baker pointed out the contradictions in finding good red teamers: "you bring someone on board who is used to being the smartest person in the room, but now they aren't, and they have to be willing to listen and learn." Moreover, "you want to hire people who are outsiders and think differently, but haven't given up on the institution yet."[20]

In addition to how they function internally, red teamers should be able to interact with the employees of the targeted institution in a manner consistent with the employees' standards and values. If the red team is comprised of people from the targeted institution, as is the case with Army and Marine decision-support red teams that are embedded within command units to mitigate groupthink and provide alternative analyses, or the CIA's Red Cell, this is a simpler task. As one senior Red Cell analyst described the sort of person who tends to flourish: "Smart people who are bureaucratically savvy. They know not to step on toes, or when to step on toes, and whose toes it is okay to step on."[21] For external red teams, particularly those conducting vulnerability probes, you want people who can temporarily internalize the goals and values of the targeted institution, understand the learning style of that institution, and relay their findings in a manner that is practical and actionable. The legendary penetration tester Chris Nickerson—a leading voice and conscience in the security industry—compares his role to that of a therapist, explaining to potential clients at a targeted institution that they should be open and honest with him about whether they are looking for a short-term security assessment or a more comprehensive overview that requires time, patience, and humility. Nickerson tells clients, "You can have a therapist who gives you a bunch of pills that let you walk around hammered, or have someone who will talk to you and educate you to make a decision on your own."[22] When red teamers lack such honesty and sensitivity, they should be isolated from the employees of the targeted institution—several heads of white-hat-hacking teams noted that many hackers simply did not deal well with people in the non-virtual world.

Though particular backgrounds and personality types lend themselves to being more effective red teamers, the approaches and techniques can be taught. Your author was fortunate to learn some red-teaming basics while attending a two-week course at the University of Foreign

Military and Cultural Studies (UFMCS) at Fort Leavenworth, Kansas, described in chapter 2. The greatest impact of this experience was the repeated exposure and awareness to metacognition—or how to think about thinking. Until you are forced through readings and lectures to understand how the mind processes information through lenses and biases, you are not conscious of the blinders that hinder ordinary problem solving. While taking a red team course, students repeatedly practice how to use what are called "liberating structures" to critique plans and inform strategic decisions. For example, UFMCS uses 1–2–4–Whole Group in which participants begin by personally reflecting on an issue and writing down their thoughts or positions, then share those ideas, first in pairs, then small groups, and then with the whole group.[23] Initially, exercises like these appear too simplified and even pedestrian to support decision-making in a real-world setting. However, upon repetition and refinement, the student soon recognizes how group decisions are often routinely derailed by the same barriers to honest communication and an unwillingness to rigorously identify and evaluate the assumptions underlying options or consider the values and interests of competitors.

However, no matter how many courses they take or how hard they try, some people are simply incapable of being red teamers. Some military planners are unwilling to engage in premortem analyses that evaluate every way that their operational plan could fail; usually this is because of a belief that doing so might introduce unnecessary doubt that could impact the execution of the plan. Cyber-security "blue team" members—usually responsible for defending an institution from hackers—have sometimes been unable to participate fully in penetration tests when they are assigned to take the opposing side. They simply try the most obvious hacks rather than model the attack of a motivated and creative adversary. Raymond Parks, who was a founding member of the Information Design Assurance Red Team (IDART) at the Sandia National Laboratories described in chapter 4, recalled at least one example in which a red team member had to quit a project that was evaluating the killing of US troops because "he just couldn't participate in that."[24] Bill Greenberg, a retired Army lieutenant colonel who oversees the curriculum development at the

UFMCS, described the inherent predilection to be a red teamer by curling his tongue like a taco: "Some people can do this, but others simply can't, no matter how hard they try."[25]

But even those adept at red teaming probably cannot, and should not, do it forever. Even the best practitioners will eventually, inevitably, become captured by institutional biases. Intelligence analysts serve on the CIA's Red Cell for an average of two years, after which time they return to their home offices. Within the Army and Marine Corps, red teamers are generally assigned to a command staff for one to two years at most, and then are reassigned to a different position related to their military occupational specialty. In the cyber-security world, white-hat hackers tend to be overwhelmingly younger, and then become members of the in-house blue-team security later in their careers: very few can do white-hat hacking their whole professional careers due to the unsteadiness of the occupation.

A subsidiary consequence of how red teams operate within these fields, and others, is to expose—several used the phrase "infect"—everyone with the approaches and techniques that red teaming offers. In practice, this means changing how they think about their home institution, taking into account the values and interests of potential adversaries, and responding to unexpected challenges. Ultimately, the goal is to make them mini-red teamers either after they leave a red team or witness one's impact from the outside. Ellyn Ogden is the worldwide polio eradication coordinator in the US Agency for International Development (USAID), and her exposure to the red teaming of polio eradication strategies is detailed in chapter 6. She noted of her in-depth experience with red teaming: "It definitely changed me. It helped me envision failures, and made me more confident and bold to raise matters with seniors. . . . There's this internal pressure on myself to speak when nobody else will."[26] By serving on a red team, or merely observing how an effective one operates, you begin to perceive the processes and challenges at your job differently, ideally with a more open mind toward potential improvements and solutions. Red teaming can thus change not only an institution, but also the thinking and acting of the people who work there.

4. Have a Big Bag of Tricks

By nature, red-teaming practitioners must be eclectic and broad-minded. The approaches and techniques that a red team applies cannot become routine and anticipated, or else the red team simply becomes subsumed in an institution's normal plans and processes. To avoid predictability and institutional capture, good red teamers must have a large and well-honed toolkit.

The techniques or approaches have to be fresh from the target's perspective because, when repeatedly used, they become predictable, expected, and thus easily gamed. A targeted institution will soon disregard the physical penetration tester who tries to get in via the door from the employee smoking area over and over again. Similarly, intelligence analysts who recycle structural analytical approaches repeatedly will find that some of their analyses are no longer "must reads" for policymakers. In addition, good red teamers should never reveal all of their tactics and tricks during their first engagement with a new targeted institution. Retired Marine Colonel Mark Monroe likes to say that when leading a red team engagement, "Never show all your cards, and always leave them wanting more."[27]

Moreover, a good red teamer should have the flexibility and adaptability to apply different techniques during the engagement when the initial plan of action is not getting traction, or is failing to achieve the sought-after dynamic. In such instances, the engagement needs to be reframed on-the-fly with a new approach or technique. The chief of the NYPD's Counterterrorism Bureau who helps prepare and run the commissioner's tabletop exercises, James Waters, noted that during the bureau's scripted scenarios, if the situation does not evolve in the manner anticipated, it will not introduce a challenge that appears in the script once that challenge becomes inapplicable. Waters declared that one of his mottos is: "Don't fight the scenario."[28] Having been a rare outside witness to an NYPD simulation in October 2014, as discussed in chapter 4, I can attest to how participating police commanders and New York City officials anticipated the consequences of an unfolding terror-based scenario and proposed the correct responsive actions. Rather than adhering rigorously to the script—in this case regarding potential catastrophes occurring during the New York City Marathon—Waters would jump to the next unexpected challenge, or "inject." Finally, the very best red teamers can recognize and acknowledge when the engagement with a targeted institution was unsuccessful, why it was unsuccessful, and what the red teamers can do to avoid this the next time around. This realization requires a rare combination of self-awareness and humility.

An expanding part of the red teamer's toolkit is the adaptation of technologies to conduct simulations, vulnerability probes, and alternative analyses. In Afghanistan, the "effects cell" in an Army Brigade Combat Team would conduct an audit-like alternative analysis, which it termed "an honesty analysis," of Afghan Army security patrols. This entailed asking an Afghan unit commander where and for how long he had conducted a patrol, and then comparing that to the data provided by GPS tracking devices placed on Jeeps or Humvees used by that unit. Mark Chussil runs quantitative strategy simulations—that take months to design and build—for businesses facing a consequential decision, in order to envision how their competitors will likely react to different strategic options. Similarly, law firms hire the Silicon Valley legal consultancy Lex Machina to run computer simulations that model and predict potential litigation outcomes for cutting-edge technology clients who face patent challenges. These technologies, and others, help to inform and quantify the red-teaming process, but they are pointless without humans capable of flexibly adding them to the red teamer's bag of tricks and adapting their findings in a way that is useful to the targeted institution.

5. Be Willing to Hear Bad News and Act on It

The findings and recommendations that flow from the red team cannot just sit on a shelf. They must be heard, acted upon, and implemented to the greatest extent that the boss deems possible. Some red teaming does not lead to concrete recommendations, but rather is conducted to identify unstated assumptions and to evaluate them in order to assist in a decision-making process. For example, many senior US government officials are avid readers of the CIA Red Cell's alternative-analytical products, even though these reports rarely influence decisions at the top of the officials' agenda. When they are asked why they willingly read them, given their finite time, they respond, "I wanted my mind stirred," or "They were different than everything else that came across my desk." In these cases, the officials' willingness to listen to the red team is unsurprising because it does not require them to make a tough decision or do anything differently. It is not "bad" news, per se, but rather novel news.

The vast majority of red teaming, however, features unsettling or disturbing news about an institution's strategies, plans, or procedures. One way that firms avoid or minimize such bad news is to "game" or "cook" the engagement. This happens when information or access to analysts is denied, which has been the case at times for Army and Marine decision-support red teamers. Similarly, a chief security officer (CSO) might increase the number of security guards that are committed to defending a facility during a vulnerability probe to ensure that his team "succeeds." Jeff Moss, known in the hacking world as The Dark Tangent and formerly the CSO of the Internet Corporation for Assigned Names and Numbers, recalled that since many cyber penetration tests happen at night, information technology directors have occasionally taken machines off-line to avoid being exposed to such trials.[29] Finally, senior leaders will introduce limitations or artificialities into a simulation to ensure that their preferred strategies or ideas are validated during the simulation; the 2002 Millennium Challenge concept-development exercise featuring Van Riper's red team, described in detail in chapter 2, is one glaring example of this. In these instances, the exercise is rigged, and the red team is prevented from faithfully "grading the homework" of the targeted institution.

Willingness to hear the potentially bad news requires listening to the summary briefing of a tabletop exercise or reading the embarrassing after-action report of a physical penetration test. Every red teamer can provide stories of senior vice presidents, three-star generals, or CSOs who stubbornly denied the existence of a shortcoming even after it was brought to their attention. One white-hat hacker relayed that his team had identified the same network control access vulnerability at a Fortune 100 technology firm for more than a decade. After each penetration test, the same vulnerability was reported to the firm's cyber-security firm, along with a plan for how it could be repaired or mitigated at limited cost. In spite of the repeated warnings, the firm has simply never addressed this much-documented shortcoming. In this instance, as can be the case in all three types of red teaming, the targeted institution is going through the motions, but refusing to learn and improve.

The targeted institution needs to have the absorptive capacity to act on what the red team has told it. Not only must the boss and the affected employees listen and connect with the red team's findings, the institution must see it through. This might require additional funding or people, and, in most cases, some potentially painful changes in standard operating procedures. In fact, there should be some prioritized work plan that can be implemented, and a monitoring and evaluation process to determine whether this has happened on the timeline required. A red team exercise that is conducted and ignored, or woefully misapplied, can be far worse than one that is never conducted at all. The senior leadership in the targeted institution thinks that its strategy or security system was scrutinized and validated by an outside source, when, in fact, it was not.

6. Red Team Just Enough, But No More

Yet just as important as heeding the lessons of the red team's findings is not repeating the exercise more frequently than is practical for the institution. For institutions facing a scheduled event or a consequential decision, red teaming can and should be a one-time effort. One such example of stand-alone red teaming is the alternative analyses described in chapter 3 used to assign statistical probabilities that Osama bin Laden was living in a compound in Abbottabad, Pakistan, in the spring of 2011.

Alternately, for those institutions for which red teaming is not a process with a definitive end point, there is nevertheless a limit to beneficial red teaming—which should be calibrated to the needs of an institution. If red teaming is done too often, the institution will never have enough time to implement a red team's most recent findings and recommendations. As James N. Miller, who was exposed to and led red-teaming efforts in the Pentagon and the private sector, puts it: "You can't red team everything to death, or else you won't get anything done. But for big important projects, getting independent eyes on it can be invaluable."[30] There is an acronym that military red teamers use to convey when it is time to put an end to their efforts: GICOT, or Good Idea Cut Off Time.

Moreover, the frequent evaluation or testing of an institution's day-to-day plans and processes by an outside or semi-independent red team may quickly demoralize a workforce. Red teaming can be a highly stressful event for the affected employees within the targeted institution. People tend to react negatively to being tested, or to having their judgment questioned in front of their peers or their boss. Moreover, the continuously repeated process of red teaming, especially very late in the development of a strategy or plan, will lead to the creation of a high wall of mistrust between the targeted institution's employees and the red team itself. Finally, a red team can warn senior decision-makers about blind spots or unforeseen challenges that they need to focus on immediately. However, if they are wrong too often about those challenges, or too certain in their judgments that turn out to be incorrect, they may be dismissed in the future. Robert Gates, who championed alternative analysis as a younger CIA analyst of the Soviet Union and later as the director of central intelligence, has found: "You only have to be wrong three times in a row for people to stop paying attention to you; to start thinking you are just Peter crying 'wolf'."[31]

On the other hand, if red teaming is done too infrequently, the institution becomes hidebound and complacent. How often an institution should utilize red-teaming techniques depends significantly on how static or dynamic its operating environment is. An institution that faces relatively few new threats or challenges, or is not contemplating a bold new direction, does not need to do it often. An institution that faces a highly competitive environment, uncertainty, and potentially catastrophic threats should red team more frequently. Ben Gilad recommends that multinational companies commission an external alternative analysis or war game of their strategy at least once every five years. Meanwhile, the Nuclear Regulatory Commission requires that each US civilian nuclear reactor be subjected to force-on-force inspections—vulnerability probes with a "composite adversary force" that is modeled upon the most likely threats—at least once every three years.[32] Jayson E. Street, who conducts physical penetration tests of banks, hospitals, and other supposedly secure facilities, believes that such tests should be done about once per year.[33] Alternatively, a company that faces advanced persistent threats from hackers to gain unauthorized access to its computer networks might require manual penetration tests quarterly, or even more often, according to white-hat hacker Catherine Pearce.[34]

The need to carefully calibrate how often a targeted institution engages in red teaming stems from its two most critical impacts. First are the concrete changes in the strategies, plans, or processes that are based upon the red team's findings. Second is the impact that the red team has on those exposed to its process and results. Witnesses to red teaming overwhelmingly describe how it makes them more conscious of their thought processes (in the case of alternative analyses), or more security-aware (as a result of vulnerability probes). Moreover, it elevates the importance of the issue that was red teamed within the targeted institution. After a red team engagement, conversations continue in the hallways, and bosses and employees become primed to remain vigilant about some particular issue. However, red teaming is ultimately a snapshot in time, and institutions are dynamic to varying degrees—eventually both the process and cognitive impacts will atrophy. In any truly competitive environment, even the best-laid plans and security procedures will eventually sprout problematic shortcomings and vulnerabilities, which those working in the targeted institution will most likely fail to uncover, or decide not to report, due to the normal institutional pressures and biases that inevitably reemerge.

The Overarching Best Practice

As stated at the beginning of this chapter, the overarching best practice is to be flexible in the adaptation of best practices. Red teamers are resistant to the very idea of best practices for a good reason—adherence to dogma is antithetical to truly effective red teaming.

With that lesson in mind, an institution should be ready to accept and adopt elements from each of the six best practices: 1) the boss must buy in; 2) outside and objective, while inside and aware; 3) fearless skeptics with finesse; 4) have a big bag of tricks; 5) be willing to hear bad news and act on it; 6) red team just enough, but no more. Of most vital importance is the "boss buy-in"—the absence of which greatly diminishes the value of the other five. These practices should generally be conceived of as complementary and reinforcing because they tend to work best when used together.

Red teamers often say that their profession is more of an art than a science. While that is true, it is also neither strictly abstract expressionism, nor a paint-by-numbers exercise. Rather, the art is found somewhere in between and should be unique to the background, temperament, and proficiency of each red teamer. Similarly, the degree to which the targeted institution recognizes the need for the red team, supports its work, and listens to its findings varies widely. As such, both the red team and the targeted institution must play their respective roles to properly implement these six interrelated best practices. In the following chapters, the stories and vignettes will provide instances where these best practices were largely adhered to, and where they were either never adapted or were ignored.

TWO

ORIGINS: MODERN MILITARY RED TEAMING

When I pinned on my fourth star in December of '08, I had a four-star coming through the receiving line to congratulate me and he leaned over and he whispered, "You realize that, from this point forward, no one will ever tell you the truth again."

—General Martin Dempsey, Chairman of the Joint Chiefs of Staff, 2011[1]

It is no accident that red teaming as we know it was refined and codified in the US military—if there is one institution that can benefit from the introspection and counterintuitive thinking that red teaming can provide, the military is it. Military decision-making has tremendous costs in terms of the potential loss of lives, money, and political capital. Presently, this includes deciding how to apportion the roughly $534 billion in annual defense spending in fiscal year 2016 to train and equip 1.3 million active-duty troops and 826,000 more in the National Guard and Reserves; planning and conducting military operations that risk the lives of service members; and recognizing when a military campaign is failing to achieve its intended objectives and making the necessary corrections.[2] Since many strategies, plans, and day-to-day operations of the US military are immensely consequential, there is tremendous pressure to think through, challenge, and test every significant decision.

Yet, paradoxically, even as the US military has the widest range of requirements for red teams, it also faces the greatest difficulty in faithfully supporting, conducting, and listening to their findings. Presently,
some version of red teaming is conducted within all armed services and
combat-arms branches. Moreover, the concept and need for it is widely
known and acknowledged among uniformed officers. Although, it would
appear that the military presents a perfect environment in which red
teaming should flourish, red teams nevertheless have faced profound difficulties becoming established and heard in this setting.

Though, as described earlier in the book, the concept of the devil's
advocate dates back to the thirteenth-century Vatican, as best as can be
determined, the very term "red team" originated within the US military
during the Cold War. It can be traced to the early 1960s, emerging from
game-theory approaches to war-gaming and from the simulations that
were developed at the RAND Corporation and applied by the Pentagon's
"Whiz Kids"—a derisive term for über-smart policy analysts—to evaluate strategic decisions.[3] The "red" referred to the color that characterized
the Soviet Union, and more generally to any adversary or adversarial
position.

Of course, red teaming was used within the US military well before
it was given the label, but the Cold War was clearly when the concept
came into its own. A May 1963 article by columnist George Dixon discussed how Secretary of Defense Robert McNamara formed a blue team
and a red team to assess the awarding of a $6.5 billion TFX (tactical
fighter experimental) aircraft contract. As Dixon colorfully described
it: "A weird game in which the innings are being played backwards, is
being waged at the Pentagon." The blue team assumed the role of General
Dynamics, which was awarded the contract, while the red team made the
case for why Boeing should have won. Dixon wrote: "McNamara must
have steeped himself in the classics. He called members of his Red Team
'Devil's Advocates'."[4]

A September 1963 article in the *Journal of Conflict Resolution* described a similar simulation from two years earlier. This one featured a
structured arms-control game between a US blue team, and a "red team"

modeled on the Soviet Union. The goals were to study leaders' decisions and identify their consequences for arms-control-treaty provisions. The red team abided by the provisions of the disarmament agreement, but because there was no contact between the teams, the blue team was unaware of the red team's strategy. In the end, the civilian leader identified the military leader as a threat monger, while the military leader thought the civilian leader was soft on national security.[5] While the findings of the study were not intended to inform decision-making or processes, they did expose the utility of red teaming and its applicability for use in comparable future simulations.

Red teaming continued to be used in an organic way throughout the Cold War and afterward, though it was not until after 2000 that its innovations were widely documented and its vernacular codified. One person partially responsible for the growth of interest in red teaming was James Miller, who from 1997 to 2000 was the defense official responsible for reviewing operational plans, including differing estimates of how potential adversaries respond. Prior to the NATO airstrikes against Serbia in 1999, he was tasked with assessing the motivations for Yugoslavian President Slobodan Milosevic's actions in Kosovo in hopes of determining what might change his decision-making calculus. Miller was startled when he received very different predictive estimates from two intelligence community (IC) organizations about what Milosevic would do: "I basically got to red team two different analytical groups within the IC."[6]

Miller's interest in the phenomenon was piqued. Upon leaving the Pentagon, he took the lead on a pilot project at the defense consultancy Hicks & Associates called the Defense Adaptive Red Teaming (DART). The DART featured retired general officers—including General Anthony Zinni and Lieutenant General Paul Van Riper (more on him later)— who both emulated adversaries in tabletop exercises of war games and conducted alternative-analysis reviews for war-fighting concepts under development. The project also published working papers that examined aspects of red teaming, including historical examples and best practices, for the small Advanced Systems and Concepts Office in the Pentagon. The DART papers, as well as a few similar ones written at the Institute for Defense Analyses (IDA), provided some of the foundational understanding for how interested military officers thought about and described red teaming.

The next milestone came in September 2003, when the Defense Science Board (DSB) released a report on "The Role and Status of DOD Red Teaming Activities." The report was produced by a ten-person task force established at the request of the Under Secretary of Defense for Acquisition, Technology and Logistics (AT&L), Edward C. Aldridge Jr., who saw a growing need for red teaming in light of 9/11, particularly to better understand new adversaries and their asymmetrical tactics. The task force, co-chaired by Theodore Gold and Robert Hermann, had been asked to examine the use of red teams in the Department of Defense, and to identify obstacles to and criteria for their productive uses. It found that red teaming was underutilized and suggested that expanded red team efforts might deepen the understanding of US adversaries in the war on terrorism and guard against complacency. In its report, the task force stated that attention from high-level officials was necessary, and suggested that then-Secretary of Defense Donald Rumsfeld, in particular, propagate the practice of red teaming throughout the department by issuing a memorandum of guidance, tasking the Office of the Under Secretary of Defense for AT&L with outlining red team procedures and best practices, and incorporating red teaming in educational institutions and activities. It also recommended that the secretary establish red teams for critical issues, such as maintaining the nuclear weapons stockpile and finding elusive terrorist leaders.

Characteristically, the US military is careful to define every last term and concept to promote a "joint" understanding of their meaning throughout the armed services. To that end, it has its own standard definition for red teams: "Organizational elements comprised of trained, educated, and practiced experts that provide the JFC an independent capability to conduct critical reviews and analysis, explore plans and operations, and analyze adversary capabilities from an alternative perspective."[7] These red teams are distinct within US military doctrine from a Red Cell, which is commonly thought of as a unit that exclusively performs threat emulation of some defended system by assuming the role of an unco-operative adversary.[8] While variations on the same principle, a red team supports a more expansive range of activities, most noteworthy the objec-tive of rigorously assessing the targeted institution to which it is attached.

Red teaming within the military presently takes the form of vul-nerability probes, simulations, and alternative analyses. Vulnerability probes in particular are a constant necessity, given that there are so many US-based and overseas installations and communications networks that motivated adversaries or insiders can attack, disrupt, or infiltrate. The Pentagon is estimated to own or control more than 4,800 properties around the world, relying upon approximately fifteen thousand different computer networks.[9] The National Security Agency's (NSA's) Tailored Access Operations (TAO) program consists of geographically dispersed elite hackers tasked with "getting the un-gettable" from foreign com-puter networks.[10] However, its members also serve as the cyber-opposi-tion force (OPFOR)—which is a vulnerability-probe red team—to test the network security of regional combatant commands, like Southern Command, which is responsible for everything south of Mexico; and Pacific Command, the Hawaii-based command that covers the Asia-Pacific. Brendan Conlon was a TAO member who participated in several penetration tests, where the OPFOR employed tactics and techniques that potential adversaries were assumed to have, based upon open-source information and intelligence reporting. In order to be faithful to the likely adversary, he recalled of himself and his NSA colleagues: "We had to totally de-skill ourselves to do what they could realistically do."[11] Some combatant commands valued hearing the shortcomings that were revealed by the penetration tests while, more frequently, others downplayed them, convinced that the TAO red teams were simply un-realistic in how good they were.

Red team simulations take the form of tabletop and live-fire exercises, which themselves date back to the *Kriegsspiel* war games invented by the Prussian Army's Baron von Reiswitz and adopted by the US Army in the late-nineteenth century, when Major William R. Livermore of the US Army Corps of Engineers and Lieutenant Charles A. L. Totten of the 4th

Artillery Regiment each developed a war game based on von Reiswitz's. In 1884, the Naval War College codified rules for an "American Kriegs-spiel" and incorporated war gaming into its curriculum three years later. Today, there are robust war-gaming units in all of the armed services, the joint staff, and the combatant commands. These have moved far beyond poring over terrain maps—although those are still used—to include advanced computer models, such as the Army's Warfighters' Simulation, which simulates potential enemies' courses of action in response to future US campaign plans and operations. Joint concepts and doctrine about how the military will fight in the future, what equipment and training will be required, and how allies and adversaries might react are routinely simulated in lengthy exercises, such as Unified Vision, Expeditionary Warrior, and the Millennium Challenge exercise in 2002 described later in this chapter.

Each of the armed services also employs highly realistic pretend or live-fire simulations to prepare service members for overseas deployments. For example, the Army's Fort Irwin National Training Center located in the Mojave Desert in Southern California features thirteen meticulously reconstructed tribal "villages," one populated by Iraqi- and Afghan-Americans, to test and refine the counterinsurgency competencies of US troops before they are deployed overseas. Senior officers acting as observer/controllers monitor how junior officers' units adapt to unexpected insurgent tactics and cultural challenges and correct the inevitable missteps through repetition.[12] The leading advanced training program for pilots is the US Air Force's Red Flag, which entails exercises held several times a year at Nellis Air Force Base in Nevada. The red forces are coordinated by the 57th Adversary Tactics Group, which oversees seven aggressor squadrons comprised of potential adversaries like MiG-29s flown by Chinese pilots, or Su-27s flown by Russians. Only highly qualified Air Force pilots become certified "aggressors," which requires them to pass several examinations and closely monitored check rides. To ensure that they realistically emulate the air-to-air threats that US forces would face in combat, Red Flag aggressors are permitted to use only known adversarial tactics and techniques, which are based upon the latest intelligence, and include, for example, Chinese or Russian fighter aircraft's performance characteristics and tolerable G-force, its missile payload, and radar capabilities.[13]

Military alternative analyses assist senior officials and commanders to challenge assumptions and think through the consequences of strategic decisions and operational plans. The costs of not subjecting a military operation to such a rigorous evaluation by an empowered and semi-independent red team can be catastrophic. In April 1980, a hundred eighteen US troops famously attempted to rescue fifty-two Americans being held hostage in post-revolutionary Tehran, Iran. The mission, Operation Eagle Claw, was aborted when three of the US Navy helicopters malfunctioned for various reasons, leaving them one helicopter short of the six required to deploy the team to Tehran. While the rescue forces were waiting at a staging area in the Iranian desert for a lift back to Navy ships in the Persian Gulf, a C-130 transport plane and an RH-53D helicopter accidentally collided creating a massive fireball.[14] Eight service members were instantly killed, the US hostages remained in Tehran, and Jimmy Carter's presidency suffered as a result. Ronald Reagan was elected in a landslide five months later.

The operation was among the riskiest to ever be authorized by a US president: the Pentagon estimated that fifteen hostages as well as thirty of the rescue forces could have been killed or injured in a *successful* operation.[15] Nevertheless, the odds of Eagle Claw succeeding were unnecessarily decreased because the plan was never red teamed. Soon after the hostages were taken, a few dozen planners met in a windowless, secluded suite of offices in the Pentagon, and continued to meet regularly for six straight months. Operational security concerns prevented them from seeking out the kind of critical evaluation that a red team alternative analysis would have provided. Their plans were shared with only a few senior officials, including the secretary of defense, secretary of state, Joint Chiefs of Staff, and President Carter's chief of staff.[16] According to the Eagle Claw after-action review, led by retired Admiral James L. Holloway III, "planners—in effect—reviewed and critiqued their own product for feasibility and soundness as they went along." Moreover, "the hostage rescue plan was never subjected to rigorous testing and evaluation by qualified, independent observers and monitors short of the Joint Chiefs of Staff themselves." Holloway concluded that a red team would have improved the mission's likelihood of turning out well: "There is little doubt regarding its potential value: a comprehensive and continuing review capability impacts directly on almost all other issues. Such a plans review element could have played an important balancing role in the dynamic planning process that evolved, conceivably making a critical contribution to ultimate mission accomplishment."[17]

The inherent need for such red team "independent observers" stems from the hierarchical structures and insular culture that exists within command staffs. Authority rests in the hands of a commander, who relies heavily upon their personal staffs for support. The commander has tremendous power not only in issuing orders, but also in establishing the "command climate" for how the unit is expected to function and what tasks are prioritized. Command staffs are thus susceptible to groupthink, a phenomenon that often prevails within institutions characterized by rigid hierarchy and shared values, and comprised of people who work in dangerous and high-stress environments. By design, they conceive of themselves as part of a team working in a unified manner toward achieving a common objective. In such an environment, criticism can put the team effort and mission at risk. Finally, because they have identities and cultures distinct from the civilian world and have shared educational experiences, most military officers approach challenges and conceive of solutions in a similarly inward-looking manner. In fact, years of US Army War College surveys of lieutenant colonels and colonels show that the most successful officers score much lower than the general US population on being open to new ideas.[18] Though officers often highlight examples of lone dissenters within command staffs, the vast majority of them also acknowledge the rarity of such individuals. In short, the military's unified chain of command provides clear lines of authority, accountability, and discipline, but this also diminishes dissent and alternative perspectives.

There have been sustained efforts to try to ameliorate this problem. Junior officers are taught to "speak truth upwards" in classrooms throughout the various steps in their professional military education. However, this is much more difficult to do in practice. There is an inherent tension between tolerating divergent thinking in the military and rewarding it because the military is such a strongly hierarchical institution. Junior officers do not simply follow orders, but also adhere to the command climate and conventional wisdom set by their superior officer and that officer's personal staff. As one Marine officer described it: "Your ability to mind read is more praiseworthy than your ability to think critically."[19] Superior officers wield tremendous power over the daily lives and careers of those serving beneath them: from funding a junior officer's initiatives to granting him or her personal leave, to playing a role in the recommendation reports scrutinized by promotion boards that decide which officers rise to fill an increasingly limited number of slots. The adjectives that a superior officer does or does not use to describe a junior officer, and the phone calls they make or do not make on their behalf, significantly advances or limits an officer's career. Moreover, everybody is well aware of this power dynamic. In this environment, it is normal for junior officers to adopt the preferences and norms of their superiors, and to refrain from voicing opposition while under their command.

In the last ten years, there has been a growth and proliferation of permanently embedded elements within commands that do (or believe they do) a limited amount of red teaming. The Combatant Commands' Commander's Initiative Groups, the service Chief of Staff's Strategic Studies Groups, and the Chairman of the Joint Chiefs of Staff's Chairman's Action Group are all purportedly intended to mitigate groupthink and provide independent analyses as one of their many day-to-day activities. The scope of activities and effectiveness of the actual red teaming that these groups do depends overwhelmingly on the demonstrated interest of the commander. Some openly embrace dissenting viewpoints and routinely make scheduled time to receive them. Other commanders ignore those staff members directed to red team, or make red-teaming efforts the sole responsibility of their deputy or chief of staff, or simply make it a responsibility of a staff section where it often becomes subordinate to the organization that it was intended to challenge. In circumstances in which the director of the red team group is perceived as being less influential, they might become captured by the everyday tasks required by the commander's staff, or the group might be denied access or information from the heads of other staff sections, who are usually senior to the group's director to begin with. Basically, all four-star commands now have some form of a specialized "group" like those mentioned above. However, their ability to be permitted and empowered to consistently red team the plans, processes, or products of the commands has been decidedly mixed.

To better grasp the origins and current state of the art of red teaming, this chapter looks to four US military case studies. To grasp the fundamentals of red teaming, it is important to focus attention on the University of Foreign Military and Cultural Studies (UFMCS), more commonly known as Red Team University—which was established in 2004 to expand on General Peter Schoomaker's objective of transforming the classroom experiences of the service, and adapting it over time to remain a valued resource for the Army and nonmilitary agencies. UFMCS red team methods can then be seen in action, by turning to a red team exercise used to analyze a Chairman of the Joint Chief's Capstone Concept for Joint Operations in 2012. An overview of red teaming in the US Marine Corps exposes the struggles it has faced to gain traction since its formal institutionalization in 2010. A look at the 2002 Millennium Challenge war game will show how war games can be corrupted, and red teaming itself can be neutralized, if leadership is unwilling to listen to their results. Lastly, an examination of three notable military red teams outside of the United States—including in the Israeli Defense Forces, the United Kingdom's Ministry of Defence, and NATO headquarters—will show how red-teaming approaches and techniques have spread beyond US borders.

Red Team University

In the summer of 2003, Peter Schoomaker was a happily retired four-star Army general when he received a phone call from someone claiming to be Secretary of Defense Donald Rumsfeld. Though Rumsfeld had met Schoomaker only a few times, he knew his reputation well, and considered him to be the person best equipped to transform the Army into a leaner, more flexible, and more expeditionary fighting force. Before Rumsfeld had a chance to ask him to come out of retirement to become the thirty-fifth chief of staff of the Army, Schoomaker swore and hung up the phone, believing one of his buddies was playing a practical joke. Fortunately, he eventually took the Pentagon chief's phone call and accepted the job.[20]

Schoomaker knew how desperately the institution needed to change. Commissioned in 1969, during his training as an armor officer, he had experienced just how broken and deficient the Army had become in the shadow of the Vietnam War. The demoralization was based upon what Schoomaker considered to be the "regimentation and institutionalization of mediocrity." Enlisted personnel wasted their days awaiting orders and following irrelevant guidelines. West Point cadets learned the same lessons and read the same books as their forefathers. The same unrealistic set-piece tank maneuvers were still being taught at the National Training Center at Fort Irwin years after they had outlived their usefulness. Schoomaker found an Army becoming increasingly irrelevant to the threats it faced, and blinkered by process, doctrine, and tradition. "While there are good things in traditions, they can also blind you to your problems." As he recalled disparagingly of the post-Vietnam War Army: "In many ways we had become the Soviet Red Army."[21]

Schoomaker's source of inspiration for how to transform the Army came from his distinguished career in the special operations world. After eight years of going through the motions of preparing for tank battles, he was set to retire and instead join the Federal Bureau of Investigation (FBI), when suddenly he was offered the opportunity to join a new unit that nobody could tell him anything about: "A real collection of misfits and weirdoes." This would turn out to be the super-secret counterterrorism team 1st Special Forces Operational Detachment-Delta, popularly known as Delta Force, of which Schoomaker was among the original twenty-two members. He later commanded every special operations force for which he was eligible: Delta Force, Joint Special Operations Command (which includes the Navy SEALs), Army Special Operations Command, and, before his first retirement, US Special Operations Command (SOCOM), which oversees all of the armed services' special operators.[22]

One of the formative missions of Schoomaker's career was the tragic, failed hostage mission, Operation Eagle Claw, in 1980 in Iran, for which he led one of the three Delta teams. Everywhere he was posted throughout his career, he brought with him a framed photograph of the burnt wreckage in the Iranian desert with the warning: "Never confuse enthusiasm with capability."[23] The lessons passed down from Eagle Claw helped establish a distinctive mindset among special operators. It engendered such principles as: never stop learning about the enemy; imagine every conceivable scenario for an operation; and thoroughly question everything. Schoomaker sought to transfer and institutionalize this mindset into the conventional army, to the greatest extent possible, by improving critical thinking, language skills, and cultural exposure.

Upon his Senate confirmation in July 2003, Schoomaker repeated the same strategic guidance to seemingly every senior officer that he encountered: "Shake up the Army." It was under his guidance that red-teaming practices became firmly established within the Army, and later within other armed services, and beyond. To channel these transformation efforts, Schoomaker authorized the establishment of several issues to focus on, one of which, Focus Area XVI, evaluated actionable intelligence matters under the direction of Deputy Chief of Staff (G-2, or "intelligence") Lieutenant General Keith B. Alexander. Focus Area XVI included the recently retired Army Colonel Steve Rotkoff, a planner of the land component of the US-led invasion of Iraq. Throughout the campaign-planning process, Rotkoff and his superior officers heard from exiled Iraqis and country experts who repeatedly warned about the near-certainty of an insurgency once Saddam Hussein was toppled. In fall 2002, when asked how long the US military should plan to be in Iraq, a prominent Shia imam, Sayyid Abdul Majid al-Khoei, told Rotkoff, Major General James "Spider" Marks, and Major General James D. Thurman:

"two generations; as long as you are in Germany." As Rotkoff recalled, the military commanders and planners simply ignored these troubling predictions: "We were all engaged in mission lock; we were going to take down Saddam and the Republican Guards. No matter how many people told us things would go wrong, we failed to listen to them. Instead, we listened to our chain of command."[24] Had there been a red team empowered to analyze and present warnings like those provided by al-Khoei, they would likely have been considered during the planning process.

Serving on Focus Area XVI a year later, as the accurately predicted Sunni insurgency in Iraq intensified, Rotkoff proposed establishing a position equivalent to an ombudsman within planning staffs. Ideally, this person would operate separately from the staff and be empowered to encourage dissent and better ensure that alternative perspectives were heard and considered. It was precisely this type of decision-support red teaming that had been intermittently heard, but totally ignored, in the run-up to Iraq. Alexander endorsed the concept and took the proposed initiative, along with a handful of others, to Schoomaker, who enthusiastically endorsed it. The Army was then formally directed to train a small red team cadre that would be embedded within brigade-level planning staffs. As part of this effort, Alexander told a Senate hearing in April 2004: "This will expand to include the establishment of a Red Team University for training within the Army education system."[25]

The home for this education initiative became the University of Foreign Military and Cultural Studies (UFMCS), located in a converted military prison overlooking the Missouri River in Fort Leavenworth, Kansas. In 2004, retired Army Colonel Gregory Fontenot was named the director of UFMCS. In the mid-1990s, while commanding an armored brigade in Bosnia-Herzegovina, Fontenot had experienced his own self-described "Saul on the road to Damascus" moment when he realized how poorly equipped his soldiers were to understand their operating environment. "Our pre-deployment training was almost exclusively how to out-shoot the bad guys once we got there." Fontenot and his small team sought to capitalize on Schoomaker's broad strategic guidance by creating an institution that would forever change how the Army thinks. Fontenot recalled that his initial strategic objective for UFMCS went far beyond Rotkoff's notion of having an ombudsman, to no less than "permanently changing the brains of the Army's future leaders."[26] However, before they could teach the art of red teaming, they had to develop a curriculum and syllabus from scratch.

While the instruction methods developed in 2004 and 2005 have been refined and updated over the years, the essence of how red teaming is taught at UFMCS has remained consistent, even as instructors are given latitude to emphasize those areas they deem most important. The courses run in six-, nine-, and eighteen-week sessions, although there is also a two-week short course. The foundational assumption for all incoming students—regardless of their background, education, or professional experience—is that they do not know how to think. The initial days are spent exposing students to awareness and understanding of their own thought processes through the works of behavioral psychologists such as Daniel Kahneman and Amos Tversky. Next, students are taught the basics of cultural empathy and semiotics (i.e., the philosophical study of signs and symbols), without which a red teamer cannot identify and understand the values and interests experienced by those within a targeted institution. This component includes visiting the Nelson-Atkins Museum of Art in Kansas City, where military officers engage in a "Fifteen Minutes of Looking" exercise that forces them to observe, document, and describe their impressions of a contemporary or modern work of art; making for a distinctly uncomfortable moment for some students.

Another central component of instruction is groupthink mitigation, which is needed because most students will ultimately return to some sort of a hierarchical command structure. Students are taught how to identify the common symptoms of social conformity, and the "mind guards" and "blockers" who enforce it, and learn strategies to overcome it. This includes forcing group participants to precommit to a position by writing it down before they hear from anybody else, leveraging anonymous ideas and feedback, and enforcing the rule of "nobody speaks twice, until everyone has spoken once." Finally, tabletop exercises and negotiation sessions are used to instill these future red teamers with the muscle memory and flexibility required to provide independent and critical analysis once sent back to their daily jobs. This includes teaching "liberating structures"—semi-structured brainstorming techniques used to generate innovative ideas and break conventional thought processes. As of 2015, UFMCS had compiled fifty-three of these methods and tools that have been borrowed from several sources and disciplines.[27] The four pillars that UFMCS curricula are based upon are critical thinking, groupthink mitigation, cultural empathy, and self-awareness.

Beyond the UFMCS curriculum, the Army's requirements for red teaming have changed since 2003. It no longer seeks to establish an independent ombudsman within brigade-level planning staffs because, in the long term, that initiative proved too expensive. Now, rather than creating standing red teams, the Army bestows a red-teaming Additional Skill Identifier (ASI) upon individuals who have been formally trained in red team approaches and techniques. Then, whenever a commanding general or chief of staff requires an independent alternative perspective, they can pull together a focused red team from staff members who have earned that ASI. Here, hierarchy turns out to be advantageous—senior Army leaders view having a red team ASI as good for one's career, meaning that the certification trickles down to midgrade and junior officers, ensuring that the techniques of red teaming are widely known and, in principle, rewarded.

The objectives of UFMCS have changed as well. The new goal is not necessarily to change the Army, but rather to tailor instruction to the needs of the students, as Rotkoff, who took over from Fontenot in 2012, describes it. Consequently, the curriculum has been partially modified for courses targeted specifically to members of SOCOM, Cyber Command, the Defense Intelligence Agency, the US Agency for International Development, or Customs and Border Protection. UFMCS also created and refined a 240-page *Applied Critical Thinking Handbook*, formerly known as *Red Team Handbook*, now in its seventh version, which is freely available online. It remains the closest thing to doctrine that is relied upon by almost all the prospective military and business red teamers interviewed for this book.[28]

UFMCS officials and staffers struggle internally about whether their efforts have been successful and how to measure their impact on the Army and the military more broadly. In no small part, this is compounded by the nature of their profession: as red teamers, they look upon even their own work with a critical eye and deep skepticism. Yet, there is evidence that UFMCS is having an impact. First, there has been a significant growth in the number of attendees. The first UFMCS red-teaming class from January to May 2006 was comprised of eighteen students: two from the Marine Corps and Navy, and the rest from the Army, including members of the National Guard. From 2007 to 2013, an average of 300 students per year enrolled at UFMCS, with the number reaching 800 in 2014.[29] Second, in surveys, graduates described the instructions as a positive educational experience, and 89 percent said they would recommend it to their colleagues.[30] (I took the two-week short course, and enthusiastically agree.) Finally, a growing number of Army general officers—from the former commanders of US Forces Korea to the Army's 25th Infantry Division in Hawaii, and the US Army Medical Command—have witnessed the first-hand benefits of having their plans or processes subjected to red teaming.[31]

However, even a full decade after Schoomaker first approved the UFMCS red-teaming initiative, it is still too soon to know if it has been impactful. In early 2014, when a staffer informed Army Chief of Staff General Ray Odierno about the red-teaming instruction provided at the Leavenworth school, he was unaware of it.[32] Nevertheless, once Odierno learned more about UFMCS, he approved the school to become one of four "broadening" institutions dedicated to promoting strategic thinking within the Army's future leaders. Moreover, the fact that UFMCS has survived successive rounds of budget and personnel cuts demonstrates that the Army and its users recognize its value. UFMCS has the added advantage of turning a profit each year because it can charge other branches of the military, the US government, and foreign militaries that send staffers and officers to take courses.

As of December 2014, Rotkoff found that he no longer needed to sell people on red teaming, but rather needed to make sure the school receives the funding needed to continue teaching. Military educational initiatives such as UFMCS are proposed and later eliminated on a regular basis. But the fact that Red Team University has survived for a decade, grown substantially, and adapted to meet the changing needs of the targeted institutions (Army and other military command staffs), suggests its viability—after all, the aspects of the military it was designed to mitigate are still plainly in evidence, as will be seen.

Card Tricks: Mitigating Hierarchy and Groupthink

As discussed earlier, two phenomena that regularly restrict the free flow of information and stifle open debates are hierarchy and groupthink. Several red team techniques taught at UFMCS mitigate these factors by using a facilitator to encourage dissent by eliciting ideas through moderated discussions and anonymous feedback. However, these techniques are not always applied early enough in the planning or decision-making process to be listened to, as subsequent chapters will show.

In the spring of 2012, the Joint Staff's arm for thinking about and writing military doctrine ("the J-7") was updating the Chairman of the Joint Chief's Capstone Concept for Joint Operations (CCJO). Among the Pentagon's many directives, this framing document plays an important role as the overriding guidance from the chairman—the most senior uniformed official—for how the military should train and equip itself, and fight in the future. It also informs all subsequent joint-doctrine publications, which fundamentally guide everything the US military does, from counterinsurgency operations to mortuary affairs. To review and critique what was written in a draft of the CCJO, the J-7 formed an eight-person red team, consisting of one major, one lieutenant colonel, and two colonels (each from one of the four armed services), along with four civilians, all of whom had PhDs: a retired Air Force lieutenant general, a national security affairs professor, an anthropologist, and a cyberwar expert.

The director of the J-7, Lieutenant General George Flynn, asked UFMCS to provide two experts to red team the CCJO during a daylong exercise. The UFMCS team, Steve Rotkoff and Mark Monroe, received a draft of the document beforehand to prepare a plan of action. On the day of the exercise, the red team—most of whom had never met—gathered in an office in Alexandria, Virginia, to participate in a series of moderated discussions. The red team sat in the middle of the room, while senior officers from the J-7 and twenty-seven members of the CCJO's writing team watched. Rotkoff and Monroe began with a premortem analysis to consider all of the ways that the CCJO could lead to failure against a series of hypothetical or real-world adversaries. Next, the UFMCS facilitators led them through an assumptions analysis to identify the document's explicit assumptions that were not validated, and the implicit assumptions that needed to be made explicit. Finally, the red team participated in a "four ways of seeing" exercise to compel them to see the chairman's concept document through the eyes of Congress, allies, potential enemies, and others.

Throughout the day, dozens of suggestions emerged for how to redraft the CCJO, which were compiled on whiteboards and easels. To filter and evaluate all of the ideas, Rotkoff and Monroe employed one of their "card tricks," known as Weighted Anonymous Feedback. Each of the eight red teamers were handed three five-by-eight-inch cards and instructed to list their three most consequential and actionable ideas that the writing team should incorporate into the following draft. Everyone anonymously wrote down their best three ideas. The cards were then collected, shuffled, and handed back to the red teamers, who were told that the most brilliant ideas should be awarded a five, while the poorest scored a one. Everyone graded all of the cards, which meant that of the twenty-four generated ideas, each could have a total score of between eight and forty.

Rotkoff and Monroe then selected only those ideas that earned a score of thirty-two or higher—of which there were seven—and wrote them on a white board at the head of the conference room. After discussing why the seven suggestions were so important and how they might inform a subsequent draft of the CCJO, their sources were asked to identify themselves. This soon revealed that none of the PhDs, including the retired three-star general, saw their ideas listed. In fact, all three ideas provided by the most junior person in the room, an Air Force major, made the board. It turned out that the most senior people—in terms of rank, education, and experience—had produced what the red teamers collectively thought were the worst ideas. Had the J-7 simply gathered eight smart people in a room to review the CCJO, without red teamers trained to elicit suggestions and use groupthink-mitigation techniques, this sort of outcome would have been inconceivable.[33] In the absence of red teaming, a senior leader's ideas, which were the worst in the room, would have won the day, as they often do.

Unfortunately, the overall impact of this one-time red team event on such an important document was minimal. This was primarily because the request for the UFMCS-led effort came far too late in the writing process, and the guidance on what the CCJO should look like was already very clear. Several members of the J-7 writing team recalled that the draft had been worked over extensively in the previous six months before Rotkoff and Monroe led the red team review. By then, all of the thoughts and recommendations that had been offered by senior officers from all of the armed services and various outside reviewers had already been integrated into the CCJO. One senior civilian official involved in the drafting process noted that the final version was largely finished, and "unless [the red team] came up with some 'oh my Gods' that we hadn't thought of, the text probably wouldn't change at that point."[34] Nevertheless, this official thought it was still somewhat useful because it made the writers more comfortable with the overall process that resulted in the document. Meanwhile, several of the writers themselves later admitted that the main reason they attended the daylong exercise was to watch the red teamers from UFMCS employ their trade, and for the most part they came away impressed and better informed about the potential value of red teaming.

Moreover, one of the J-7 red team members—who had previously served on staff-level red teams—thought the process was "done as a matter of course," but overall was "too formalized and ritualistic to have much practical value."[35] The dilemma for Rotkoff and Monroe, however, was that while they had sought to elicit more radical ideas challenging the CCJO's core assumptions, it's less likely that those ideas would have been integrated into a subsequent draft. There simply was too much time and too many resources dedicated to wrapping up the writing process, and too much guidance from senior officials and outsiders. Serious, truly divergent thinking was not feasible so late in the game.

The practical lesson from the J-7's effort is that a red team engagement must happen early enough in the process to make a difference in the outcome. Or, as Rotkoff likes to say in regard to defending the perimeter of a military base: "You cannot red team the mortar team when the enemy is already in the wire."[36]

Marine Corps Red Teaming: Challenging Command Climate

In October 2010, upon becoming the thirty-fifth commandant of the Marine Corps, General James Amos sought to institutionalize red teaming within the Corps. In the initial planning guidance that he issued to all of the military and civilian members of the Corps, he attempted to make clear to the rest of the Marine Corps the value that he placed on red teaming by making it one of his top priorities to "develop a plan for instituting a red cell at each MEF [Marine Expeditionary Force] and in each deploying MEB [Marine Expeditionary Brigade] . . . The purpose of this cell is to challenge prevailing notions, rigorously test current [tactics, techniques, and procedures] and counter groupthink."[37] Along with ordering the establishment of red teams within the Corps's two main combined arms task forces, Amos formed his own commandant's red team comprised of five Marines who had served the previous two years on the Army Directed Studies Office—a red team that had resided in the Army chief of staff's office from 2006 to 2010. The commandant's initiative would collide with the very bureaucratic resistance and hierarchical axioms that had made the Marine Corps seem so ripe for red teaming.

Based on his personal experience, Amos was well aware of the utility of red teaming. Amos witnessed its worth firsthand when he commanded the 3rd Marine Aircraft Wing (3rd MAW) from August 2002

to May 2004. The 3rd MAW provided air support for the ground invasion of Iraq, and was responsible for countering the Sunni insurgency in
the al-Anbar province after Saddam Hussein was toppled. Amos's red
team—called the 3rd MAW Fusion Cell—consisted of an eclectic mix
of fifteen mostly field-grade officers with diverse backgrounds and areas
of expertise. They were directed to "be the CG's [Commanding General's] Napoleon's Corporal; continually assess how we are doing business;
if it doesn't make sense—say so; and offer alternatives to the CG."[38]
The Fusion Cell received access to all of the reporting and intelligence
it needed, and it briefed Amos almost daily.[39] One Fusion Cell leader
recalled that Amos sought "frank assessments and open discussion that
challenged conventional thinking."[40] The 3rd MAW Fusion Cell's most
critical contribution was in analyzing insurgent motivations, tactics, and
likely responses to US counterinsurgency operations. In particular, after the unit had suffered six helicopter shoot-downs, they conducted an
alternative analysis of the methods and tactics for using Cobra attack
helicopters to provide air support to ground troops.[41] Recommendations
stemming from the analysis included shifting flight patterns, with one
aircraft shooting and the other as overwatch, to avoid being patterned
by the Iraqis, and relying primarily upon fixed-wing aircraft for flights
over Baghdad. The Fusion Cell's recommendations significantly reduced
lethal insurgent attacks and helicopter shoot-downs.

Both current and former Marines acknowledge the need for red
teaming within command staffs, especially during wartime. A retired
Marine colonel, who served on the planning staff for the I MEF before
the Iraq War, recalled that one of the biggest constraints to the critical
appraisal of an operational plan was "the tyranny of time." He described
life during the planning process in 2002 and early 2003: "A normal day-
to-day is 0530 to 2200. Then, after 2200 you would deal with whatever
administrative or personal things you couldn't get done. That was a normal day, seven days a week, for thirteen months straight. You have no
time to step back and look at things. It's not that you fall in love with
the plan, but you are the plan." This colonel now mentors junior Marine
officers who are selected to be red teamers responsible for challenging

strategies and plans before they are authorized and implemented. Because, he notes, when serving on the planning staff itself, "It's nice after an event to say, 'well we should have thought about this, and that,' but in reality you are unable to."[42]

The new red teams were forced to confront this inertia head-on. Despite the mandate from Amos that MEFs and deploying MEBs integrate red team elements into their command staffs and the readily apparent need for them, efforts were decidedly mixed in the initial years. The perception among many informed Marines is that several commanders, or their closest aides, had viewed the commandant's initiative as an unwanted, externally imposed requirement, and they had subsequently "slow rolled" the initiative to a large extent. Lieutenant Colonel Brendan Mulvaney, who directed the commandant's red team during its first three years, recalled that when his unit met with MEFs to describe the red-teaming initiative there was resistance from colonels who were the leaders of staff sections responsible for specific issues, such as personnel, intelligence, operations, and so forth. "They are all type-A guys, who would say 'if I did all of this to get where I am, why would I need to learn anything from a red team?'"[43]

Other commanders and their senior staffs contended that Marines, by nature, are independent and critical thinkers, and that creating an additional element dedicated to fostering even more independence and critical thinking would be not only unnecessary but potentially disruptive to unit cohesion and mission effectiveness. In particular, they believed that they were already effectively self-reviewing plans and policies, that they were self-red teaming—a fallacy common to many institutions. Still other Marine officers contended that although red teams can play a useful role, the style and temperament of some red teamers in practice is simply insulting to staff. Colonel Timothy Mundy, who led the II MEF red team in Afghanistan described below, warned that the initiatives can fail when the personnel are wrong. "We are the really smart guys who can think critically and independently, and the rest of you are just a bunch of oafs."[44] Of course, any red team should include personnel able to adequately communicate findings.

The Marines bureaucracy twice attempted to eliminate the roughly fifty personnel billets set aside for red teamers through the Force Structure Review Group process. In each instance, Amos had to personally order that the positions be protected. The following year, the commandant's own red team requested that Amos explicitly signal to the senior members of the Corps that the initiative was a worthwhile priority and that most people supported it. Amos found it necessary to do this twice before senior Marine officials at the General Officers' Symposia. One of these officials, Lieutenant General John Toolan, recalled: "The commandant was very frustrated, and I was the brunt of some of that frustration. It took a while for him to shake lapels before we got what red teams were, including my own lapels."[45] Additionally, the commandant's red team prepared a white paper that would have clarified the roles and missions for which MEFs and MEBs would utilize red teams. However, after being written and then rewritten over the course of two years to take into account concerns raised by various arms of the service, it was never published.

It is not unusual for a tradition-bound institution that emphasizes individual initiative and decisiveness to be skeptical of the utility of red teaming, especially in an era characterized by static defense budgets and declining personnel numbers. Nevertheless, it is rare for military and civilian Marine Corps officials to openly contest the wishes of the commandant. The most common reason that officials seemed to distrust and resist red teaming so strongly was their unfamiliarity with the process and their belief that it was unnecessary. "We'd been pretty successful in places like Anbar [province in Iraq] and Helmand [province in Afghanistan], so why do we need a red team?" was how one colonel paraphrased this sentiment.[46]

In the face of this uncertain environment, a small but growing cadre of junior officers was directed to fill the MEF and MEB red team billets. Before joining their assigned command staffs, they received basic instructions in red-teaming approaches and techniques, either through six-week courses at UFMCS or Marine Corps University (MCU). Several majors and lieutenant colonels serving in these positions reported that some commands openly accepted their role, while others said, as one put it, "thanks, but we will make you a special projects officer." Lieutenant Colonel Daniel Geisenhof, a red team instructor at MCU, noted that commanders already have an Operational Planning Team (OPT), a core group of planners that is responsible for developing and evaluating potential courses of action for the command. "The common perception you hear is, 'I'm getting this outsider, and what exactly is he doing in my planning cell?'"[47] Though in its earliest stages, these Marine red teamers quickly recognized that the only way to make their acceptance more likely was to make it clear that they were there to contribute to the mission's overall success. However, the dilemma is that the most effective way to make an impact within a command staff is by acting with subtlety, without leaving any fingerprints. Trying to overtly demonstrate that their efforts had a demonstrable impact would only make future receptivity to the red team's findings more difficult.

One early, but illustrative, example of the challenges faced by Marine Corps red teams occurred in 2011 when a six-person team was deployed to support the II MEF (forward), whose area of operations focused on Afghanistan's southwestern Helmand and Nimruz Provinces.[48] According to one member, the unit "was almost entirely marginalized" from the very beginning. Red teamers came to refer to themselves as the "kids at the card table at Christmas." They were led by a confrontational British Royal Air Force weapons engineer and situated within the Future Plans (or "5") section of the command. They nominally reported to the 5's head, who also happened to be a British officer, but who, according to his aides, never received clear guidance on how to employ the red team. However, in practice, the head of the Operations (or "3") was a Marine colonel who was, by far, the most powerful command staff, and who disregarded the red team's efforts to provide independent analysis. In retrospect, having a British officer head the red team—and receiving tasking from and reporting to another British officer—was unwise because it caused the Marine staffers to perceive the red teamers as unnecessary outsiders.

The effects of these dynamics could be seen in debates over what replacement crop Afghan farmers could grow rather than the opium poppies that were heavily taxed by the Taliban. The Marine colonel insisted the farmers grow wheat, while the red team contended quinoa was actually better suited for the soil and climate of the area. After being presented with the quinoa option one final time, the colonel declared to the staff: "They can red team whatever they want, provided everyone agrees that the villagers are growing wheat." What the red team did not know was that there already were extensive wheat-growing programs and contracts were already well underway, which basically meant that there was no longer a viable alternative. Regardless, the colonel's outright rejection of the red team's findings suggested an intolerance for alternative points of view—anathema to the very spirit of red teaming.

This red team also suffered from poor composition. Beyond the British officer, the II MEF red team was comprised of military and civilian personnel who were not seen as major players moving up the promotion ladder to important assignments. This essentially signaled to command staff that they need not be listened to. One member also noted that "the Red Team initially, at least, did not have a very clear idea of how staff actually worked." It was only after Mundy, officer-in-charge of the Enhancement Assessments Group for II MEF, arrived to serve as the leader of the red team that he found, through trial and error, a way to provide some value to the staff by providing independent alternative analysis. (It probably did not hurt that Mundy is the son of General Carl Mundy, the Marine Corps commandant from 1991 to 1995.)

Mundy made it his first priority to understand the problems that the Marine colonel leading the operations section needed assistance in addressing. After listening and observing the day-to-day operations, various staff sections—often informally during evening hours—would approach individual red team members for advice and editorial feedback on written products that were eventually read by the II MEF commander. (Major Jose Almazan refers to these secretive and unofficial contributions as the "Chaplain Effect" of red teamers.[49]) Though this was not the initial purpose of the red team, its members' adaptability to meet the unforeseen analytical needs of the II MEF command gave them some sense of accomplishment in what was otherwise a low-impact and low-morale experience.

Troubled as this team's mission was, it does not reflect a universally negative reaction to red teaming within the Marines. In fact, a later Marine Corps red-teaming effort showed much greater promise.[50] In January 2014, the I MEF began a deployment to assume command for the southwest area of Afghanistan—the last major Marine Corps command that deployed to that country. The I MEF red team was also located within the "5" plans section, but was led by a Marine Corps lieutenant colonel. Most importantly, team members reported and were tasked directly to the I MEF commanding general, who was openly enthusiastic about the red team. It was directed to challenge the assumptions of the planning staff as it developed plans for advising and supporting the Afghan security forces—rather than doing so after the fact. In addition, the red team provided an alternative assessment of the command's internal processes—specifically safety and security procedures and combat stress management programs. In June 2014, the I MEF red team was enhanced with three additional red team-trained Marines to provide an independent assessment of the plans for the scheduled withdrawal from Afghanistan.

It is an open question as to whether future Marine Corps red teaming will resemble the II MEF experience in 2011, the I MEF in 2014, or even if it will survive at all. As the Marine Corps reduces its congressionally authorized size from 202,000 to 182,000 active-duty Marines between 2010 and 2015, several senior officers have expressed the belief that Amos's red-teaming initiative will not survive. Generally, the operational specialty positions that the Marines have prioritized for preservation are those that take the longest to grow (pilots, logistics, and communications), while those that can be reconstituted quickly should the need arise have been targeted for elimination (infantry). Toolan, for one, believes that red teaming is "vitally important" for the Marine Corps, and that it should make it a priority to grow "premier red teamers who are rewarded for their efforts and work."[51] Amos's initial successor, General Joseph Dunford, appeared to be less willing to fight continuously to promote and preserve red teaming. Indeed, in his own commandant's planning guidance released in January 2015, red teams—which had been the second-highest priority under Amos—were not mentioned at all. Yet, neither were other comparable activities, as the unpredictable budget environment has made such detailed guidance largely impractical.[52] Dunford was nominated to become the chairman of the Joint Chiefs of Staff in May 2015, and it remains unclear if his replacement, General Robert B. Neller, can preserve red-teaming billets, or whether the Marine Corps will lose the unique alternative challenging and perspectives provided by red teaming. Lieutenant Colonel Brian Ellis, who replaced Mulvaney as the director of the commandant's red team, has found that, as the red team infrastructure has become further established, it has become more widely accepted among midcareer and senior officers. As long as the existing red team initiatives and billets are protected, "we are running with it and putting everything in place until someone tells us to stop."[53]

Even as the bureaucracy has imposed constraints, Marine officers have continued to spread the techniques and awareness of red teaming. In 2013, Lieutenant Colonel William "Razz" Rasgorshek accepted a teaching position at Red Team University, making him the first Marine Corps instructor at Fort Leavenworth. Actually, in keeping with the general Marine Corps resistance to the concept, when other Marines at Leavenworth learned that Rasgorshek would be moving to the Army post, they tried to have him work for them rather than at Red Team University, but were overruled by senior officials from Marine Corps Headquarters, where Amos worked. As an aviator with a quarter-century of active-duty service and multiple combat tours, Rasgorshek was another Marine officer who, by his own admission, believed himself to be a critical thinker. After going through two six-week courses on red teaming, "my brain got completely altered, and it made me question what I had been doing in the past twenty-seven years in the Marine Corps." With several classes of Marines having come through his course, he has found that there is great demand for the red-teaming perspectives that he teaches, but that once those officers are assigned to various commands they have trouble getting traction as red teamers, and command staffs struggle with integrating them into their day-to-day operations. Within the Marine Corps, the boss's buy-in, in the form of the commandant, has been present but the process has been inadequately and inconsistently structured within command staffs.[54]

To drive home what red teaming can accomplish, Rasgorshek draws upon an analogy from his experiences as a combat pilot, many of which happened at night and required using night vision goggles. Due to the absence of cones and rods (the two types of photo receptors in the eye) in the area near the optic nerve, each eye has a natural blind spot. The human binocular field of vision, which is 120-degrees vertical and 200-degrees horizontal, prevents an object from being in the blind spot of both eyes simultaneously.[55] However, for pilots wearing night vision goggles that only provide a 40-degree field of vision, a "night blind spot" can appear under conditions of low ambient light—causing pilots to lose sight of an object 5 to 10 degrees wide of the center of their field of vision. As the eyes tire, a pilot's focus will start to degrade and the blind spot will emerge undetected. Thus, in their training and safety refresher courses, pilots are taught to offset this inevitable problem by scanning from side-to-side so that they can see what they are looking at. "Similarly, there are certainly blind spots in our brains. It is a matter of educating people how blind spots develop, showing them that they exist, and then educating them so they can practice in order to control the interference of the blind spots. That is what red teaming can do."[56]

Millennium Challenge: "The Significant Butt-Kicking"

The Millennium Challenge 2002 (MC '02) was intended to be the largest, most expensive, and most elaborate concept-development exercise in US military history. The exercise was mandated by Congress to "explore critical war fighting challenges at the operational level of war that will confront United States joint military forces after 2010."[57] Developed over two years at a cost of $250 million, it would grow to include 13,500 service members participating from seventeen simulation locations and nine live-force training sites. It was intended to be an assimilation of live and simulated events, with 80 percent of the exercise consisting of forty advanced computer models, and the remaining 20 percent involving actual troops and equipment maneuvering in the field. MC '02 was developed under the direction of the Norfolk, Virginia-based Joint Forces Command (JFCOM), which was then the Pentagon's lead agent for promoting military "transformation"—the top priority of Rumsfeld. This transformation envisioned and promised by senior defense officials featured "disrupted innovations" and "leap-ahead technologies" that would provide commanders with "dominant battle space knowledge" to conduct "rapid decisive operations" against future adversaries.[58]

These untested war-fighting theories, however, existed only in the PowerPoint presentations and minds of defense intellectuals and senior Pentagon officials. The MC '02 would put them to the test and would exercise and experiment with many aspects of the "revolution in military affairs," over the course of three weeks in the summer of 2002. It was considered such an important event that Rumsfeld himself visited JFCOM headquarters to enthusiastically endorse the exercise: "MC02, as I'm told it's called—sounds like fizz water in the old days . . . will help us create a force that is not only interoperable, responsive, agile and lethal, but one that is capable of capitalizing on the information revolution and the advanced technologies that are available today."[59] JFCOM Commander General Buck Kernan summarized what was no less than the expected outcome: "MC '02 is the key to military transformation."[60]

The featured activity of MC '02 would be a red team war-game simulation. The hypothetical joint experiment would feature an anti-access, area-denial scenario that was situated in the world of 2007, pitting a US blue team staffed by 350 personnel and led by Army Lieutenant General B. B. Bell, against a red team opposition force (OPFOR) of ninety personnel modeling an adversary, and initially led by the retired Marine Lieutenant General Paul Van Riper. Kernan personally selected Van Riper to lead the OPFOR, believing that, since he was a "devious sort of guy" and "a no-nonsense solid professional warfighter," he was the best possible candidate.[61] The OPFOR, widely understood to represent Iraq or Iran's military, had a carefully prepared campaign plan, for which the ultimate objective was to preserve the red team's ruling regime and reduce the presence of blue forces in the region. The blue team also had a campaign plan, which included securing shipping lanes, eliminating the OPFOR's WMD facilities, and compelling the red ruling regime to abandon its goal of regional hegemony. To most participants, the MC '02 exercise resembled much of the "Running Start" operational plan that US Central Command (CENTCOM) planners were developing and refining in the summer of 2002 to disarm Saddam Hussein of his suspected WMD program and to remove him from power in Iraq.[62]

Van Riper had participated in previous war games for JFCOM, including the previous year's Unified Vision 2001 exercise in which he played the role of a landlocked regional power. That exercise had been designed to assess the theory of "effects-based operations," which is the process of using a full range of capabilities, rather than short-term military goals, to achieve a strategic outcome. According to its proponents, these operations call for "thinking differently about how best to employ national instruments of power . . . beyond just force-on-force campaigns, battles and engagements."[63] However, from this experience, Van Riper was aware of the potential inherent unreality of some of these high-profile war games. At one crucial engagement during Unified Vision 2001, Van Riper was informed by the white cell overseeing the game that the United States had destroyed all twenty-one of the red team's deeply buried ballistic missiles, even though the blue team commander never actually knew where they were located. It was simply assumed that in the future the United States would have the real-time radar and sensor capabilities to eliminate them. After the Unified Vision 2001 exercise, JFCOM provided a report to Congress that claimed that the exercise had corroborated the effects-based operations concepts. When Van Riper complained to his JFCOM interlocutors that that was untrue, he was promised regarding MC '02 that "next year will be a free play and honest exercise."[64] On the eve of MC '02, Kernan even declared: "We have a very, very determined OPFOR, both live and simulation . . . this is free play. The OPFOR has the ability to win here."[65]

This did not mean that MC '02 was designed without built-in constraints—in fact, it is common for military simulations to test concepts that will inform future personnel, training, and procurement decisions. For example, there was only a thirty-six-hour window during which the live-fire, forced-entry component of the experiment was to occur. The participating forces—including from the 82nd Airborne Division and 1st Marine Regiment—had been called off their normal training schedules, and would only be used in conjunction with the computer-simulated maneuvers during that window. Also, both sides were permitted to reposition their forces at night, during which time neither could initiate attack. But most notably, while the OPFOR was supposed to use only a limited set of military capabilities that it was projected to have in 2007, the blue forces were allowed to have command-and-control relationships, communication networks, and military capabilities that the Pentagon in fact planned to field well beyond 2007. These included advanced weapon systems that have never been fielded to this day, such as the Airborne Laser, or others that were not deployed until 2014, such as the Standard Missile-3 Block IB. The white cell, or "control," was the architect and manager of the exercise, and also monitored events, assessed the impacts of various actions, and provided feedback to the blue and OPFOR teams. The white cell, played by retired Army General Gary Luck, also had the authority to intervene in order to ensure fair play and to verify that all the concepts were tested under the exercise's resource and time constraints.

At the start of MC '02, to fulfill the forced-entry requirement of the exercise, blue issued red an eight-point ultimatum, of which the final point was surrender. Red team leader Van Riper knew his country's political leadership could not accept this, which he believed would lead the blue forces to directly intervene. Since MC '02 took place just one month after the George W. Bush administration announced the "preemption doctrine" in its National Security Strategy, Van Riper decided that as soon as the US Navy carrier battle group steamed into the Gulf, his red team would "preempt the preemptors" and strike first. Once the US forces were within range, Van Riper's OPFOR forces unleashed a barrage of missiles from ground-based launchers, commercial ships, and planes flying low and without radio communications to reduce their radar signature. Simultaneously, speedboats loaded with explosives were deployed in swarms to conduct suicide attacks against the US fleet. The aircraft carrier battle group's Aegis radar system—which tracks and attempts to intercept incoming missiles—was quickly overwhelmed, and nineteen US ships were sunk, including the carrier, several cruisers, and five amphibious ships. "The whole thing was over in five, maybe ten minutes," Van Riper said.[66]

The red team had struck a devastating blow against the blue team. The impact of the OPFOR's ability to render a US Naval fleet militarily worthless stunned most of the MC '02 participants. Van Riper described the mood as being like "an eerie silence. Like people didn't really know what to do next."[67] The blue team leader Bell admitted that the OPFOR had "sunk my damn navy," and had inflicted "an extremely high rate of attrition, and a disaster, from which we all learned a great lesson."[68] Meanwhile, Kernan received an urgent phone call from Luck alerting him: "Sir, Van Riper just slimed all of the ships."[69] Kernan instantly recognized that this was bad news for MC '02 because it placed at risk JFCOM's ability to fulfill the remaining live-fire, forced-entry component of the exercise. The actual forces were awaiting orders to execute their mission—at Fort Bragg, North Carolina, off the coast of San Diego, and at the Fort Irwin National Training Center—and they had only thirty-six hours during which they could be employed. Kernan recalled, "I didn't have a lot of choice. I had to do the forcible entry piece."[70] Thus, to sustain MC '02, he directed the white cell to simply refloat the virtual ships to the surface. Bell and his blue team—including now the live-fire forces operating under his direction—applied the lessons from the initial attack, and were able to fend off subsequent engagements from the red team.

On day four, Van Riper's red team prepared itself for an amphibious assault by the Marines. He knew from studying publicly available US defense-planning documents that the first wave would include the V-22 Osprey, a multimission, tilt-rotor aircraft that the Marines had in the pipeline but which was not actually fielded until 2007. The V-22's twin thirty-eight-foot propellers gave the transport aircraft a notoriously large identifiable radar signature that could easily be identified and tracked with relatively crude radars and surface-to-air missiles. The red team was ready to begin shooting down the V-22s when Van Riper's chief of staff received a message from the white cell. Hostile fire against the V-22s or blue's C-130 troop transport planes was forbidden. The white cell also directed the chief of staff that the OPFOR had to position its air defense assets out in the open so the blue forces could easily destroy them. Even after some were not destroyed, the red team was forbidden to fire upon blue forces as they conducted a live airborne drop. Van Riper asked the white cell if his forces could at least deploy the chemical weapons that he possessed, but he was again denied.

Van Riper was furious. Not only had the white cell's instructions irredeemably compromised the integrity of the entire process, but also his own chief of staff—a retired Army colonel—was receiving direct orders about how the OPFOR should be deployed. When Van Riper went to Kernan to complain, he was told: "You are playing out of character. The OPFOR would never have done what you did."[71] Van Riper subsequently gathered the red team and told them to follow the chief of staff's orders from that point on. The independence that he believed a red team must be granted to do its job had been corrupted. Six days into the exercise, he stepped down as commander and served as an advisor to OPFOR for the remaining seventeen days. During that time, the blue team achieved most of its campaign-plan objectives, by destroying the OPFOR air and naval forces, securing the shipping lanes, and capturing or neutralizing the red regime's WMD assets. The OPFOR was partially capable of preserving the red regime, but it was substantially weakened and its regional influence was much diminished.

Van Riper may have stepped down from the leadership of the red team, but he was not willing to let the matter drop. He wrote up a report detailing the numerous shortcomings of the war game, how it was controlled, and how the exercise could lead the Pentagon to have misplaced confidence in what were still-untested military war-fighting concepts. He handed the only six hard copies of the report to senior JFCOM leaders, but never received any feedback. All of those reports remain classified. Having participated in many similar red team exercises, including ones for JFCOM, Van Riper had generally found them to be useful learning tools. However, unlike the other concept development exercises, he believed that MC '02 was both egregiously scripted and falsely carried out. As Van Riper recalled: "War-gaming is not normally corrupted, but this whole thing was prostituted; it was a sham intended to prove what they wanted to prove."[72]

Before MC '02 even ended, Van Riper e-mailed several professional colleagues with his concerns about the design and conduct of the exercise. He believed that what had happened was going to leak to the media because so many of his OPFOR colleagues were irate. "What I didn't want to see happen was JFCOM putting out another press release with my name on it," as it had done after the previous year's Unified Vision 2001, "validating a concept that had failed."[73] Not unexpectedly, Van Riper's e-mail was immediately leaked to the *Army Times*, which published a comprehensive account: "Fixed war games? General says Millennium Challenge 02 was 'scripted'."[74]

The reaction to the leak was swift. Senior JFCOM and Pentagon officials were livid that the retired Marine lieutenant general had blown the whistle on MC '02. They emphasized in press conferences that every major concept had been validated (there were eleven in total), while discounting what the OPFOR had been able to pull off. Kernan, who called Van Riper "a pretty slick fellow," claimed that the exercise was not about winning or losing, despite contrary statements he had made weeks earlier. Kernan also admitted: "You [have] got to be careful about the word 'free play.' And I used it, and I wished I hadn't."[75] Vice Admiral Martin Mayer, Kernan's deputy, claimed, "I want to disabuse anybody of any notion that somehow the books were cooked."[76] When Rumsfeld was asked if he believed that MC '02 was "rigged," he deflected the question to the Vice Chairman of the Joint Chiefs of Staff General Peter Pace, who declared, "I absolutely believe that it was not rigged."[77]

Yet, JFCOM itself would later conclude the opposite. The final JFCOM report on MC '02 ran 752 pages long and was not released to the public until almost ten years later in response to a Freedom of Information Act request.[78] The report detailed how the OPFOR had initially caught the blue team off guard, in large part because the blue team stuck closely to well-known and practiced US military tactics. Moreover, to the extent that the blue team was perceived to be the winner, it was predominantly due to its quantitatively and qualitatively superior military capabilities. Meanwhile, the report admitted significant limitations and artificialities that were built into the war game, and the unexpected shifts in the rules of engagement early on. "These changes brought about some confusion and potentially provided the blue team operational advantages."

Finally, the JFCOM report explicitly acknowledged: "As the exercise progressed, the OPFOR free-play was eventually constrained to the point where the end state was scripted. This scripting ensured a blue team operational victory and established conditions in the exercise for transition operations."[79] In essence, the white cell determined that once the experiment was scheduled to end, the blue team would be allowed to win.

The independent Defense Science Board was also directed to conduct a thorough review of JFCOM exercises and of MC '02 in particular. The Board concluded that "results (what actually happened in the experience) were not distinguished from interpretations, judgments, and opinions" and "were not conclusive in any sense and must be combined with interpretations and judgments to inform the way ahead. However, a more effective telling of the MC '02 story would distinguish these."[80] JFCOM never developed any such story.

As a red-teaming exercise, MC '02 was destined to experience shortcomings from the start. Both the red team and the targeted institution had preconceived objections going into the exercise. Van Riper thought that the untested concepts and the misplaced faith in then-nonexistent technologies were dangerous and unnecessarily risky for the military to pursue. Beyond being a prominent skeptic of the ongoing revolution in military affairs, he believed that some of these untested concepts would be utilized soon in the invasion of Iraq. His red team set out to win outright, and thereby demonstrate the shortcomings of these concepts.

Moreover, he doubted whether the red-teaming process itself would be faithful to the principles of fair play that he had been promised by JFCOM, which, only three years old at the time, had a reputation for conducting unrealistic and scripted concept-development exercises.

For the last five years, Van Riper has taught the red-teaming elective at MCU, of which he is also the founding president. The central lesson from MC '02 that he conveys to his Marine officer students is that they should possesses a systems view of warfare that assumes messy complexity and multiple courses of action, rather than the more linear and mechanistic vision that he believes JFCOM officials had internalized in 2002.

The targeted institutions—JFCOM, and the Office of the Secretary of Defense more specifically—were determined to validate the principles and concepts that would support the advanced technological military transformation that Rumsfeld and his senior aides had been insisting upon. Here, the red team was not correctly scoped with a clear mandate to faithfully simulate how an enemy could realistically operate. Some of the findings from MC '02 did result in concrete changes to how the armed services prepared and fought more collaboratively in the future, including the Joint En-Route Mission Planning and Rehearsal System—the web-based communication system commanders use to receive and use real-time intelligence while in flight, and collaborate with staff and other commanders through video, voice, chat, and file sharing.[81]

In addition, courses of action underutilized during the exercise were redeveloped, specifically regarding how commanders used information operations—during MC '02 they were slowly, and therefore inefficiently, employed. Moreover, it had a demonstrated effect on many of the key participants. Bell described MC '02 as "a watershed 'eureka' moment in the application of red teaming." He believed that Van Riper did exactly what he was supposed to do by attacking the blue forces 'a-doctrinally'—meaning in a manner that JFCOM was totally unprepared for—and that everybody learned from the results. Soon after MC '02, Bell was promoted to four-star general: "The military and civilian leadership must have figured out that, after the significant butt-kicking I had experienced, I must have learned something."[82] Bell became one of the most outspoken proponents of red teaming, and estimates that he directed the formation of at least twenty distinct red teams—especially simulations of an adversary's motivations and likely behaviors—while in command positions in Europe and on the Korean Peninsula before retiring in August 2008.

However, a different enduring impact was on the minds of the senior military officials who were deployed from the United States to Afghanistan and Iraq or provided support in the years that followed MC '02. There, the inherently messy realities of combat negated the aspirational acronyms that conceptual development exercises were supposed to prove. Even during MC '02, Kernan recalled that many of the participants were understandably more focused on getting ready to go to war than on the exercise, which probably harmed the process itself. "I told Rumsfeld afterwards, 'If you want to do this again, you have to properly resource it, and if national priorities change, you have to be willing to scrub it'."[83] Yet, Rumsfeld and other senior Pentagon officials were unable or unwilling to hear the bad news that came out of Norfolk.

Ironically, Millennium Challenge 2002 has become a shorthand reference for denigrating the cutting-edge and unrealistic notions of military transformation that characterized the Rumsfeld era. A red team simulation that was intended to socialize the military around the inevitability of a leap-ahead, futuristic transformation ultimately left precisely the opposite impression. That it required a $250 million red team simulation, and a motivated and justifiably angered former Marine lieutenant general officer, to make this apparent, suggests that it was a highly useful experiment after all. Unfortunately, leaders were unwilling to hear the bad news in the case of MC '02, and did not correctly frame the scope of the activities. Those who might employ the techniques of red teaming both in the military and the private sector should heed these lessons.

Military Red Teaming Abroad

This chapter has focused domestically as a matter of practicality and access, but also primarily because contemporary red-teaming approaches and techniques have largely originated in and been disseminated from the United States. However, red teaming's benefits have led to its being readily adopted and institutionalized overseas, especially within foreign militaries that have learned from and emulated the US experience. Not coincidentally, these are all military headquarters- or command staff-established red team units, and many officers from the following three countries and institutions received instruction and socialization in red teaming from UFMCS.

Just as the military has been the institution that has most widely and frequently used red teaming in the United States, this is also the case overseas. Three of the most prominent red teams for which there is publicly available information are the Israel Defense Forces' red team conducting alternative analysss of intelligence, the UK Ministry of Defence's Development, Concepts and Doctrine Centre (DCDC) red team working for civilian and military agencies, and the NATO Allied Command Transformation AltA cell facilitating critical thinking for headquarters and command elements. A close examination of these examples will provide a sense of the increasingly global sweep of military red teaming.

In the days before the outbreak of the 1973 Yom Kippur War, Egyptian troops massed along the Suez Canal—outnumbering Israel forces one hundred thousand to one thousand—as Syrian troops assembled in the Golan Heights. Yet, these troop movements failed to raise alarms for Israeli military intelligence because they mirrored drills conducted on a regular basis. Major General Eli Zeira, head of military intelligence at the time, later said, "When an officer who is analyzing the matter looks into it for the fourth time, in October 1973, he does not take the data as data of war, but as data of a drill."[84] Zeira ignored an October 1 warning from Ashraf Marwan, an Egyptian source, who claimed that Egypt intended to go to war, discrediting it as unreliable. He subsequently chose not to authorize an additional intelligence assessment or mobilize Israeli reserves. "[Zeira] was in charge of the national assessment, but it was essentially a single person's opinion," said Zvi Zamir, head of the Mossad.[85] Minister of Defense Moshe Dayan later reflected, "I never once heard an estimate that disputed that of the Military Intelligence head. . . . They were all of one mind: that war is not likely."[86]

Just ten hours before the first strike on October 6, Israel realized that the threat of war was imminent and authorized the complete mobilization of reserve forces, which required two to three days for full deployment.[87] Five days after Marwan's warning, an ill-prepared Israel was surprised by the Egyptian-Syrian attack that commenced the Yom Kippur War, which would lead to more than 2,500 Israeli deaths. The incident is one of Israel's greatest intelligence failures.

Seven weeks later, the Agranat Commission, established by the Israeli government to investigate the shortcomings of the Israel Defense Forces (IDF), "reached a unanimous decision that the chief of staff bears personal responsibility for what happened on the eve of the war, both with regard to the evaluation of the situation and to the preparedness of the IDF." It also found that the IDF's Directorate of Military Intelligence's (DMI) analytic framework was the root cause of the intelligence failure, and called for the removal of the IDF chief of staff based, in part, on the fact that he did not conduct an independent analysis of the intelligence. It also recommended that new mechanisms be implemented to avoid similar strategic disasters in the future.[88] According to an anonymous senior Israeli intelligence officer, this led to the creation of, "within the military intelligence framework, an internal function, which would independently review and criticize the intelligence assessment product published by the Military Intelligence Research Unit."[89]

This intelligence failure spurred the creation of the IDF's own red team, Mahleket Bakara, which is Hebrew for "department of control."[90] Known informally as Ipcha Mistabra—Aramaic for "it turns out that the opposite is correct"—the unit is an independent and autonomous group within the DMI's research department. "We are the ones preventing people from being caught up in the conventional wisdom," the head of the unit has said.[91] Led by a colonel or brigadier general, it is composed of a limited number of respected, senior production officers who serve for two- to three-year terms. The unit both conducts alternative analyses of products written by other intelligence divisions and self-generates its own topics and questions. In addition, the director of military intelligence will request specific analyses. The Mahleket Bakara employs a method that translates into "the opposite may be true," through which officers consciously and intentionally reach the opposite conclusion of another division. Their alternative-analytical products—which can be a few dozen per year—go directly to the DMI but are also routinely shared with high-level officials and relevant members of parliamentary committees.[92] The briefings are described by one knowledgeable source as "exhausting," in that "they require the officers to forcibly argue with more powerful people all the time."[93] Over time, the unit has grown more reputable and reports to the head of military intelligence, Major General Herzl Halevi, rather than just to the head of the DMI research department. Like many other red teams, Israeli military and intelligence officials acknowledge that it is difficult to demonstrate the impact of the alternative analyses produced by the Mahleket Bakara. However, it remains a highly prized assignment for military intelligence officers and its analyses are widely admired by civilian and military officials.

Another country where red team principles have been recently embraced by its military is the United Kingdom. Much like US Army and Marine Corps units, British red teams are embedded within command staffs and headquarters that operate parallel to, but outside of, normal operational planning teams to challenge the norms and assumptions of the staff and ultimately improve the quality of a plan.[94] However, the leading-edge unit responsible is located in the Ministry of Defence's (MOD's) semi-independent think tank—the Development, Concepts and Doctrine Centre (DCDC), which is located in a small building on the UK Defence Academy campus in Shrivenham, near the city of Swindon. Among the roughly ninety DCDC personnel is a red team in the Development, Analysis and Research Team (DART) that since 2009 has conducted one-off engagements for military and civilian government agencies—as well as for NATO, specifically for concept-development documents and Strategic Foresight Analysis framework. Much like the US Army, the unexpected challenges and complexities of combat in Iraq and Afghanistan motivated the MOD's senior leadership to establish the red team. The traditional protocols for developing military concepts and plans were perceived to be inadequate and outdated, and new approaches were needed to stimulate creative thinking and generally make the bureaucracy uncomfortable.[95]

The DCDC red team is led by retired Army Brigadier Tom Longland and consists of a dedicated group of ten to twelve military officers and civilian analysts, who are supplemented by outside-issue-area experts on a case-by-case basis.[96] Without advertising their services, the red team accepts engagements based upon its available time and its belief that red teaming can improve a document, policy decision, or course of action for a targeted institution. Whether this is possible can often be determined quickly during initial scoping conversations with the person who approached the DCDC red team. When sponsors from the targeted institution cannot clearly articulate what idea or process they want red teamed, or what their ultimate objectives are, then they are not ready. As Longland notes: "If we don't have the time, or it is clearly just a check the box exercise, or they don't have their ideas well enough developed, we decline the job." Once an initial agreement is reached, an issue-specific red team is formed, which can include two people working for one day, or up to twenty reviewing papers and concepts over the course of three weeks. The red team will employ a series of techniques as needed, including information-quality checks, document-weighting analysis, and logic mapping, and it will conduct analysis and mapping. The DCDC red team is guided by three golden rules: 1) The red team must be able to brief somebody senior enough to make a difference; 2) The quality of the final product that is presented is the most important component; 3) If it is late, it is useless; if that final product is briefed to senior officials only after the targeted institution can use it, then it will not make a difference.[97]

Similar to US military practitioners, Longland has found that particular personalities and backgrounds lend themselves to being good red teamers, while, alternatively, "there are some people who will never be red teamers as long as they draw breath." The challenge for military establishments is that the type of people who are the best red teamers are rarely the best Army officers since, especially in peacetime, "every military system wants a safe pair of hands, so that's who gets rewarded and promoted." Moreover, as Longland observes, the most proficient red teamers might go unnoticed because they are awkward people to work with and are subsequently placed in jobs that require limited social interaction. "[Red teaming] requires a fringe effect of minor autism. They don't realize that what they are saying isn't in tune with the rest of the world; though it's logical and correct, the social implications are hidden to them." Some techniques that the DCDC unit uses to promote creativity and the free flow of ideas—which unknowingly resemble those of other red teams that tend to be successful—include the prohibition of hierarchy (the leader's primary responsibilities are administrative), banning of military uniforms, or use of first names rather than military rank as a form of address. According to Longland, the best red teamer he ever witnessed was a twenty-two-year-old female civilian who was a DCDC intern while studying international relations. She possessed a clinical ability to diagnose problems, possessed none of the hang-ups that characterize typical male, mid-forties military officers, and was totally fearless in expressing her opinion and pointing out how even the most senior military officers were wrong. And because of the uniqueness of her age and gender, her ideas were greeted with both stunned silence and receptivity.[98]

In order to collate best practices and offer general guidance for other red teams, the DCDC red team has published two editions of a *Red Teaming Guide* to counter biases, emotions, and the human tendency to simplify complex problems through assumptions and models, and to "identify the dynamics that can lead to faulty analysis and conclusions." The guide offers seven commonsense guidelines for good red teaming, which align closely with those taught at UFMCS, and borrows liberally from UFMCS's *Applied Critical Thinking Handbook*. The guidelines include "plan red teaming from the outset," "provide clear objectives," "fit the tool to the task," and "poorly conducted red teaming is pointless; do it well, do it properly."[99]

Finally, a more recent example of military red teaming abroad is the Alternative Analysis (AltA) cell formally established in April 2012 at the NATO Allied Command Transformation (ACT) headquarters in

Norfolk, Virginia.[100] AltA facilitators are trained to lead group discussions for headquarters or command elements at the request of a commanding general who recognizes that a decision or the development of a new operating concept requires critical thinking that cannot be internally generated. Fifteen to thirty-five new facilitators, taken from various ACT departments, are trained in a weeklong course once every six months. After spending a year at ACT headquarters, staff members begin AltA awareness training through educational events, after which they may be nominated to receive additional training to become facilitators. Johannes "Hans" de Nijs, branch head of operational analysis at ACT and leader of the cell, described the facilitators' goal: "We didn't want to have a team inside that says, 'Hey, I know better.' It is the expertise of the staff itself that has to come out."[101] This facilitated process, coupled with awareness training, allows AltA to socialize its purpose throughout the organization, while maintaining separation from other headquarters staff.

As is true with other red team engagements, trained facilitators have found that the most essential component is understanding exactly what the commanding general needs help with before moderating a semi-structured conversation to uncover solutions that would not otherwise have been revealed. Recalling the first time that he requested AltA, ACT Chief of Staff Lieutenant General Phil Jones admitted, "I absolutely did not know what the problem was. I knew there was a problem and I needed someone to look at it because I wasn't getting the answers I wanted from the organization itself."[102] This is often the case, and a facilitator's role is to use "intellectual intelligence" to encourage dialogue between the "problem-owner" and other stakeholders to elicit the best decision collectively identified by participants. At the close of each exercise, AltA facilitators distribute a short questionnaire for participants to fill out in order to develop a database for every setting in which AltA has been applied to evaluate its own overall effectiveness over time. Because the participants complete the questionnaire, the results convey only their perceived value of the process and methodology. Han de Nijs acknowledged, however, that they can never really prove that an AltA engagement resulted in any particular outcome. Success for AltA, according to Lieutenant General

Jones, will only be realized when critical thinking becomes a routine process throughout the organization's "mindset and culture."[103] While this transformation of all staff members into "mini-red teamers" is frequently championed, it inevitably remains unobtainable. Military concepts and tactics that are demonstrated, or believed, to work tend to spread and be adopted and tailored for other countries' militaries. The speed and depth with which red teaming will become further established overseas will depend highly upon the extent to which US military red teaming is endorsed by senior American commanders and perceived to have a positive impact by their foreign counterparts.

Conclusion

The US military's current manifestations of red teaming, as well as those of the UK and NATO, largely reflect the shared difficulties of those responsible for the planning and conduct of the second Iraq War. Retired Army Colonel Kevin Benson, a Red Team University instructor since 2007, has found that "red teams as an integral part of the design and decision-making process give commanders and staffs the opportunity to think the unthinkable—ask 'what if?', and challenge assumptions and facts."[104] Benson was a lead planner for the Coalition Forces Land Component Command (CFLCC) from June 2002 to July 2003. "I accepted as fact that we, CFLCC, could recall the Iraqi Army immediately after we took control of Baghdad. I never considered what would happen if this 'fact' did not come true."[105] The present challenge is how to justify funding and staffing a red team while the overall size of the active-duty force has decreased 5 percent from 2009 to 2014, with another 2.5-percent decrease scheduled before 2017.[106] However, as Toolan acknowledged: "If the commander wants and uses a red team, manpower concerns would be dealt with. If I needed it, I would find the personnel."[107] Whether red teams remain similarly supported and resourced by senior commanders after US military forces are fully withdrawn from Afghanistan remains uncertain. As does whether they will become less of an institutionalized devil's advocate presence within command staffs, or more of a nice-to-have capability for select commanders, like the 2007 red team exercise requested by the director of the J-7 to analyze a Chairman of the Joint Chief's Capstone Concept for Joint Operations.

The Millennium Challenge 2002 exercise was partially told from Van Riper's point of view in Malcolm Gladwell's book *Blink: The Power of Thinking Without Thinking*. That story emphasized how the Marine red teamer "created the conditions for successful spontaneity" with a decision-making style that "enables rapid cognition."[108] It was a deserved characterization of Van Riper's unique, and possibly unmatched, capacity for a senior officer to truly think like a motivated adversary. However, Gladwell did not reveal anything about the built-in structural limitations and motivations placed on JFCOM by Congress and the office of Secretary of Defense Rumsfeld. This caused Gladwell both to omit the critical background story of earlier JFCOM red-teaming efforts, as well as to overlook the limitations imposed by politicians and the Pentagon, who were simply executing the MC '02 exercise on the scale and timeline that had been carefully developed over the previous two years.

The art of red teaming took an unnecessary hit because of the constrictions and design of the Millennium Challenge, the compromised manner in which it was subsequently run, and how the press reported it. Leveraging conversations with other senior participants and the JFCOM after-action report—only made public in 2010—provides a historically accurate account of this particular concept-development exercise. The red team units and examples highlighted in the following chapter shift the focus from devil's advocates in military command staffs and simulations of future military enemies, to alternative analyses that overcome the challenges of biases and institutional pathologies that characterize the US intelligence community. The US military has benefited from red teaming when it has been championed by senior commanders and appropriately organized, and when a team's members have been empowered to speak the truth to their higher-ups and their unit. But its continued support and proliferation will always find resistance from the inherent conservatism and hierarchy that characterize military institutions.

THREE

ALTERNATIVES: INTELLIGENCE COMMUNITY RED TEAMING

A better channel should be established to convey speculative and/or unorthodox views of experienced analysts to the upper echelons of the various intelligence agencies. This might be done by means of gists of only a paragraph or two. Acquaintance with such views could provide officials with a better grasp of Soviet options and also serve to warn them of possible Soviet actions or intentions.

—Robert Gates, CIA analyst of the Soviet Union, 1973[1]

The US intelligence community (IC) comprises seventeen different organizations collectively staffed by roughly 100,000 full-time employees and is budgeted $54 billion per year for the National Intelligence Program and $18 billion per year for the Military Intelligence Program.[2] Everyone knows about the Central Intelligence Agency (CIA), these days most likely for its covert drone strikes in Pakistan and Yemen. The National Security Agency (NSA) is also broadly well known, especially since the disclosures revealed by former IC contractor Edward Snowden leaking highly classified documents. However, at its most fundamental level, the IC has not historically been as committed to operations abroad or data collection, as it has been devoted to analysis. "The absolute essence of the intelligence profession," as the former Director of Central Intelligence Richard Helms put it, is analytical—compiling all of the available information and making sense of it for officials and policymakers.[3] As summarized by then-senior CIA analyst and official Paul Pillar: "The analyst's task is akin to sifting through a large trash bin to reach conclusions about what is going on inside the building from which the trash came—a necessary and sometimes fruitful task . . . but a messy and time-consuming one as well."[4] Analysts produce "analytical products" in the form of short memos, longer research papers, congressionally mandated reports, and oral briefings.[5] Intelligence analysis is intended to forecast emerging global trends over decades, anticipate upcoming crises or opportunities, respond to breaking events, or simply answer an outstanding question posed by a policymaker.

The enduring challenge for intelligence analysts is to know—and better yet demonstrate—that their ideas made a difference. Normal authoritative analytical products created by mainline offices include "setting the scene" of the political dynamics before an upcoming election and estimating the likelihood of a certain event happening. One example of the latter was the IC warnings provided to the Obama White House about the likelihood of a Russian military incursion into the Crimea region of Ukraine in March 2014. According to the head of an IC organization, various memos and reports characterized the political protests by Russian-speaking Ukrainians in Crimea, described the massing of Russian military forces in detail, and estimated how and whether Russia might attempt to assume control of Crimea. The official noted that it was impossible to know if the warnings went unread, were read and dismissed, or, more likely, were read and taken seriously, but not acted upon because the Obama administration was unwilling to take the costly policy steps that may have prevented this outcome. Nevertheless, such analytical products are intended to inform senior officials about events in Russia and Crimea in accurate detail, not to develop policy options.[6]

The overwhelming majority of traditional analytical products developed by IC organizations every day are supposed to provide accurate, clear, and timely information about real-world events and conditions for policymakers. Whether the products monitor, estimate, or warn, their fundamental contribution is toward a better understanding of the world. This is the routine work of each "line office" for its specific area of focus. The CIA, for example, has ten line offices, four of which concentrate on political or economic issues, and six on transnational matters.[7] Such line offices within the CIA and elsewhere in the IC rarely engage in in-depth alternative analysis to provide the sort of "speculative and/or unorthodox views" that Robert Gates called for in 1973, and which are the sorts of red team analysis that are the focus of this book.[8] In response to the 9/11 terrorist attacks and the Iraq weapons of mass destruction intelligence failures, analysts have been trained since the mid-2000s in alternative-analysis techniques like structured brainstorming, "what ifs," and pre-mortem analysis. However, according to many current analysts, almost all of what they produce remains normal analytical products, which are referred to as "traditional" and "authoritative," or "mainline" analysis. This is the expected work that analysts are required to produce by their bosses, and only a limited amount of time is set aside for unconventional or alternative analysis.

Ultimately, for all of their mystique and the reverence in which they are held, intelligence agencies are simply hierarchical bureaucracies staffed by human beings. Analysts are susceptible to the same cognitive and organizational biases that limit the effectiveness of any institution. The impacts of cognitive biases on analysts are well documented and widely acknowledged. IC organizations make efforts to train analysts to identify and mitigate these issues, but, nevertheless, bias is understandably prevalent—and three types are most commonly identified by current and former officials.[9] First is the tendency to overestimate the likelihood of a high-consequence event—such as Iran developing or testing a nuclear weapon—in order to reduce the likelihood of backlash should this occur. Second is the natural socializing influence that makes it highly difficult for analysts to come to conclusions that are significantly different from their colleagues with whom they spend every workday. Andrew Liepman, an IC analyst for more than thirty years, found that there is a "homogenization of people, behavior, and products at the CIA. There is a way of thinking that seeps into your mentality, and to really fit in well you have to accept a certain group mentality."[10] And third is the dilemma of what many intelligence officials and analysts independently described as "the tyranny of expertise" among analysts, whereby they become anchored in their narrow, though deep, knowledge base about an issue. Carmen Medina, who retired after thirty-two years in the CIA as the head of the Center for the Study of Intelligence, where she led an Agency-wide lessons-learned program, recalled that "in the generalists-versus-experts debate, I favored generalists, and believed that they made the best red teamers." She explained that "the very best analysts have a tremendous sense of curiosity of the world, but truly curious people don't spend ten to fifteen years becoming an expert in something."[11] Gregory Treverton, chairman of the National Intelligence Council and scholar of intelligence matters, noted of subject-matter experts: "These people are least likely to think differently and see discontinuities."[12]

Organizational biases include segmentation, as will be seen in the case of the Al Shifa pharmaceutical factory, which occurs when analysts who lack the requisite knowledge are called upon to provide an estimate. Or, because of operational-secrecy concerns, outsiders might never actually subject authoritative analyses to a red team analysis before providing them to policymakers. Another prevalent organizational bias involves coordination problems. Though different agencies and even individual analysts can come to differing conclusions, products that are disseminated outside of the IC are generally coordinated among all of the contributing agencies to ensure that policymakers are presented with one consistent position on crucial issues. The dynamic of synthesizing various conclusions into one authoritative analysis can at times result in watered-down and generalized language that everyone within the coordinating group can agree to. Since the product is likely an updated version of an earlier one, they will often rely heavily upon whatever the previously agreed-upon language was. As former CIA Director Michael Hayden described it: "The coordination process requires sandpapering the rough edges, and sometimes the truth is found in those rough edges. I've seen many times where it diluted the product."[13] Or, as one Office of the Director of National Intelligence official described them: "Coordinated products are very boring and very obvious, by necessity."[14]

Authoritative, coordinated products are generally unsurprising as well as uninteresting to policymakers. Michael Morell joined the CIA in 1980, was President George W. Bush's intelligence briefer on 9/11, and retired as the acting director in 2013. Over the course of his experience, he found that "every policymaker intuitively understands the traditional line products. Policymakers read the sources, read what's reported in the press, and so when they read traditional analysis they aren't surprised at all."[15] This presents challenges for the intelligence analyst producer and the policymaker consumer. Analysts must somehow "break through" with unexpected findings to get a policymaker's attention. In the year prior to the Arab Spring of 2011 the CIA produced four hundred reports "that basically described the concerns that we saw in this region that had the potential for disruption," according to then-CIA Director Leon Panetta.[16] Nevertheless, once the Arab Spring broke out in earnest, policymakers complained that they had not been adequately warned far enough in advance to develop preventive options. Policymakers, meanwhile, often privilege intelligence reporting that varies from what they have come to expect, and welcome frankness about what confidence level an analyst assigns to their conclusions. Finally, there is no rigorous or systematic methodology applied throughout the IC to evaluate the accuracy or utility of various forms of analysis—not even for predictive estimates.[17]

This chapter examines several instances of red teaming, or the lack thereof, within the US intelligence community. The focus is on alternative analyses that are distinctive and different—in terms of authors, process, and final product—from the normal authoritative analytical work. First is the Team B competitive-analysis exercise that was commissioned by the CIA in 1976 to independently evaluate the strategic intentions and military power of the Soviet Union. Second is a case where red teaming was undoubtedly needed, but never requested: the 1998 bombing of the Shifa Pharmaceutical Industries Company (Al Shifa) in Khartoum,

Sudan, based on intelligence that supported the claim that it was involved in chemical weapons production and was owned or controlled by Osama bin Laden. Third is an in-depth examination of the CIA's Red Cell, created two days after 9/11 with the exclusive mandate to do out-of-the-box alternative analysis, and how it has evolved into its present-day form. Fourth is the three distinct red team probability estimates in 2011 that were developed to assign a numerical likelihood to whether bin Laden was living in a compound in Abbottabad, Pakistan. The IC has a particular need for red teaming to mitigate the cognitive and organizational biases that often weaken its analytical products, which thus have a diminished impact on the thinking of policymakers.

Team B: "Reflecting the World as They Saw It"

Within the US government, the crown jewel of all intelligence products is the National Intelligence Estimate (NIE). It is the epitome of a mainline analytical product. Typically drafted by a highly respected senior analyst and based on the latest raw data, NIEs are developed through months of coordination between all IC organizations, and then disseminated in top-secret form to inform policymakers about important trends and developments regarding particular countries, regions, or issues. Since they represent the collective judgment of the IC, NIE's findings can be highly influential in establishing the basis for foreign policy and military goals. They also risk strong criticism—among those holding security clearances—when key findings do not support a Congressional member's or an official's preferred policies. They may even be completely wrong. Famously, three weeks after the first Soviet Union nuclear test in August 1949, the CIA issued Intelligence Memorandum No. 225, which stated "the earliest possible date by which the USSR might be expected to produce an atomic bomb is mid-1950 and the most probable date is mid-1953."[18] Throughout the Cold War the NIEs that were most widely read among policymakers and, consequentially, had the greatest impact on foreign policy and US military force levels unsurprisingly dealt with

Soviet military power. Through the mid-1970s, over two hundred such NIEs were produced as new products or updated versions.[19]

In November 1974, an NIE was published that drew particular attention as it addressed a controversial foreign policy debate: whether and how to pursue détente with the Soviet Union. There were intense disagreements in and out of government about trends in the relative military positions of the United States and Soviet Union. If the Soviet Union were only building its strategic nuclear arsenal to reach a level of parity with the United States and its allies, then it would be worth pursuing arms-control agreements that froze this position between the two superpowers. However, if the Soviet Union was actually racing ahead and building up its ability to launch surprise attacks on the United States, then the policy of détente and arms-control agreements would place the United States in a position of relative weakness.[20] The November 1974 NIE, titled "Soviet Forces for Intercontinental Conflict Through 1985," expressed doubt as to whether the Soviet Union had "firmly settled on either acceptance of parity or a decision to seek a clear-cut strategic opportunity," and concluded that it was still seeking strategic superiority, but based on how the United States would react. The Army, Navy, and Air Force offered dissenting opinions, stating that they foresaw a "decisive shift of the strategic balance" in favor of the Soviet Union, which was exploiting the policy of détente to stall US advances while strengthening its own power.[21]

Members of the President's Foreign Intelligence Advisory Board (PFIAB)—established by President Dwight D. Eisenhower to provide analysis on and conduct independent evaluations of foreign intelligence programs—were particularly concerned about this NIE's findings. National Security Advisor Henry Kissinger asked them to present their concerns directly to President Gerald Ford at an August 1975 meeting, during which PFIAB member John Foster, a scientist who was former director of the Lawrence Radiation Laboratory and assistant secretary of defense research and engineering at the Pentagon, recommended, "The community should have two teams doing independent, competitive analysis." Foster told the president to "just tell the intelligence community you want a competitive estimate," to which Ford astutely replied: "I doubt you can get that kind of competitive judgment."[22] Nevertheless, the IC would undertake the effort and learn a lasting lesson about the potential politicization of red team composition and processes.

Ford directed Kissinger to issue a presidential directive to red team the NIE process. Director of Central Intelligence William Colby was ordered to "establish an independent analysis group composed of intelligence community and nongovernment representatives which would produce an experimental estimate on the capability of Soviet strategic forces, independent of NIE 11–3/8–75."[23] Colby flatly refused to comply, telling Ford, "It is hard for me to envisage how an ad hoc 'independent' group of government and nongovernment analysts could prepare a more thorough, comprehensive assessment of Soviet strategic capabilities . . . than the intelligence community can prepare."[24]

The PFIAB red team proposal was essentially shelved for the next seven months, until Colby resigned at the request of President Ford and was replaced by George H. W. Bush.[25] After reviewing the concept with Ford's senior national security advisors, Bush soon reversed Colby's judgment and authorized the experiment with "[L]et her fly. OK, GB."[26] The PFIAB then commissioned the experiment, in which outside experts would perform a red team alternative analysis to compete with the CIA intelligence assessment and see if they reached different conclusions. Thus, there would be an annual update to the November 1974 NIE through the normal process by an internal "Team A," as well as a review of its work by three external B Teams.

Team A was composed of IC analysts already working on the updated estimate, while members of the B Teams (Air Defense Panel, Missile Accuracy Panel, and Strategic Objectives Panel) were chosen by Bush and the NIE Evaluation Committee (a PFIAB committee created in response to enduring concerns with NIEs, and chaired by Robert Galvin, chairman and CEO of Motorola). Each of the B Teams was composed of ten outside experts who either had, or were given, the necessary security clearances and were directed to "work independently from the intelligence personnel and organizations involved in putting together the NIE," given access to all relevant information available to the US government, and instructed to follow Team A's production schedule.[27] The final product would be a report of their findings, to be studied and discussed by the PFIAB, and then reviewed and critiqued by a select panel of senior civilian and military consumers. Robert Gates, who was a Soviet analyst at the CIA at the time, believed that "the members of the PFIAB who wanted it done didn't care too much about Team A. They wanted a Team B to come up with answers that they thought reflected the world as they saw it."[28] Team A was tasked specifically to update the prior NIE, but, as is discussed below, the Team B red team was established without well-defined scope and objectives.

What became known as the "Team B" was the Strategic Objectives Panel, led by Harvard professor of history Richard Pipes. At the end of the day, this Team B's work would prove most controversial. Although the ground rules were established in a letter from Leo Cherne, the chairman of the PFIAB, to Bush, it was not until after the analysis was complete that participants discovered there was no clear conceptualization of Team B's purpose, task at hand, and ultimate goal or product. The structures and scope of what they were supposed to do was unclear to the red teamers themselves, as well as the targeted institution (the CIA). Pipes later recalled there was "no fixed definition of this team's mandate."[29] Team B reviewed all of the prior NIEs going back ten years to develop its own assessment, which the CIA neither intended nor expected it to do. Team B was also unaware that yet another additional panel—the NIE Evaluation Committee—would review and critique its findings.

During the first meeting between Team A and Team B—intended to give the teams time to exchange and comment on each other's drafts—it became clear that Team B was intent on discrediting Team A analysts. According to Pipes, "This outcome was at least due in some measure to the Agency's unwise decision to field against senior outside experts a troop of young analysts, some of them barely out of graduate school, who . . . could not help feeling intimidated by senior government officials, general officers, and university professors."[30] Major General Jasper Welch, a member of the Strategic Objectives Panel Team B under Pipes, recalled that disagreements stemmed from how the CIA's analysts were assigning meaning to the "scraps of information that came out of the Politburo" about Soviet aspirations. "We saw weak sourcing, and we had a fit. We were very critical of their regular work product, and we let them know 'you guys haven't done your homework'."[31] The teams met, revised their assessments based on conferring together, and then presented their findings to the PFIAB on December 21. The briefing was more of "a lecture by Pipes, and then technical talks on particle beams [circular error probability], and the backfire bomber," according to retired Admiral Daniel Murphy, deputy director of central intelligence.[32]

The red-teaming process had been seriously compromised. At issue, in part, was the inherent politicization of the experiment. Pipes, chosen primarily based on Foster's recommendation, selected the team members, though many names came from lists prepared by Foster and Paisley. Members were supposedly "selected from among experienced political and military analysts of Soviet affairs known to take a more somber view of the Soviet strategic threat than that accepted as the intelligence community's consensus."[33] However, based upon their published writings and public commentary, most were staunch anti-Soviet hardliners, who were openly predisposed to oppose the policies of détente. Melvin Goodman, head of the CIA's Office of Soviet Affairs, later reflected: "Team B represented the hard right on U.S. foreign policy; this group consistently labeled the Soviets an aggressive imperialistic power bent on world domination. Team B estimates were drafted in order to reify this worldview."[34] Even the members of the PFIAB, who had called for a Team B, admittedly had an overt agenda.[35]

Team B's final report reflected these hard-liner views, stating that the CIA had consistently underestimated the Soviet threat. The report claimed that past NIEs were based on Soviet capabilities rather than intentions and the Soviets were distinctly offensive-oriented, and accused the CIA of "mirror imaging" the United States in past NIEs, despite the fact Team B engaged in mirror imaging itself.[36] Ultimately, Team B's depiction of the Soviet Union disregarded any possibility that the Soviets might change their motivations or behavior in the future. When Bush released the NIE that was produced by Team A in the normal authoritative

IC analytical process, he attached a letter registering his opposition to aspects of the Team B experiment:

> The experiment in competitive analysis that was begun with this *Estimate* has not been completed, and any final judgment on its utility cannot be rendered. Nevertheless, there is a negative aspect that is already clear and which concerns me deeply; namely, the selective leaks regarding the details of the process and, worse, the substantive conclusions developed by the "Team B" panel that was concerned with Soviet strategic objectives. Inspired by these selective leaks, allegations have appeared in the press that the judgments appearing in this official *Estimate* were shaped by pressure from the "Team B." There is no truth to such allegations. The judgments in the attached *Estimate* are the best that can be made on the basis of the analysis of the available evidence.[37]

Indeed, the leaks began just two days after Team A and Team B met, with a story of the experiment appearing on the front page of the *Boston Globe*. David Binder from the *New York Times* was promised the full story, including an interview with Bush, if he waited until the experiment was complete. After Binder's article appeared on the front page of the *Times* on December 26, the story spread, exacerbating the politicization. In a *Washington Post* article one week later, Richard Pipes and anonymous government officials and Team B members gave a "laudatory and self-serving account of their work." The leaking and actions of Team B members led to inquiries by congressional committees. By February 1978, the Senate Select Committee on Intelligence (SSCI) issued a report titled "The National Intelligence Estimate A-B Team Episode Concerning Soviet Strategic Capability and Objectives." Pipes claimed that a draft of the report "accused [Team B] of coming up with preconceived notions, working with PFIAB, and [implied] that the purpose was to force Carter to increase DOD expenditures."[38]

The final version of the SSCI report found that Team B's contributions were "less valuable than they might have been" because the process was too heavily structured by the PFIAB and the director of central intelligence, resulting in a narrow analysis that paid too much attention to criticizing past NIEs.[39]

Though Bush appeared in the media to defend the process, he later wrote a memo to Cherne on his last day as the director of central intelligence stating that Team B had set "in motion a process that lends itself to manipulation for purposes other than estimative accuracy."[40] The Team B report would not be declassified for eighteen years, making it difficult to refute its conclusions that were leaked to the media. Moreover, the hardline views of the Team B members would soon find a home in President Ronald Reagan's administration. Of its ten original members, six held positions under Reagan while another served as his presidential campaign's military advisor.

As a red team initiative, the Team B exercise did little to provide a useful alternative-analytical perspective for policymakers. Welch thought that the three primary points of contention—Soviet air defense expenditures, ballistic missile accuracy, and global intentions—would always be contentious issues no matter what the outcome of the exercise was.[41] Although Bush and other high-level leaders apparently bought into and supported the initiative, and Team B was given full access to information necessary to perform its duties, other aspects of the process contributed to its ineffectiveness. The CIA and White House were unable or unwilling to act on Team B's findings—even if they were flawed. When Bush was asked what to do with the Team B results, he replied, "Nothing. I have to go along with my own guys."[42] Moreover, the composition of the team lacked much variety or any truly divergent thinkers. The rushed manner in which it was initially approved, misunderstandings about the scope of its activities, and manner in which the Team B members acted ensured that the only enduring process impact that the initiative had was to make sure that "Team B" was never replicated. Gates, who served in the CIA for another fourteen years including as deputy director and then director of central intelligence, recalled: "Team B wasn't embraced by the Agency, because everyone saw it as a pretty naked attempt to get the answers they [the PFIAB] wanted. It also cast a pall on alternative analysis for years."[43] In fact, when alternative-analytical concepts reemerged in the early 2000s, the term "alternative analysis" became commonplace, rather than "competitive analysis" due to bad memories of Team B.

In 2009, Representative Pete Hoekstra, the senior ranking member of the House Permanent Select Committee on Intelligence, declared that the 2007 NIE on Iran's nuclear weapons program was flawed: "Our intelligence analysts seem to be stuck in an analytical rut and unwilling to alter their corporate line on Iran's nuclear program. . . . I propose this problem be addressed by establishing a 'red team' of independent experts to challenge the career intelligence analysts' assessment of the Iranian nuclear program."[44] The director of national intelligence, retired Admiral Dennis Blair, did not offer any response, and Hoekstra's calls, despite being restated three years later when the International Atomic Energy Agency released a report detailing unresolved questions of Iran's nuclear program, went unmet. Though a select number of conservatives—including Team B member Paul Wolfowitz while serving as deputy secretary of defense in 2001—periodically resurfaced the idea of a Team B analysis, the proposals never gained traction for fear of repeating the prior failed experiment in red teaming that had been characterized and inherently flawed by its politicized composition, unclear objectives, and inevitable leaks to the press.

Al Shifa: A Missed Opportunity

Just as bad as misused red teaming are situations where red teaming is needed to challenge groupthink but is never undertaken. Soon after the August 7, 1998, bombings of the US embassies in Tanzania and Kenya—killing 224 people, including eleven Americans—the CIA was convinced it had correctly identified the perpetrator. Based upon the lengthy monitoring of a terrorist cell in Nairobi, Kenya, responsibility was placed squarely upon Al Qaeda and its leader Osama bin Laden. Using a metaphor that later became infamous by his conclusion that Iraq possessed WMD, Director of Central Intelligence George Tenet actually told Bill Clinton and

his senior aides, "This one is a slam dunk, Mr. President."[45] To reduce
the likelihood that US response options could leak and thus tip off members of Al Qaeda, these intelligence reports were presented exclusively to a
self-described "small group" of roughly one dozen senior US officials who
maintained their daily schedules so as to not raise suspicion and met in the
White House situation room. The small group soon endorsed a military
retaliation against targets in multiple countries simultaneously, simply in
order to emulate the embassy bombings themselves, to demonstrate resolve against the transnational terrorist organization, and to attempt to
kill bin Laden and other senior Al Qaeda leaders. However, it would later
be discovered that one of the strikes was based on woefully inadequate intelligence and that dissenting opinions from within the IC were not taken
into consideration by the small group, though even a cursory red teaming
of that intelligence would have likely uncovered its glaring flaws.

In the months prior to the embassy bombings, senior policymakers—
including those who would comprise the small group—had been primed
by repeated intelligence warnings from the CIA about Al Qaeda's alleged
efforts to acquire WMDs. Two CIA analytical reports concluded that
the Al Shifa factory was owned by or connected to bin Laden and was
involved in the production or shipment of chemical weapons based upon
the alleged existence of a nerve gas precursor. The physical evidence consisted of a single soil sample obtained nine months earlier by a European
citizen operative of Middle Eastern descent who told his CIA handlers
that he had evaded security guards to get onto the factory's grounds.[46]
Analyzed at a Department of Energy (DOE) laboratory, the clump of soil
was found to contain two-and-a-half times the normal trace of O-ethyl
methylphosphonothioic acid (or EMPTA), a chemical precursor used in
the production of deadly VX nerve gas. Relying upon more circumstantial evidence that had been prepared by the CIA just two days before
the embassy bombings, National Security Council (NSC) staffers also
concluded that bin Laden "has invested in and almost certainly has access
to VX [nerve gas] produced at a plant in Sudan."[47]

By chance, the day after the embassy bombings, the CIA received
strong evidence based on communication intercepts and a human source

inside Afghanistan that bin Laden had ordered a meeting be held at the Zhawar Kili training complex in Khost Province, Afghanistan, on August 20. Tenet told the small-group members that perhaps two hundred to three hundred militants and Al Qaeda leaders, including some arriving from Pakistan, were planning to attend. Upon hearing this information, the small group soon reached a consensus to attack the gathering.[48] With just this one retaliatory target ready for final authorization from President Clinton, the CIA, US Central Command (CENTCOM), and the Joint Staff in the Pentagon were directed to develop additional Al Qaeda-affiliated targets outside of Afghanistan, per the small group's agreement soon after the embassy bombings that a military retaliation must include targets in two countries. As Bruce Riedel, who was the senior director for Near East and South Asian affairs in the NSC, said: "You got the Christmas tree effect—what else do you want to go after?"[49] Eventually, roughly twenty additional targets in three countries—five in Sudan, others in Afghanistan, and more than one in a Persian Gulf country (probably Yemen)—were put forth.

Based upon the information that Tenet presented, the small group mistakenly believed that the Al Shifa pharmaceutical factory was linked to both chemical weapons production and bin Laden, and thus, it overwhelmingly endorsed destroying it with a cruise missile strike in conjunction with the attack on the Al Qaeda gathering in Afghanistan on August 20. One additional target, a tannery, also in Khartoum, that bin Laden had received from the Sudanese government as partial payment for a massive road-building project was also included in the final list submitted to Clinton, who had left on August 18 for a previously scheduled vacation in Martha's Vineyard. According to his autobiography, Clinton "took the tannery off the list because it had no military value to Al Qaeda and I wanted to minimize civilian casualties."[50] On the morning of August 20, the President gave his final approval to retaliate. US Navy warships launched thirteen cruise missiles to destroy Al Shifa, and sixty-six more, which severely damaged the training complex in Afghanistan. Though perhaps twenty to thirty suspected Al Qaeda militants were killed, bin Laden and all his senior aides survived.

What Clinton and the small group did not know was that CIA reporting about Al Shifa was weak and inconclusive. Due to the overriding operational security concerns, the intelligence had never been subjected to a red team competitive-intelligence assessment to test or evaluate its sourcing, assumptions, or conclusions. Moreover, for reasons that remain unclear, the analysis was done exclusively by the Counterterrorism Center (CTC) rather than by experts within the CIA's Nonproliferation Center, which was supposedly the CIA's primary collection-and-analytical unit for all WMD issues, including the coordination of WMD-related assessments across the IC agencies. Senior members of the Nonproliferation Center only learned about the proposed military operation thirty-six hours beforehand, and they immediately voiced concerns about the sourcing and analysis of the soil sample, in particular. By coincidence, the director and deputy director of the Nonproliferation Center ran into Tenet in the Agency's cafeteria on August 19, and warned him "you know, there are some real issues about the Al Shifa facility." Tenet assured them that those issues were being worked through.[51] However, the CTC did nothing of the sort, and the Nonproliferation Center's assessment of the intelligence was never requested. Deputy Director of the CTC Jami Miscik recalled: "This was a case where the compartmentalization within the CIA would really hurt us."[52]

The subsequent dissent against what the CTC analysts had prepared, and Tenet had presented, was immense. Mary McCarthy, the NSC senior director for intelligence, had worked at the CIA for a dozen years, including as an analyst for Africa affairs, and was the White House's lead interlocutor with the Agency. She found Tenet's briefing unpersuasive, and his conclusive judgment regarding the evidence in need of further refinement. McCarthy wrote a memo on August 11 to National Security Advisor Sandy Berger that warned: "The bottom line is that we will need much better intelligence on this facility before we seriously consider any military options." This memo was not shared with the small group, which would not have been unusual, but Berger never asked her to elaborate on her concerns. She would not be told about the cruise missile strikes until late on the evening of August 19.[53]

Like other IC agencies, analysts from the State Department's Bureau of Intelligence and Research (INR) were not asked to review the Al Shifa intelligence. Only one INR analyst, "Steve," a senior Middle East expert, was directed to come to the White House on the evening of August 19, and only to help prepare diplomatic cables that would be sent out after the missiles had been fired. Soon after the attack, INR analysts collectively told their boss, Assistant Secretary of State Phyllis Oakley, that the CIA's evidence was insufficient to tie Al Shifa to bin Laden or to claim the existence of chemical weapons. Oakley recalled that not only were the INR analysts' opinions not sought before the attack, but she also believed the small group "didn't vet the information at all. And then didn't prepare for the negative public reaction that followed."[54]

There was also disagreement, beyond the Nonproliferation Center, within the CIA itself about Al Shifa. The month prior to the Embassy bombings, in a three-page memo, analysts had questioned what definitive conclusions could be drawn from the soil sample, and recommended covertly obtaining additional samples from Al Shifa, ideally using a different vetted operative.[55] This never happened. According to *New York Times* journalist James Risen, three additional senior CIA officials, including Deputy Director for Operations Jack Downing, "believed that the attack was not justified."[56] Even before Tenet gave his final White House briefing about bin Laden's connections to Al Shifa, a group of senior CIA officials met with him and held a straw poll about whether to support the attack; the majority warned: "Don't do it." The analysts' worries about the soil sample, Downing's concerns, and the straw poll results were never shared with the small group.[57]

Finally, General Anthony Zinni, commander-in-chief of CENTCOM and officially in charge of the cruise missile retaliation, recalled that the CENTCOM intelligence staff had never heard of Al Shifa before the CIA nominated the target for destruction. After Zinni retired, he worked as a consultant for the CIA, where he conducted a thorough review of the Al Shifa intelligence portfolio. As Zinni recalled: "You could see right away there were problems with it."[58] Moreover, every member of the Joint Chiefs of Staff—other than its chairman, General Hugh Shelton—were only informed about the Al Shifa bombing the day before it occurred. They unanimously and strongly opposed the operation.[59]

However, the small-group structure that was used to debate a military retaliation against Al Qaeda prevented dissenting opinions from reaching decision-makers. Though the rationale understandably was to prevent a potential military operation from leaking, IC officials nevertheless contended that a red team competitive-intelligence assessment could have been done with just a few analysts. The likelihood of a leak in such an instance would have been extremely low. Moreover, there were more than five days between August 14 and 19, during which time a small red team—ideally comprised of WMD experts from the Nonproliferation Center or a DOE laboratory that had not conducted the initial soil sample analysis—could have completed an assessment and presented its findings to the small group. Finally, such a red team estimate could have been decisive in persuading the small group, and ultimately Clinton, not to attack Al Shifa because debates about its target-worthiness extended well into the evening of August 19. At one point, a senior White House official tried to contact Tenet—who was told to make himself available that evening—to get further clarity about the intelligence regarding Al Shifa on behalf of Attorney General Janet Reno. When his security director answered the phone, he simply replied, "The director has retired for the evening," and refused to wake Tenet up.[60]

The bombing of the Al Shifa factory was a diplomatic disaster. It turned out that bin Laden had no connection to the targeted factory. In fact, the CIA had no knowledge of the actual owner—a Sudanese businessman named Salah Idris—until after the attack. Moreover, the soil sample that allegedly contained the nerve gas precursor was actually obtained across the street from the factory four months before Idris bought it. The factory was neither a highly secretive site, nor was it heavily guarded, as Clinton administration officials had first claimed. Additionally, the designer of Al Shifa, an American who built pharmaceutical plants around the world, said it contained none of the equipment required to make nerve gas—worse, the CIA only contacted him to inquire about the factory's capabilities one week after missiles had already destroyed it.[61] During the weeks following the strikes, Clinton administration officials were forced to publicly backtrack from almost all of their initial claims. Eventually, the Treasury Department unfroze all of Idris's US-based assets; a tacit acknowledgment that he was in no way connected to Al Qaeda or WMD production.

Writing in his memoirs nine years later, Tenet acknowledged: "You can still get a debate within the intelligence community on how good a target al-Shifa was."[62] In reality, there was little to no debate among all of the analysts and officials interviewed for this book. Though some could understand why the small group felt compelled to bomb any target that could be connected to Al Qaeda and WMDs, nobody thought that the underlying intelligence that supported the CIA's central claims was valid. These analysts and officials also acknowledged that they would have gladly put forth their dissenting opinions in the requisite time frame if they had ever been solicited. Moreover, having such a debate *after* the intelligence was used to inform policymakers was pointless. The purpose of conducting a red team competitive-intelligence assessment before August 20, 1998, would have been to test, verify, and refine an authoritative analytical finding.

Of course, there is no guarantee, had the intelligence been red teamed, that either the small group or President Clinton would have changed their minds. However, the closed structure of the decision-making process and the compressed time frame made meaningful red teaming nearly impossible, and thus could not have ultimately improved the outcome. Intelligence estimates, whether authoritative or alternative, are a critical component of a policymaker's calculus, but they are not always decisive. The small group had been conditioned by extensive earlier reporting about Al Qaeda's interests in and potential acquisition of WMD, and was concerned about the potential political consequences of inaction if there were a lethal attack on an American city. It was also forced to come up with a second military target, because officials believed that emulating Al Qaeda by bombing two targets in two countries simultaneously would somehow demonstrate America's resolve and deter the terrorist organization from undertaking any similar attacks.

Nevertheless, a red team would have at least made them aware of the strong dissenting viewpoints from within the Agency that were not represented, as well as those from non-CIA IC analysts. At a minimum, it would have compelled them to demand further clarifying information about Al Shifa before endorsing its destruction. However, they never heard the bad news from those analysts who had enormous doubts about the intelligence, and instead were unknowingly overconfident about the conclusions based upon that intelligence. As small-group member Secretary of Defense William Cohen later wrote about Al Shifa: "The intelligence community at the highest level repeatedly assured us that 'it never gets better than this' in terms of confidence in an intelligence conclusion regarding a hard target."[63] The small group should never have held such a high degree of certitude.

Jami Miscik, who was given the unenviable task of compiling the talking points used by senior officials to justify the bombing of Al Shifa, believed that "if the Nonproliferation analysts had been brought in to review the intelligence, it would have given a fuller and richer assessment of the estimate for the decision-makers."[64] And if they still required a second target, the tannery in Khartoum was as plausible a candidate as any because it was actually owned and controlled by bin Laden. As Under Secretary of State Thomas Pickering, who only learned of the small-group decision on August 19, recalled, "a red team assessment would have been helpful, and it was a mistake not to have had it."[65] In this case, it was a self-inflicted mistake by both the small group and the IC to have refrained from red teaming. The small group was led to believe by Tenet that the intelligence was reliable and, because it was set upon retaliatory strikes against the most viable Al Qaeda-connected targets, never considered establishing a red team, despite repeated warnings from IC analysts about the validity and conclusiveness of the underlying intelligence.

Inside the CIA Red Cell: "I Wanted My Mind Stirred"

Around midnight on September 12, 2001, Director of Central Intelligence George Tenet summoned his chief of staff, John Moseman, and the CIA's deputy director of intelligence ("the DI"), Jami Miscik, to his seventh floor office in the Old Headquarters Building.[66] In the confused aftermath of the previous day's unprecedented terror attacks, senior White House officials were confident that there were additional plots against the US homeland, and that the CIA needed to better anticipate the range-of-threat scenarios that officials should be prepared for. In response, Tenet decided to form a group of contrarian thinkers to challenge the conventional IC thinking within the intelligence community and mitigate the threat of additional strategic surprises through alternative analysis. Tenet later wrote: "I wanted people so far out of the box they would be in a different zip code." On that evening his instructions were simple: "Tell me things others don't, and make seniors [officials] feel uncomfortable."[67]

The following morning, Miscik and two senior analysts formed the CIA's Red Cell, which has been a semi-independent alternative-analysis unit within the Agency ever since. It was intentionally not called a "Red Team" because the unit was intended to have a much more expansive purview than a traditional red team, which was understood to focus solely on an adversary's intentions and capabilities. Furthermore, the term "cell" was chosen by Tenet personally since he believed it sounded more alluring and conspiratorial. Though there had been units that did alternative analysis before, such as the Strategic Assessment Group, they had had limited time and freedom to truly think outside the box. If nothing else, the Red Cell has succeeded in having an unmistakable cachet and in having cultivated an air of mystery, and its products are widely perceived by non-IC officials as having a unique and unmatched ability to make them think. David Petraeus, CIA director from 2011 to 2012, characterized the Red Cell in a manner that was representative of the sentiment heard from other officials: "They were phenomenal at questioning and challenging the conventional assumptions, but they could do it with the right balance of not getting voted off the island."[68]

At its outset, and unsurprisingly, the Red Cell dealt exclusively with terrorism-related issues, producing three-page memos bearing titles such as "How Usama Might Try to Sink the US Economy" and "The View from Usama's Cave," in which analysts speculated on what might be going through bin Laden's mind. None of the Red Cell's initial four or five analysts were terrorism experts, and only one was a Middle East specialist. In this case, members were individually selected for their analytical capabilities, creativity, and mindset. They were a mix of junior analysts, one GS-12 (a midlevel federal employee), as well as senior CIA analysts, a National Security Agency analyst, and a CIA case officer. Though the Red Cell aligned with the typical national security discourse among Washington policymakers, one senior analyst, Carmen Medina, thought that the Red Cell was "way too masculine and way too white in its early days," which "means they were certainly missing out on some developing world perspectives."[69] Miscik recalled that the goal was to get fresh sets of eyes to reconsider the range of terror threats: "We wanted creative people who could take the existing reporting and put it back together in different ways."[70] Or, as Paul Frandano, who codirected the Red Cell during its first four years, put it more directly: "Tenet charged us to piss off senior analysts. If we weren't doing that, we weren't doing our job."[71] Some senior analysts indeed were pissed off that nonexperts were questioning their work, while others later acknowledged they were simply jealous of the Red Cell. Meanwhile, others never saw the point. As Philip Mudd, the deputy director for analysis in the Counterterrorist Center at the time, recalled, "I didn't object to what they wrote, but I would always ask 'so what exactly do you want me to do with this?'"[72]

From its earliest days, the Red Cell has been distinct from mainline directorate of intelligence units in several consequential ways.

First, its directors personally select most of the analysts that serve on the Red Cell from many well-qualified applicants within the IC. Directors seek people who are analytically fearless, excellent writers, and deeply knowledgeable about history and world affairs. Harder to find, but nevertheless necessary, are individuals with the characteristics of "playing well in the sandbox with others," checking their rank and ego at the door, being bureaucratically savvy, and having the ability to laugh at themselves daily.[73] Red Cell analysts contend that such traits are meaningful because—when compared to other IC offices—the development of ideas and final products is done through a much more collaborative process of constant dialogue and feedback. Analysts generally serve on the Red Cell for between three months on short-term projects and the more standard two-year terms before they return to their mainline units within the CIA or other IC agencies. The reason for this rotational practice is both to keep the Red Cell fresh and also to expose as many analysts as possible to alternative-analysis techniques. "We wanted to make them atypical in their analytical approaches," described one senior CIA official.[74]

Second, the Red Cell generally sets its own agenda and primarily self-tasks the issues and countries or regions it will focus on. It is largely insulated from the daily requirements of answering tactical questions, drafting speeches, and briefing policymakers downtown. Moreover, unlike other CIA offices, the National Intelligence Priorities Framework guidance does not apply to the unit. Roughly 75 percent of its work is self-tasked, and is based upon analysts watching the calendar of upcoming events, scanning Twitter, blogs, and op-eds, or open-endedly brainstorming topics with colleagues and invited outsiders from the IC and other government agencies, policy wonks, or academics. One biannual brainstorming session is referred to as "Idea-Palooza," which looks retrospectively at how the world has unexpectedly changed and how the Red Cell might help policymakers think about possible surprises in the upcoming months. A Pentagon official who participated in several of these sessions gushed: "There's a crackling kind of energy as soon as you walk into the room."[75] Several members claimed that the most memorable products covered issues that they had wrestled with for years, but could only write about with the time and freedom provided during their tenure with the Red Cell. Before analysts pursue such solo projects, they must first get approval from a director, and it is generally granted.

The Red Cell is also occasionally tasked as a formal requirement from an IC official or perhaps the White House. This occurs more often informally through open-ended questions posed during morning meetings or by the directors of mainline analytical offices, who ask if the Red Cell could take a fresh look at an issue or country that confronts them. For example, a regional national intelligence officer may request that the Red

Cell reanalyze one of the countries they are responsible for covering, and ask it to make the case for how the countries could experience a sudden state failure. In one example, a March 2010 memo assessed how policy-makers could sustain Western European support for the ISAF mission in Afghanistan, recommending specifically that appeals from President Obama and Afghan women could potentially overcome the growing public skepticism for the war.[76a]

Third, the Red Cell's analytical products are themselves often phys-ically different from those produced by mainline offices. In 2001, before the first reports were distributed, a label was added on the left side of the title page alerting readers that it was not, and should not be considered, an authoritative analysis of the subject. The warning was later standard-ized: "This memo was prepared by the CIA Red Cell, which has been charged by the Director of Intelligence with taking a pronounced 'out-of-the-box' approach that will provoke thought and offer an alternative viewpoint on the full range of analytic issues." That text appears on a secret February 2010 Red Cell special memorandum: "What if Foreigners See the United States as an 'Exporter of Terrorism'?"—which was pub-lished in its entirety by WikiLeaks. The three-page memo, which was representative of Red Cell products at the time, broke with conventional wisdom by discussing the impact of emigrants from the United States, or Americans themselves, who take part in terrorist activities abroad. The memo stated that this could become a more widely held perception, leading terror groups to actively recruit Americans, or countries to request the rendition of US citizens whom they claim to be terrorists.

The Red Cell has evolved over time from a hastily assembled group focusing on terrorism that made senior officials feel uncomfortable, to one that has become more structured, dedicated to broader global cov-erage, and more widely accepted within the IC. It was more formally established in the 2004 Intelligence Reform and Terrorism Prevention Act, which includes legislative language that Red Cell members them-selves played a strong role in shaping.[76] It has also more than doubled in size, with roughly a dozen analysts presently serving at any one time, and has become a highly desirable posting for aspiring or even senior IC analysts. "It's where the action is," is a description commonly used by IC officials and staffers.

With the caveat that its products are distinct and already strongly endorsed by most directors of intelligence, the Red Cell has been creative in how it catches the eyes of senior officials who are otherwise too busy to read intelligence analyses. In September 2012, Petraeus directed the Red Cell to "take on our most difficult challenges" and "shock us."[77] In attempting to shock senior IC officials and policymakers, at times its analyses have been *too* creative.

Former National Security Advisor Stephen Hadley routinely opposed what he believed were the Red Cell's conclusory and eye-catching titles. He recalled telling more than one CIA director: "Please don't give me eye-catching titles, because they alone will stick in people's heads and may not be supported by the piece."[78] To enhance the likelihood its content is read, the Red Cell openly borrowed best practices from the publishing world. In April 2012, its members met with staffers from *Foreign Policy* magazine to learn how the editors capture readers' interest through catchy headlines, "listicles," and photographic slideshows. As Blake Hounshell, *Foreign Policy*'s managing editor at the time, recalled of discussions with the Red Cell: "I didn't realize that we were in the same eyeballs business, but they wanted to know how our stuff went viral. The techniques that we considered to be 'click bait' were what they were most interested in."[79] One Red Cell product was turned into a graphic novel, as an experiment, but it was never formally distributed. It is notable that several of these techniques first adopted by the Red Cell have been utilized to frame and package other IC mainline analytical products.

The Red Cell is now less confrontational and more transparent with its mainline colleagues and others in the IC. Before tackling an issue or region, the Red Cell might now alert the relevant group chief ahead of time (though they have no say in what the Red Cell pursues or publishes), and even let them know when the product will be released so they will not be surprised. Close watchers and consumers of the Red Cell also contend that its work has become less "alternative" and speculative in nature, and more actionable and responsive to current events. A rare critique of the Red Cell's recent work is that it has become reminiscent of journalists or bloggers, who have to come up with something to write about even when the topic might not be worth pursuing. This criticism is met by most other observers, who contend that the Red Cell's work has become more analytically rigorous, and, like most IC products since the disastrous Iraq WMD misdiagnosis, more willing to show the homework and sourcing supporting an analyst's assumptions. Also, line offices have been authorized to do an increasing (though still limited) number of their own alternative analyses over the years, which officials say has eaten into the Red Cell's work. The requirement to show more homework, the growing length of Red Cell products, and the red-teaming competition from line offices, help explain why the Red Cell has produced fewer products over time despite having a larger staff.

Another consistent observation that consumers offer is that once you get past a catchy headline, the Red Cell's analysis is not that unique or unusual. But rather its work should really be viewed in comparison with the normal dry, generic, or boring intelligence analytical products often associated with those of mainline offices. As secretary of defense, Robert Gates made a point to read every Red Cell analysis that came across his desk. "I never skipped past one of them. . . . I found their analysis pretty useful because, while they were an alternative perspective, I never found that they had fallen off the edge of the world."[80] A senior intelligence official outside of the CIA, who otherwise praised the Red Cell's ability to consistently reframe an existing topic, also thought that "in some respects, their work gets read specifically because it is produced by the Red Cell, not necessarily because it is value-added."[81] Michael Hayden, the CIA director from 2006 to 2009, found the Red Cell's work "a little too much like science fiction at times," but also insisted that, "I read everything it produced closely because I wanted to have my mind stirred."[82] He added that most of the CIA's mainline analytical products generally could not accomplish this.

Indeed, as is true of any alternative-analysis unit, evaluating the Red Cell's effectiveness in stirring minds or promoting out-of-the-box thinking is challenging because it can rarely be proven that any Red Cell product directly resulted in a new policy outcome or changed an official's way of thinking about something. Moreover, Red Cell directors and members note that it is often impossible for mainline offices to demonstrate the significance of their own standard analytical work. But the demand for the Red Cell's work has been high and sustained since September 2001, and, for most intelligence analysts, having one's work sought-after and read by senior officials is the ultimate professional goal and demonstration of relevance. Demonstrating the ultimate boss's buy-in, President George W. Bush read almost every one of the Red Cell's products, and would routinely question Red Cell analysts personally in the Oval Office, telling them: "I am going to ask tough questions, but I'm not going to ask you to change your views. I want to understand what you're telling me."[83] Senior NSC officials in both the Bush and Obama administrations have also been avid readers. In part, this is because policymakers become conditioned by reading authoritative analytical products, and, unsurprisingly, are then interested and even enthusiastic when the IC produces something unexpected and original.

While the Red Cell was created in the wake of 9/11 to deal exclusively with the prospect of additional terror surprises, its ability to adapt to the needs of its consumers strongly demonstrates the utility in supporting and resourcing an enduring alternative-analysis office. Beyond the demand from policymakers to read what the Red Cell produces, its impact has also been felt within the CIA and the broader IC. Alternative analysis is now more widespread and accepted in large part because the Red Cell was established and endorsed by successive CIA directors. Moreover, these directors have wisely allowed the unit to change and evolve over time to answer the perceived demands of policymakers. They have also made the Red Cell a "safe to fail" environment, which has fostered unconventional and challenging analytical products—of mixed quality and utility—that would have never been created otherwise. One Red Cell member described their "hit rate" at "50/50"—meaning having an impact on policymakers' thinking—observing, "If [policymakers] like us too much, we're failing at our mission."[84] Providing a similar assessment, Michael Morell, who read hundreds of Red Cell products before he retired in 2013 as the acting CIA director, described the unit as resembling a home run hitter for whom you learn to live with the strike-outs. "For every seven duds, you get three brilliant pieces. So you have to learn to live with the duds, and not try to smother [the Red Cell] with traditional oversight that would kill its creativity."[85] This batting average far surpasses the impressions that mainline analysis customarily has on senior officials. Of course, whether a Red Cell product compels officials and policymakers to change a policy remains completely up to them.

Osama bin Laden's Compound: From Zero to Fifty Percent

The hunt for the most wanted man in the world, Osama bin Laden, has been exhaustively retold in articles by investigative journalists, interviews with Obama administration officials, a memoir written by one of the US Navy SEALs directly involved in the raid, and even an Academy Award-winning movie, *Zero Dark Thirty*. The story captures President Obama's commitment to finding bin Laden, and the subsequent pains-taking work of IC analysts, combined with a little luck, that led them to a high-walled compound in Abbottabad, Pakistan, where the Al Qaeda leader was believed to be living with several family members. Despite the vast resources that were directed toward spying on the compound and the multiple streams of circumstantial evidence, prior to the raid, the IC could not definitively confirm whether bin Laden was there. In early March 2011, during his initial presentation to President Obama and all the senior aides, CIA Director Leon Panetta acknowledged that there was no conclusive evidence that bin Laden was at the Abbottabad compound and that he, personally, estimated the probability to be no greater than 60 to 80 percent.[86]

The prospect of deploying twenty-three Navy SEALs, their inter-preter, and a search dog 100 miles into Pakistani territory only to fail to achieve their intended objective was daunting. The operation risked the further deterioration of relations with Pakistan, whether it succeeded or not. In response, the Pakistani government could have reduced its counterterrorism cooperation with the United States, denied overflight rights to CIA drones operating in the Federally Administered Tribal Areas, and hampered Afghanistan war operations by further limiting access to overland supply lines or vastly increasing its support for the Taliban.[87] The absence of conclusive evidence, likely harm to diplomatic relations and counterterrorism cooperation with Pakistan, risks to the Navy SEALS, possibility of collateral damage, and domestic political consequences if the operation failed collectively made the CIA's initial judgment an ideal candidate for alternative-analysis red teaming.

Most of the analysts (primarily with a task force from within the Counterterrorism Center [CTC]) who tracked down the person they believed to be bin Laden had been on the case for years, some for more than a decade. Their deep immersion in the search made them susceptible to tunnel-vision bias, whereby preconceptions and heuristics cause people to choose or privilege evidence that supports a desired outcome, while suppressing or ignoring information that disproves it. Moreover, according to several officials, the task force was an exceptionally confident group, given their experiences in the preceding years at capturing or killing senior Al Qaeda leaders. For example, one of the CIA's lead analysts—an actual person who was portrayed as "Maya" by Jessica Chastain in *Zero Dark Thirty*—told her colleagues that she was 95-percent confident that bin Laden was there, and later informed the SEAL team that her confidence was "one hundred percent."[88] The senior manager of Maya's analytic unit fixed his certainty at a lower, but still robust, 80 percent.[89] Subsequently, to ensure that a final decision was not based on biased analysis, as Senator Diane Feinstein, chair of the Senate Select Committee on Intelligence, aptly characterized the alternative analyses applied to the bin Laden intelligence: "They red-teamed it, and red-teamed it, and red-teamed it."[90]

There is an inherent tension in empowering an external group to review the intelligence for such a sensitive military mission. On the one hand, the more people who know about—or are "read in"—to a top-secret activity, the greater the likelihood that it could leak into the public domain and upend the entire endeavor. On the other hand, if only a limited number of senior officials are permitted to be aware of the activity, they will be unable to debate and discuss the matter with trusted external advisors who might provide vital alternative insights. Moreover, an insulated group could unknowingly produce a flawed intelligence estimate that has not been even cursorily challenged by informed outsiders. As the Al Shifa episode demonstrates, this latter possibility has indeed been an unfortunate reality for the United States in recent history.

Tragic or embarrassing episodes such as the destruction of Al Shifa, the failed 1980 Delta Force raid in Iran to attempt to free American hostages held in Tehran, and the 1993 Black Hawk Down disaster in Mogadishu, Somalia, were on the minds of Obama administration officials in the spring of 2011 as they considered the evidence supporting Osama bin Laden's whereabouts. Given that capturing or killing the terrorist leader was among President Obama's highest priorities, those officials were willing to accept some uncertainty about the intelligence and the potential downsides of the military mission. Yet, they consciously accepted that there was a risk that news of the Delta Force raid would leak, in exchange for challenging the CIA's initial estimates. Moreover, there were more than two months of sustained discussions among senior officials, which permitted sufficient time for competitive-intelligence red teaming.

Three separate red teams reviewed and challenged the sourcing intelligence and potential courses of action against bin Laden. The methods and outcomes of the first two remain highly secret, though many vivid details have become public. The first was conducted by the CIA-led bin Laden task force that authored the initial estimates that placed the terrorist leader in Abbottabad. They set aside a few days to reexamine all of the data and consider whether there were any alternative hypotheses that fit. The second was done at the direction of Michael D'Andrea, the chief of the CTC.[91] He selected four trusted analysts who had not been read-in to the bin Laden collection-and-analysis effort, and sought their views separately. As Michael Morell, the deputy director of the CIA at the time recalled, D'Andrea "wanted to know what other smart people thought and whether their analysts had actually missed something."[92]

Among the other possibilities that these two red teams considered were that both Abu Ahmed al-Kuwaiti, the "courier" who led the CIA to the compound initially, and the anonymous tall individual in the compound were either warlords from Afghanistan who ran their businesses from Pakistan or were drug dealers from the Gulf who simply kept a private life.[93] The CTC analysts' red team estimates ranged from 50 to 80 percent.[94]

The final red team effort was conducted under the lead of the National Counterterrorism Center (NCTC).[95] The largely unknown story of the NCTC's efforts provides an illustrative example of how red teaming is often conducted on behalf of multiple objectives.

In this case, red teaming was done, in part, to provide historical cover for the White House in case the raid failed.[96] In March and April of 2011, President Obama's senior national security team met multiple times to review and debate the intelligence, military options, and potential political and diplomatic implications. At the end of an April meeting, Michael Leiter, the director of the NCTC, warned National Security Advisor Thomas Donilon and White House Senior Counterterrorism Advisor John Brennan: "If this goes bad, you will want to be able to point to the red team results." Leiter considered the CIA's estimates that bin Laden was in the compound as being exceptionally strong, and though he knew of the prior red-teaming efforts, he thought, "of course, the CIA could not red team its own assessments."[97] Leiter's principal deputy, Andrew Liepman, who had been the deputy chief of the Counterterrorism Center before moving to the NCTC, agreed that "you couldn't have the same people that lead the hunt, to assess whether they found the right guy."[98] It was left to Brennan and Morell to give the green light to Leiter's proposal for a final red team. Though it was perceived as a little late in the game since most of the senior intelligence officials, including Leiter, had only been read-in to the effort two weeks before the operation, Brennan and Morell thought that it would not hurt to have another group take one more look at the intelligence. Moreover, it might be useful to have a "cover your ass" competitive estimate on hand if things went wrong.[99]

Leiter then created an NCTC red team consisting of three senior analysts who had not yet been read-in to the intelligence regarding bin Laden and the Abbottabad compound—two from the NCTC and one from the CIA. Granted access to all of the IC's supporting information, they were given forty-eight hours to poke holes in the CIA's analysis and to try to prove an alternative case for who could be in the compound. They were not explicitly directed to interpret the information skeptically, as some have reported.[100] Leiter recalled that the NCTC red team "found some holes that people hadn't considered and some assumptions that were challenged." Specifically, they found that there were assumptions about the methods used to communicate with bin Laden that were almost certainly wrong if it were true that he lived within the compound. All three analysts concluded, based upon the available evidence, that there was an assumption that bin Laden was there. Leiter went a step further and individually asked each of the three analysts what percentage they would assign to the likelihood of bin Laden being in the compound: the first said 75 percent, the second 60 percent, but the third—who was the one most closely connected to counterterrorism and Al Qaeda issues in his career—said only 40 percent.[101]

It was at one of the final discussions before the launch of Operation Neptune Spear—the raid that killed bin Laden—that Leiter presented his red team's findings to Obama and his senior aides. Leiter's presentation was especially consequential, according to three participants, because the NCTC-led effort was the final red team conducted regarding bin Laden's location, and the last one that decision-makers would hear. Leiter summarized the analysts' results, but the only number that stood out was the 40-percent probability, which he pointed out was "thirty-eight percent better than we've been for ten years."[102] President Obama asked if that estimate was based upon any new information. When Leiter explained to him that it was not, Obama declared, "this is a flip of the coin" as to whether bin Laden was actually in the compound, adding, "I can't base this decision on the notion that we have any greater certainty than that."[103] Obama essentially processed and compressed all of the various probability estimates that he received into just a 50-percent likelihood.[104]

Obama asked an open-ended question to the room about why so many different intelligence analysts were independently producing such a range of estimates. Panetta turned to Morell, the number two CIA official, for an answer, who explained that the confidence variables were grounded in the personal experiences of the analysts. Those who had been directly involved in targeting the high-value Al Qaeda-affiliated terrorist for almost a decade had known nothing but success, and were subsequently very assured in their judgment. (As noted earlier, the CIA analyst referred to as "Maya" in *Zero Dark Thirty* told officials that she was up to 100-percent confident that bin Laden was there.[105]) However, those who had lived through the false 2002 Iraq WMD National Intelligence Estimate disaster were more circumspect about arriving at a conclusion with incomplete information. "Even if we had a human source inside of the compound who swore that bin Laden was there, I still couldn't offer a ninety-percent estimate, because humans lie and tell you what you want to hear," Morell later reflected.[106]

There remain disagreements about the utility of the three red team assessments. Secretary of Defense Robert Gates found that the range of estimates served as "a healthy and useful dose of realism as we did the planning." However, he added, "the thing that was the most persuasive was that, for all the shortcomings of the intelligence, we knew that it was the best shot of getting him since Tora Bora."[107] On the other hand, Mike Vickers, undersecretary of defense for intelligence, told author Peter Bergen that the final NCTC red team effort "really didn't change anything."[108] However, Leiter was more positive and believed that it "helped everyone clarify their thinking one last time," and dispelled anyone's concerns that the CIA or any single individual was mischaracterizing the intelligence regarding bin Laden.[109] Another senior administration official recalled that, while the results did not change anyone's minds, they were valuable in that they made everyone more comfortable with the ultimate decision when Obama authorized of the Navy SEAL operation on May 2, 2011.[110]

The value of competitive-intelligence red teaming is to identify the strengths and weaknesses of and refine an authoritative analytical estimate by empowering fresh eyes to reevaluate assumptions and conclusions. The analysts brought in to red team were both senior and immersed enough in the intelligence to be respected and listened to, but had been outside the mainline analytical processes when they were called upon, and were therefore more objective. In the case of the red teaming done in March and April of 2011, this was a worthwhile and successful endeavor. Analysts overwhelmingly believe that assigning numbers to what are inherently subjective estimates can lead policymakers to have a false sense of precision. And yet, even the degree of certainty in the case of the bin Laden raid, based upon multiple independent sources, was unprecedented since 9/11. As Liepman characterized that either/or estimate: "We were at 0 percent for a decade, so going from 0 to 50 percent meant a lot to everyone."[111] Furthermore, had the Navy SEALs unexpectedly found out that bin Laden was not in the Abbottabad compound, or had the operation gone tragically wrong, then the NCTC's red team would have served as proof that the White House had carefully thought the matter through.

Conclusion

The type of "speculative and/or unorthodox views of experienced analysts" that Robert Gates called for in 1973 in the opening quote of this chapter has since found sustained support in the intelligence community. Nevertheless, it remains appropriately limited since the vast majority of what the intelligence community produces is still mainline analytical reporting. As Gates acknowledged: "That's the bread and butter of intelligence, and we are very good at that. Policymakers value, depend upon, and have grown so accustomed to it that this must always be our focus."[112] The dilemma for established alternative-analytical units is to help policymakers who consume their products think about alternatives and the future in a manner that mainline analysts cannot. If this is perceived as being too implausible—and therefore unhelpful—it will be ignored. Indeed, while the Red Cell motto—"Where no idea is too bold"—is verbally appealing, if its products were truly too bold, they would not be nearly as widely read. Moreover, demonstrating the utility of alternatives to a mainline analysis is difficult—as Stephen Hadley, who was an avid Red Cell consumer for more than seven years at the White House, described: "If they can get an 'A-ha moment' that a policymaker did not have before, that seems to me a good day's work."[113] For one-time IC red team engagements, such as the 1976 Team B and the 2011 bin Laden probability estimates, the more significant challenge has been to correctly identify what issues policymakers need help thinking through, and how this particular red team can be effective to that end. In the case of Team B, the multiyear efforts of the PFIAB to challenge the National Intelligence Estimates that underlay the policy of détente with the Soviet Union, and the composition of the Team B itself, clearly telegraphed what its conclusions about the CIA's Team A National Intelligence Estimate would be. It was an example of alternative analysis with clearly premeditated and biased intent. The three distinct red team probability estimates produced to challenge the initial estimate by the CIA's bin Laden task force that the terrorist leader was in the Abbottabad compound also had obvious motivations beyond rigorously assessing the facts. The White House wanted the president and senior policymakers to feel confident in the decision-making process, and to have a "cover your ass" card to wave in case bin Laden was not there or the military operation failed.[114] Of course, the fact that red teaming was used in preparation for America's most important post-9/11 special operations mission proves how crucial it has become for the intelligence community. Finally, in the case of the Al Shifa pharmaceutical factory, red teaming by relevant experts in the CIA Nonproliferation Center or DOE laboratories could have provided the group with a better understanding of why there were widespread doubts about the soil sample and the facility's alleged connection to bin Laden. However, as many senior IC officials have made clear, intelligence is only one input that decision-makers take into account, and blanketing Al Shifa with cruise missiles was a decision that the small group and President Clinton were likely going to endorse, given that they were primed to worry about WMDs and insisted that they needed a second target to "demonstrate resolve."

While the IC's red teaming has been focused on alternative analyses and competitive-intelligence estimates that mitigate cognitive and
institutional biases, the homeland security sector has experienced an entirely different set of challenges. As the following chapter will show, red
teaming can also take the form of vulnerability probes used to assess
whether homeland security defensive measures can withstand the challenges posed by motivated and skilled adversaries.

FOUR

ADVERSARIES: HOMELAND SECURITY RED TEAMING

The one thing I learned doing red teaming was that no matter what technological barriers were in place, with just a little bit of surveillance you can figure out how to beat every single defensive system.

—Bogdan Dzakovic, former head of the FAA Red Team, 2013[1]

In the spring of 1974, Stephen Sloan was a tenured professor of political science at the University of Oklahoma, whose work primarily focused on political violence in newly independent states.[2] Field research proved to be tricky. For example, while he was conducting interviews for his doctoral dissertation on student indoctrination programs in Jakarta, Indonesia, in October 1965, the military coup that toppled President Sukarno broke out. "I had to change my dissertation subject," he later admitted, "because my interview subjects just kept disappearing."[3]

In 1974, he decided to visit Israel with his wife Roberta Raider Sloan, and write up his experiences in an eight-part series for his home state's largest newspaper, the *Daily Oklahoman*.[4] That freelance writing assignment, combined with the emerging prevalence of terrorist violence emanating from the Middle East, led him to significantly reorient his research toward what was then—with the exception of pioneers like Brian Jenkins at the RAND Corporation—an almost nonexistent academic field: international terrorism. "I was greeted by total indifference from my colleagues, who told me 'terrorism can't happen here,' or 'that does not fit within the mainstream of political science'." Sloan's initial terrorism seminar, innocuously titled "Problems in Comparative Politics," was offered in 1976, and is believed to be the first such course available at a university within the United States.[5]

The limited research into the phenomenon of international terrorism at the time had primarily attempted to answer two questions: "Who are they?" and "What do they want?" Sloan, relying upon RAND's terrorist-incident databases and those that he created with students, instead addressed the more prosaic question: "What do they do?"

It was while examining the operational aspects of modern terrorism that Sloan became motivated to develop realistic red team simulations for law enforcement and counterterrorism personnel. "I was interested in doing more than just writing about what terrorists did." Sloan's wife, who was a professor of theater, also at the University of Oklahoma, suggested that he apply improvisational techniques for the "terrorists" and "hostages" to permit responding law enforcement to train in a realistic, dynamic scenario. Participants created a character and wrote a biography for that individual, which detailed their motivations and objectives for becoming a terrorist. In more than one simulation, Roberta Sloan would herself play the role of a handgun-toting terrorist, under the pseudonym "Leila." As Stephen Sloan recalled: "The two primary inspirations for my simulating terrorism were my long-standing research into political violence and my own love affair for my wife."[6]

In September 1976, Sloan designed and led his first simulation after he convinced Bill Jones, the captain of the University of Oklahoma Police Department, to realistically test how officers would respond to a hostage-taking incident. The simulation was held at the department's shooting range, with special operations forces' reservists faithfully assuming the roles of the terrorists. It quickly became clear that the department was wholly unprepared for such an event. By the end, as Sloan recalled, "there were bodies of police officers all over the ground and Jones was swearing profusely." Two months later he led a more elaborate simulation: a hostage-taking and aborted skyjacking of an executive aircraft at the university's Max Westheimer Airport, to which the Norman Police Department was called upon to respond. Though the terrorists were able to detain several hostages and force them onto the plane at gunpoint, the hostage negotiators—who were from the New York Police Department (NYPD)—were able to deescalate the situation and end the simulation with only two people killed, which was considered a tremendous success.[7]

Throughout the 1970s, Sloan wrote several papers, occasionally in collaboration with his doctoral student Richard Kearney, describing how law enforcement personnel should conduct realistic red teaming. At the time, there was virtually no guidance or training manuals for how local law enforcement personnel should prepare and respond to the sort of violent terrorism that was frequently breaking out in airport terminals and during aviation hijackings, a routine occurrence at the time, with three skyjackings per month between 1973 and 1977.[8] The military's specialized Army Delta Force or Navy SEAL counterterrorism forces did not yet exist, much less the Special Weapons and Tactics (SWAT) units that are now ubiquitous in major metropolitan areas and on many university campuses.

Sloan and Kearney's articles appeared in less-distinguished outlets, like the *Daily Oklahoman*, *The Police Chief*, and *International Studies Notes*.[9] These culminated in what was a groundbreaking book when first published in 1981: *Simulating Terrorism*. Based on the more than fifteen simulation exercises that he had conducted over the previous half-decade, Sloan's book aggregated his observations and findings to provide detailed guidance for simulation-training techniques, thereby subsequently transforming and standardizing how law enforcement prepared for incidents of terrorism.[10] He would further refine his research, culminating in his 2012 book, coauthored with Robert Bunker, *Red Teams and Counter Terrorism Training*, which included a chapter written by Roberta Sloan on the improvisational techniques that one should use when playing a terrorist.[11]

In the four decades following the publication of his 1981 book, Sloan ran terrorist simulations all over the world for multinational companies, government ministries, military counterterrorism units, and local law enforcement. As he developed and refined his approaches, he learned that there are four factors intrinsic to an effective red team simulation. First, "you must have command support" from senior decision-makers within the institution, with those people assuming their real-life roles as they would be in a hierarchy: "I don't want captains playing colonels, or colonels playing generals." Second, the composition of the team matters tremendously. Sloan found that former special operations forces were the best "terrorists" because they could act ruthlessly and innovatively as the barely scripted scenarios unfolded. Actual actors who were unafraid to be loud and had obnoxious ideologues made excellent hostages. "I would always avoid macho guys who wanted to brag about their military or police experiences. Their lack of self-control and common sense made them a liability to the exercise." Third, multijurisdictional tensions must be built into the simulations in order to replicate the inevitable conflicts that emerge when local, then state, and then FBI forces arrive at an actual, potentially very violent, crime scene. Fourth, during the after-action briefings, Sloan would emphasize the positives and the learning that had occurred, but would also detail each shortcoming, with specific recommendations as to how they could be prevented or mitigated. He would also emphasize to the senior decision-maker that they could always choose to ignore what the red team revealed, but would then become responsible for any terrorist attack resulting in financial liability or dead people.

The red team simulation exercises that Sloan and others led the way in developing have become widespread. Sloan's ideas are now practiced by law enforcement agencies at all levels throughout the United States. Protecting people and things, and enforcing the law, are missions that lend themselves to evaluation and potential improvement that rigorous red teaming can provide. The federal lead for most such activities is the Department of Homeland Security (DHS), including the National Cybersecurity Assessment and Technical Services (NCATS) team, which conducted 384 cyber-hygiene scans in fiscal year 2014, and conducts between thirty and thirty-five cyber penetration tests for unclassified federal agencies each year.[12] This includes monthly cyber-hygiene automated scans of public access points, and two-week manual penetration tests of government agency networks upon request, on a first-come-first-served basis. Before each engagement, the red team meets with the chief security officer of the agency to scope the test and develop a plan. One government employee always leads the team, and three or four subject-area experts are hired as contractors for the two weeks.[13] During a penetration test for one agency, the team found that there were more than nine thousand computers connected to a network, when the agency previously believed it had somewhere between two and three thousand. In another instance where an agency began with five thousand public web servers, the red team was able to reduce that number to one hundred, thereby exponentially shrinking the potential pathways for a cyber attack.[14]

Besides the cyber domain, physical security can also be improved through these red-teaming techniques. The Government Accountability Office (GAO) conducts vulnerability probes of federally funded programs at the request of Congress and under the authority of the comptroller general to reveal security shortcomings and offer corrective recommendations for the relevant federal agencies. Using only information that would be available to the general public, these federal investigators successfully smuggled radioactive material across the southern and northern US borders in 2006, bomb components into nineteen unidentified airports in 2007, bomb components into federal buildings in ten-out-of-ten attempts in 2009, and a simulated explosive into a major secure seaport in 2011.[15] Before taking on an engagement, the GAO team, composed primarily of former criminal investigators, conducts a feasibility study that scopes the defenses of the targeted federal agency to determine if the team is suitable for the work. The vulnerability probe itself is then rigorously documented to show precisely how the investigators were able to gain unauthorized access to some secure facility or area. Finally, the findings are put through a quality-assurance process, given to the agency for comments, and then published in a report with recommendations.[16]

Between 2003 and 2008, the GAO conducted numerous assessments of US borders and was able to use counterfeit identification to gain entry in 93 percent of the cases—through the northern borders of Washington, New York, Michigan, and Idaho; the southern borders of California, Arizona, and Texas; and internationally through airports in Florida and Virginia.[17] By 2008, the GAO began to look at unmanned and unmonitored areas near ports of entry. In four states on the northern border, state roads near the crossing were found unmanned, and in three states on the southern border, investigators were able to cross undetected with radioactive materials and contraband. In one instance, even after border patrol agents were alerted of the investigators' suspicious activities by a citizen, the agents still could not locate them before they crossed the border.[18]

Tests conducted by the GAO between 2003 and 2007 also unearthed weaknesses in the DHS's Customs and Border Protection (CBP) document-fraud detection, when investigators were able to enter from Mexico by land and from Canada by boat without even showing identification, and internationally by air through Virginia and Florida.[19] In addition, GAO reports in 2006 revealed security weaknesses in the CBP's ability to detect cargo containing radioactive material. To address these poor findings and other vulnerabilities, the CBP's Operational Field Testing Division (OFTD), under the Office of Internal Affairs, now conducts red team testing of land, sea, and air ports of entry and checkpoints in the United States to simulate how adequately border guards prevent terrorists and radioactive materials from entering the country. Between 2006 and 2013, the OFTD conducted 144 covert operations at eighty-six locations.[20] Since 2009, CBP investigators have repeatedly crossed borders using fake passports, licenses, or documentation. Even in instances where agents were suspicious, investigators were frequently able to persuade agents to allow them to cross.[21] In an effort to address document-fraud vulnerabilities, the CBP created a "Back to Basics" training course for agents in 2010, and has since taken steps to evaluate its effectiveness, though there have not been any conclusive results. Unfortunately, the findings of CBP's covert tests have been deemed Sensitive Security Information and are not publicly available.[22]

re well versed in the layout of the substation and its communication
.es, and avoided detection by security cameras, disappearing just one
.nute before the first police car arrived on the scene. Overall, the as-
.lt was low tech because the gunmen's arsenal consisted of no more
.an wire cutters, night-vision goggles, and high-powered rifles.[25] No
.gerprints were found on the shell casings and no traceable footprints
. tire marks were left at the site, leaving law enforcement officials bereft
. leads and unable to investigate further. Power was quickly rerouted
.ound the site to avoid power outages and maintain stability of the sys-
.n, precluding a major blackout, and there were no injuries. However,
.me customers in Silicon Valley were asked to conserve power, and it
.ok nearly a month to repair the damages. Two years later, no arrests
.d been made—even after PG&E announced a $250,000 reward for
.formation about the incident—and law enforcement officials remain
.ffled by the motive of the attackers.[26] Astonishingly, the same substa-
.on was targeted by thieves in August 2014, despite PG&E's efforts to
.hance security after the April 2013 breach.[27]

Jon Wellinghoff, chairman of the Federal Energy Regulatory Com-
.ission (FERC) at the time, called the attack, "the most significant in-
.dent of domestic terrorism involving the electrical grid that has ever
.curred" in the United States.[28] US officials repeatedly warn of the vul-
.rabilities of the nation's electrical grid to cyber attacks. However, the
.tack on the PG&E substation shed light on the physical vulnerability
. the country's electrical system, whose roughly 2,000 transformers are
.onnected by three big grids: one in the East, one in the West, and one
. Texas. Though it is unclear whether PG&E conducted vulnerability
.sessments to test the physical security of the facility before the attack
.curred, the company and industry have since taken steps to address
.is gap. In June 2014, in response to the attack, PG&E unveiled a
.00 million, three-year plan to boost security at Metcalf. This happened
.ortly after the North American Electric Reliability Corporation filed a
.tition with the FERC—which regulates the United States' high-voltage
.ansmission system—to develop a standard to prevent physical attacks

Just as the GAO and DHS agencies increased their focu
tional terrorism after 9/11, the Nuclear Regulatory Commi
has sought greater security for US nuclear plants. The NRC
power plants to standards modeled after the classified Desigr
(DBT), which assumes attacks will be carried out by multi
possibly suicidal, highly trained personnel, armed with ex
intent on causing deadly nuclear fallout. To test plants' prep
security compliance, the NRC requires them to undergo f
(FOF) drills at least once every three years. These exercises ai
the DBT in order to identify weaknesses in the facility's secu
Within an agreed-upon window of time, an external mock
versary force will attempt to penetrate and simulate dama;
set" of key safety components. In 2012, the NRC condu
three FOF inspections at twenty-two commercial nuclear p
fuel-cycle facility, eleven of which were found to have perf
ciencies. One exercise "resulted in the simulated destructi
age to a complete 'target set' of vital plant components th
attack."[23] Whenever the FOF drills indicate that protecti
DBT is insufficient, plants are required to promptly implen
security measures.

The inherent challenge with red teaming that tests t
government facilities or critical infrastructure—such as
chemical facilities, wind turbines, communications netv
or highways—is to demonstrate the added value of preve
Too often this requires a highly visible or consequential bre
before these investments are made or mandated. Consid
at the Pacific Gas and Electric Company (PG&E) Metcal
Substation in San Jose, California. Just before 1:00 A.M
2013, at least two gunmen slipped into an underground v;
telephone cables, thereby circumventing the security came
sensors at the facility. In less than an hour, the attacke
than $15 million in damage by firing over one hundred ro
out seventeen large transformers powering parts of Silico
released hazardous material that later had to be contained

(including a requirement for undertaking risk assessments), devise security plans based upon evaluated threats and vulnerabilities, and conduct "third-party" verification of the assessments and plans.[29] However, the proposal does not characterize what type of threats the facilities should protect against or the defenses they should use, and it allows them to perform third-party verification for each other.[30] It is impossible to know if red teaming could have prevented the Metcalf break-in and subsequent damage, but it would have assuredly uncovered many of the substandard security procedures in place and raised security awareness among the substation's security personnel.

It is clear that homeland security is particularly well suited to red teaming—however, as will become apparent, the findings of red teams have not always been heeded, with dire results. The four case studies of red teaming in the homeland security field that follow have either never been told, or were reported in a limited and incomplete context. First is the tragic story of the Federal Aviation Administration red team that repeatedly documented and reported glaring aviation security vulnerabilities before 9/11, but whose findings did not lead to sustained improvements in those security systems. Second, a contrasting feature will look at the vulnerability assessments conducted in the mid-2000s of the threat that Man-Portable Air Defense Systems (MANPADS) posed to New York City airports, the findings of which informed the Crisis Response Plan activated by the Joint Terrorism Task Force. Third is the NYPD commissioner's tabletop exercises that senior commanders and selected New York City officials are required to participate in, without any knowledge of the high-consequence terrorism scenario that is prepared, in order to evaluate how they would respond in a real-life setting. These have contributed to NYPD terrorism-response strategies, due in large part to the buy-in from former Commissioner Ray Kelly. And fourth, the evolution of the Information Design Assurance Red Team (IDART) at Sandia National Laboratories, which has refined and promoted red-teaming approaches and techniques since its founding in 1996 and now plays a leading role in teaching and spreading an awareness of red teaming within the US government.

Pre-9/11 FAA Red Team: "A Substantial and Specific Danger to Public Safety"

Steve Elson is the kind of person who ends phone calls with the matter-of-fact warning: "Remember, your government is trying to kill you." One might dismiss this threat as a paranoid rant—until one remembers that Elson actually spent most of his professional life working for the government, devising novel ways to kill Americans.

A US Navy SEAL for twenty-two years, Elson went on to lead clandestine special operations teams that conducted vulnerability probes to test the defenses of military bases, nuclear submarines, and supposedly secure facilities where senior military and government officials lived and worked. These included stealthy, unarmed "soft attacks" on the Camp David presidential retreat in rural Maryland—"the Secret Service was astounded how many times the guy playing the president went up to presidential heaven"—or simulated force-on-force "hard attacks" in which "we would break into a commander's house and spirit them out of there, right in front of their families," Elson recalled.[31]

In 1999, after retiring from active-duty military service, Elson served on the Federal Aviation Administration (FAA) Special Assessments Team, soon commonly referred to as the "red team." The red team concept had emerged from a recommendation of the Presidential Commission on Aviation Security and Terrorism that was formed after the December 1988 bombing of Pan Am Flight 103 over Lockerbie, Scotland, which killed 270 people.[32] In that attack, Libyan operatives apparently smuggled a Semtex explosive bomb hidden in a radio cassette player inside a suitcase, which had been stored in the plane's forward cargo hold. The bomb was likely detonated by a barometric trigger device once the plane reached an altitude of 31,000 feet. No onboard passenger had checked that suitcase—rather, it had originated in Malta and either been transferred to Pan Am 103 or substituted for an innocent piece of luggage at Frankfurt International Airport. At the time there was no policy of "bag matching" to ensure that every bag loaded on the plane belonged to a corresponding onboard passenger. During an FAA inspection of Pan Am security at Frankfurt two months prior to the bombing, an agent had specifically pointed out the lack of such a tracking system for interline luggage.[33] The FAA red team, created in the aftermath of Pan Am 103, was intended to identify such shortcomings by conducting realistic vulnerability probes, and became operational in March 1991.

Yet, from the start, the FAA red team would struggle to make an impact on airport and airline security. Though it was founded in response to a clear need, demonstrated by the Lockerbie bombing, no foundational mission statement or guidance document was ever drawn up to clearly govern the conduct of the red team's operations, the scope of its activities, or the management of its findings. Interviews with early members and administrators, and reviews of strategy documents from the FAA's parent agency, the Department of Transportation (DOT), reveal that the foundation for what the red team would do was, in large part, based upon the personalities and professional experiences of the most senior people involved. This is no way to manage a bureaucracy. It was not until 1994 that an administrator first drafted a "Concept of Operations" paper, but even this document lacked specificity with regard to the type of vulnerability probes to be conducted, criteria for selecting test locations, or content of the red team's reports. Formal legislative language was equally vague—signed into law in October 1996—mandating that the FAA administrator "conduct periodic and unannounced inspections of security systems of airports and air carriers to determine the effectiveness and vulnerabilities of such systems," including "anonymous tests of those security systems."[34] Rather than guidelines codified in some sort of written document, a series of formal and informal understandings emerged between the red team and its FAA overseers. Needless to say, this resulted in confusion as red teamers and managers were replaced.

Over time, it emerged that the red team was to be independent from the FAA's day-to-day regulatory oversight of airport and airline security, and would consist of, on average, four or five elite agents. It was mandated to emulate how terrorists were believed to operate in aviation fields and to do covert testing of existing security procedures that the airline industry was supposed to have implemented. Red team members received top-secret intelligence assessments of terror groups from the FBI and CIA, but found the information to be of such poor quality that they overwhelmingly relied upon open-source information and informal law enforcement contacts as the basis for emulating terrorist tactics. Worse, the team could not self-task to decide where it would conduct a vulnerability probe, but rather had to receive written permission from a more senior official. Or, at times, the security team at a local airport could request that the FAA red team come in to review and assess its own security procedures. While it was tasked with conducting vulnerability probes at domestic or international airports—first alerting the local US embassy ahead of time for the latter—they were supposed to be no-notice tests for the evaluated security officers, and they could not ever disrupt commercial activity. This put it at a significant though understandable disadvantage because it could not interfere with the day-to-day operations of an airport, while terrorists obviously would do this intentionally.

Finally, the red team was required to document its findings in the form of reports that were shared up to the level of the associate administrator for Civil Aviation Security (CAS).[35] The data from the reports would then be shared with CAS field units that were responsible for deciding what follow-on remedial action, if any, should be taken. (The red team's findings were never shared directly with any airport or airline security officials.) This could lead to an administrative action in the form of a warning notice or a letter of correction, which included documentation of the corrective actions taken, or agreed to be taken, by the violator. Alternatively, the FAA could impose a civil penalty of a small fine of less than $50,000, which was typically reduced further through negotiations between the FAA and an airline's lawyers. In 1996, the penalties recommended by the FAA averaged about $35,600 for national air carriers, $14,400 for commercial operations, and $6,000 for individuals. However, fines were reduced in about 80 percent of the cases, resulting in an average penalty 75-percent less than the FAA's recommendation.[36] Though these financial penalties were available to FAA administrators, in practice red team findings did not directly lead to civil fines.[37] In cases of sustained and gross criminal negligence, the FAA administrator could revoke the mandatory operating certificate of a domestic airline carrier, but this never happened, nor was it ever a plausible threat prior to 9/11.

During the 1990s, a typical vulnerability probe consisted of the red team preparing a fifteen- to twenty-page operational plan detailing the timeline, movements, and objectives of the team member or outside agent who would occasionally serve as the "mule." For example, a "passenger" might check two bags onto an airplane, but then never board that flight, which might result in a bag-match violation. The red team would also conduct challenge assessments, where a team member would wander around the tarmac as a plane was being boarded to determine if someone on the ground crew would ask who they were or even look in their direction. The ground crew rarely did either. Most often, the red team would smuggle crudely disguised and poorly concealed fake bombs, simulated weapons (such as six inches of gun-barrel steel that gave off the same magnetic signature as an actual gun), and hunting knives onto airplanes. Elson, serving on the red team at this time, and his fellow members found that aviation security was consistently poor, and they smuggled who- or whatever they wanted onto planes "all too easily, all too often."[38]

All such shortcomings, and many others, were well documented in specific detail in reports. The reports were sent directly to the office of the associate administrator for CAS, but the red team was never told what letters of correction, penalties, or corrective procedures had been issued to the offending airlines or airports. Since the red team was unaware of how its findings were being put to use, even as it continued to uncover similar vulnerabilities throughout the United States and at major international hubs, it could only conclude that nothing was being done. And, as Elson observes, "The whole idea of red teaming is to find and fix the damn problem. If you won't fix the problem, don't bother."

These security failures persisted during Bogdan Dzakovic's tenure as FAA red team leader from 1995 to 2001. Dzakovic had been a security professional in the Coast Guard and the Naval Criminal Investigative Service, and was a team leader with the FAA's air marshal program beginning in 1987. When he was recruited to the red team, he already had a poor impression of the FAA's sensitivity toward the threat of terrorism, but was enthusiastic about emulating motivated terrorists in order to covertly test and improve aviation security. Dzakovic recalled, however, that from the start, "The problems that [Elson] identified in the early 1990s, I was finding the exact same problems at the exact same airports. Literally nothing was being done."

One particularly dismal outcome emerged from a five-month assessment in 1996, named Operation Marco Polo, when the red team planned to conduct sixty simulated bomb-smuggling attempts at the Frankfurt International Airport, the same airport where a suitcase bomb was checked on board Pan Am Flight 103 before its explosion over Lockerbie. Dzakovic dressed up as a uniformed baggage handler and was provided with a standard airport ID. His ID allowed him to station himself within the baggage makeup area, which is the transit point between airplanes on the tarmac and passengers in the terminals. A mule would check in a bag—identifiable to Dzakovic, but not obviously so to anyone else—and then call him on a cell phone as soon as they saw it go down the chute on the conveyor belt. Dzakovic would then casually walk toward where the bomb detection x-ray monitors were located, timed so that he passed by just as the marked luggage was being screened. Even from some twenty feet away he could clearly see the bomb components displayed on the x-ray monitors most of the time.

Dzakovic described the process and outcomes of the tests: "If they found it, I would identify myself and let them know they were part of an assessment. It turned out that they never found any of them." It was not a matter of the airport needing more technologically sophisticated equipment, but rather that the screeners simply did not watch the monitors. After thirteen failures, FAA administrators informed US carriers flying out of Frankfurt of the poor results to see if their detection performance would subsequently improve. There were thirty-one additional tests before Operation Marco Polo was terminated ahead of schedule. Eight years after the Lockerbie bombing, Frankfurt airport security turned out to be a perfect failure. Of the red team's forty-four total bomb-smuggling attempts, not a single one was detected.

Similarly, though less alarmingly obvious, red team vulnerability probes uncovered a range of security deficiencies at virtually every airport in which they were conducted. Moreover, the red team's findings were replicated in the day-to-day security assessments conducted by other FAA agents. In November 1999, the DOT inspector general reported to Congress the results of audits by its Special Emphasis Assessment teams, which conducted far less sophisticated vulnerability probes than the red team. During the audits, teams got access to secured areas in 117 of 173 tests at eight major US airports. Once they gained access, they boarded aircraft operated by thirty-five different carriers. "Employee failure to carry out security responsibilities was found to be the primary cause of access-control weaknesses."[39]

Successful as the red team was at exposing vulnerabilities, Dzakovic nevertheless believed that the process itself was becoming corrupted over time. The red team documented instances in which FAA administrators tipped off local FAA security managers about upcoming inspections in regard to tests of CTX explosive detection machines. The administrators later admitted having done this on purpose, in order to make sure that the CTX machines were working and being maintained by a qualified operator on-site when the red team's test occurred. According to Dzakovic, FAA administrators also instructed the red team not to write up security shortcomings, specifically regarding the reliability of a relatively new x-ray imaging software program.[40] Overall, red team members developed the impression that they were slowly working themselves out of a job, because once they found vulnerabilities in an airport's security procedures or some screening technology, they were often told not to conduct any more probes of that procedure or technology at that airport.

Meanwhile, the absence of feedback continued. As Dzakovic acknowledged: "I don't know what the managers did, or how they thought about these issues." The red team was tasked with identifying problems, which it easily did, but it could never compel the higher-ups to do anything about them. In August 1998, Dzakovic even made his concerns known in a detailed sixteen-page letter he sent through his chain of command to the FAA administrator and the secretary of transportation.

Nevertheless, reflecting on his time as the red team leader he recalled, "There was not one single instance that I am aware of in which action was taken to correct these security loopholes."

After Elson retired to private life, he and Dzakovic—who remained the red team leader—launched a campaign to warn the US government about the vulnerabilities that the red team was uncovering. In 1999 and 2000, they gave alarming briefings to the DOT inspector general, GAO investigators, and senior Congressional staffers in committees responsible for overseeing the FAA and aviation security. Elson would fly from his home in New Orleans to Washington, DC, at personal expense, often making a point to go behind customer-service counters to steal passenger-manifest lists and baggage-claim tickets to bring to the briefings, just to show how easily it could be done. Though officials and staffers would listen with genuine astonishment to the alarming concerns raised by Elson and Dzakovic, they admitted that there was very little that they could do, especially since the aviation industry exercised tremendous influence on Capitol Hill and within the FAA itself.[41] FAA administrators later told the 9/11 Commission that major domestic carriers and industry trade groups essentially limited security regulations and also ensured that Congressional appropriators cut additional funding for the expansion of rigorous and realistic security-assessment testing. Indeed, the red team itself had initially been intended to consist of eighteen people, but it would never grow beyond eight, thereby limiting the number and scope of vulnerability probes that it could undertake.

In February 2001, after failing to get traction through the FAA chain of command or Congressional overseers, Elson and Dzakovic decided that the time had come to publicize their findings. *U.S. News & World Report* described how Elson got through three screening checkpoints at the New Orleans International Airport with a serrated hunting knife tucked in his pants, and Dzakovic was anonymously quoted as warning that his team was able to get access to secure areas in major airports 95 percent of the time from 1998 to 1999.[42] As a historical reference, in 1978 airport screeners detected 13 percent of prohibited, dangerous objects—such as firearms and explosives—during less-realistic compliance tests;

and, in 1987, it was 20 percent.[43] Elson also orchestrated a security assessment, which was conducted by another recently retired FAA field agent, Brian Sullivan, of the Boston Logan International Airport on behalf of the local Fox television affiliate. That investigative news report, which aired on May 6, 2001, revealed the inability of passenger and luggage screeners at Terminal B to find prohibited weapons, even though the Fox affiliate informed Logan security officials that those same screeners had failed previous covert tests. Dzakovic hand-delivered a copy of the report of the findings to a senior staffer in the office of Senator John Kerry of Massachusetts, but he never received a response.[44] The 9/11 hijackers began to conduct surveillance runs later that month, including one by the group's leader, Mohamed Atta, in late-June 2001 from Logan itself.[45] On September 11, United Airlines 175 and American Airlines 11 flights, which were hijacked and flown into the World Trade Center towers, both departed from Terminal B at Logan International Airport.

It was not until after 2,996 people tragically died on 9/11 that the security lapses repeatedly identified by Elson and Dzakovic finally received the long overdue attention they merited. The 9/11 hijackers took advantage of the overall security culture that characterized domestic airlines and airports that the red team had flagged time and time again, and that FAA officials had done little to address. Several days later, the FAA grounded the red team. Dzakovic and Elson went back to Capitol Hill soon afterward to speak with many of the same Congressional staffers they had warned before 9/11. This time, the staffers were listening much more closely to what had to be done to improve aviation security and prevent future attacks. At the end of the meetings, Dzakovic would ask, "When will there be an investigation into what went wrong and who is responsible?" In each instance, the staffers replied similarly: "Our bosses will do everything that they can to prevent an investigation into 9/11."[46]

Fearing nothing would be done again, Dzakovic filed a whistleblower disclosure with the Office of Special Counsel (OSC) against his employer. The OSC is the independent federal agency that, in theory, protects whistleblowers from retaliation. The central charge that he made in the more-than-four-hundred total pages that he submitted to the OSC office was that the FAA itself had posed a gross threat to public safety. "The FAA red team was the only entity in the entire federal government that actively tried to prevent 9/11. And we were actively ignored," Dzakovic charged.

The subsequent investigation—which was actually conducted by the DOT inspector general (a likely conflict of interest)—could not corroborate some of Dzakovic's claims, including that the associate administrator for CAS deliberately covered up or suppressed the red team's findings. However, the investigation found that while FAA administrators and CAS local field units did, at times, issue letters of correction and fines to airlines and airports, there was no system in place to disseminate and track the violations, which "hindered CAS's capacity to affect coordinated remedial action." Moreover, "these follow-on actions were not readily visible, and, given the consistently poor results of testing over time, the intended outcome of sustained improvement in airport security was not apparent." It was the March 2003 OSC letter to President George W. Bush that explicitly summarized the investigation's findings: "the FAA's Red Team Program was grossly mismanaged and . . . the result was the creation of a substantial and specific danger to public safety."[47]

In 2003 and 2004, the FAA red team received a brief flurry of media attention with the results of the 9/11 Commission's public hearings and the publication of its final report. Dzakovic testified before the Commission in May 2003: "What happened on 9/11 was not a failure in the system, it was a system designed for failure. FAA very conscientiously and deliberately orchestrated a dangerous façade of security." As a consequence of his whistleblowing efforts of FAA mismanagement, he was assigned to menial tasks for several years, now as an employee of the Transportation Security Administration (TSA), which took over responsibility for aviation security from the FAA in 2002. Eventually, Dzakovic was able to secure a transfer to the Midwest, where he works from home as a "principal security specialist" in the TSA's general aviation section, though his extensive expertise as a security professional is not utilized—"I'm a sophisticated clerk" is how he describes it.

Elson continued to help local news outlets smuggle prohibited items through airport security checkpoints for several more years, sending letters—in ALL CAPS—documenting security lapses to anyone in authority who might read them. When he flies, he still thinks like a motivated terrorist, identifying what he believes are unnecessary vulnerabilities. For example, Elson said it baffles him that at Washington, DC's Ronald Reagan International Airport anyone can sit down with a cup of coffee directly across from the security checkpoints of several terminals and simply watch the tactics, techniques, and procedures used by the security personnel—the perfect opportunity for a terrorist scouting how to get themself or an item through security. Once through screening, he has found that anyone can pretend to put on their shoes for as long as they want to and watch how the screeners operate from the other side. He remains friends with Dzakovic, who calls Elson "the most extremely situationally aware, calm, and smartest security guy I ever saw," and "an actual American hero" for the travails he experienced as a federal whistleblower. Likewise, Elson describes Dzakovic as "Fearless. Dedicated to country, family, and friends. Has an instinctive grasp of how to keep people from getting killed."

Even though the red team had completely proved its value, the strict FAA red team concept was not reconstituted in the post-9/11 homeland security overhauls. The TSA began its own revamped covert testing program in September 2002 under its Office of Inspection (OI). Rather than operate as a stand-alone red team, the OI standardizes a purportedly rigorous testing regime across a wider scope of airports and airlines. Without informing TSA officers, small inspection teams try to smuggle dangerous items through screening checkpoints or in checked baggage, and try to gain access to secure areas. In the days after the test, the leader of the inspection team meets on-site with the tested personnel to discuss the results and vulnerabilities. The inspection team then provides its results to TSA managers who decide what additional corrective actions or civil penalties might be required. In 2013, TSA Administrator John Pistole labeled the testers as "super-terrorists, in terms of court testing," while Dzakovic derisively refers to them as "pink teams" that are simply "a testing regiment that fits within the confines of the bureaucratic needs."

Nevertheless, in vulnerability probes concluding in 2015, DHS auditors successfully smuggled weapons and fake explosives past TSA checkpoints a stunning sixty-seven out of seventy attempts at multiple airports.[48]

Truly, no matter how rigorous the testing of aviation security is today, even the best defenses cannot defend against every method of attack that a creative criminal or terrorist can conceive of. Moreover, the security procedures are continuously updated based upon the threat information gathered from suspected terrorist organizations. For example, based upon intelligence about a new threat—such as a nonmetallic bomb that uses an electronic device as a shell and could go undetected through standard screening procedures—the TSA introduced new additional screening measures in July 2014. Passengers traveling on US-bound flights from certain overseas airports are now required to turn on their electronic devices before boarding. Devices that cannot be powered on are not allowed on the flight and the passenger may be required to undergo additional screening.[49] But even these standards might never be sufficient. In 2012, Evan "Treefort" Booth demonstrated—with step-by-step videos he posted online—how easy it is to build extremely lethal weapons with items that are available for retail purchase exclusively after the security screening at airport terminals, and one small multipurpose tool that passengers are allowed to bring onto airplanes. These included a powerful, remotely triggered suitcase bomb, and a functioning "gun" constructed out of a hair dryer, hair band, magnet clip, 9-volt batteries, magazines, tape, dental floss, and aluminum, using 8.4-ounce cans of Red Bull serving as ammunition.[50]

Despite the Lockerbie bombing, findings of high-level commissions, and the repeated and growing warnings of terrorist threats to commercial airlines, aviation security was simply not a priority of the US government before 9/11. The FAA was the lead agency assigned to execute this mission, but it was given limited authority and funding. This was the intentional result of the influence of aviation industries on Capitol Hill, and of the close relationship—some would claim cooption—between industry and senior FAA officials. The red team's dismal findings were not necessarily "covered up," but they were discounted by administrators who believed that, overall, aviation security had improved over time, or at least as much as was possible given the limited power that the FAA possessed.[51] As the 9/11 Commission summarized the opinion of Bruce Butterworth, director for policy and planning at the FAA, about the red team: "Butterworth implied that it was the air carriers and other stakeholders that reluctantly accepted the information provided by the testing. They did not want to know."[52] Clearly, in fact, security never improved sufficiently to address the level of the terrorists' threats to commercial airliners. During the ten years of its existence, the FAA red team repeatedly demonstrated and documented this, and appropriately reported it to their managers, who completely failed to adequately address the red team's troubling findings. Bosses at multiple levels did not buy in to the red team's mission and, subsequently, the bureaucracy was unreceptive to any of the bad news that was repeatedly uncovered. The pre-9/11 FAA red team is a cautionary tale of the extreme peril of failing to heed a red team's findings, though most examples of red teaming in the homeland security field are not so fraudulent and dire.

How to Shoot Down a Plane: MANPADS-Vulnerability Assessments

On November 28, 2002, Al Qaeda-affiliated terrorists fired two shoulder-fired SA-7 surface-to-air heat-seeking missiles at an Arkia Israel Airlines' Boeing 757 civilian airliner as it took off from the Moi International Airport in Mombasa, Kenya. Though both missiles missed—possibly because of countermeasures that were built into the 757—it marked the first missile attack on a civilian airliner outside of a conflict zone. Had the terrorists succeeded, all 271 civilians would very likely have been killed. The attack elevated the perceived threat of the weapon the terrorists had used, the Man-Portable Air Defense Systems, or MANPADS. At the time, there were an estimated 750,000 MANPADS around the world. Available on the black market for as little as $5,000, many thousands of them were believed to be under the control of a few dozen non-state actors.[53] The potential physical threat to civilian passengers, and psychological threat to what was a $100-billion-a-year industry, was stark. Secretary of State Colin Powell warned in October 2003: "No threat is more serious to aviation."[54]

In December 2004, Congress passed the Intelligence Reform and Terrorism Prevention Act, which specifically mandated that the Department of Homeland Security (DHS) conduct MANPADS-vulnerability assessments at all 440 US commercial airports and report its findings to Congress.[55] DHS then directed the TSA to take the lead on this effort. This initial requirement was, in essence, a red team simulation of how a motivated terrorist group would try to shoot down a civilian airliner with a shoulder-fired missile. The TSA-coordinated assessment teams were comprised primarily of FBI, US Secret Service, and Department of Defense representatives. The assessment teams prioritized their initial efforts at the eighty Category X and I airports—the largest and most highly trafficked airports within the United States, and those that were believed to be at the highest risk of attack. Between fiscal years 2004 and 2008, ten airports received two such assessments, two of which were New York's John F. Kennedy International Airport and LaGuardia Airport.[56] Unlike the FAA red team before 9/11, the MANPADS-assessment red team would find a much more receptive audience among local and federal law enforcement agencies for its findings and corrective recommendations.

The four-person red team tasked to undertake the first two MANPADS assessments for these New York City airports began by internalizing the motivations and goals of a terrorist group that might launch an attack against a civilian airliner. The red team's fundamental supposition was that such a complex and consequential operation would not be attempted impulsively and without tremendous preparation. The most likely terrorist operatives would be rational and strategic actors with apparent political motivations. This initial step was needed to help narrow down the most likely shooting zones from which terrorists might bring down a civilian airliner with a missile. In theory, the shooting zone from which terrorists could potentially hit a plane taking off, landing, or circling above a major airport with the widely available SA-7 missile is a few hundred square miles. For more advanced MANPADS, such as the SA-18, that zone increases to a few thousand square miles.[57] For either weapons system, the potential launch point was simply too large—and encompassed too many law enforcement jurisdictions—to plausibly assess or defend against. Therefore, the red team made four key assumptions about the most likely terrorist perpetrators that significantly shrunk the probable shooting zones, so as to zero in on areas that deserved the greatest enhanced-security focus.

The first assumption was that the attackers would be comprised of a small multidisciplinary team, which included a security element to protect the shooter and a video element to capture what they had done. Whoever actually pulled the trigger would be a uniquely valued and highly trained individual, probably have extensive combat experience, but also be smart and adaptable enough to enter the United States undetected. Subsequently, the terrorist organization would want the shooter to be safely extracted, and thus would protect the shooter with a heavily armed security element and conduct the shoot-down from an area near viable escape routes.

Second, the terrorists would have political objectives, which meant that they would not attack just any target of opportunity, but would likely aim for an Israeli or American domestic carrier rather than an airline affiliated with an Arab or Muslim country. This would require that the terrorists be capable of differentiating planes that took off and landed by remotely monitoring the air traffic control information. By 2003, it was already possible to listen to live air traffic control feeds from most major airports over the Internet.[58]

Third, it would have to be a planned attack, which meant that the terrorist group would conduct extensive surveillance of the airport's take-off and landing patterns—which vary based upon wind directions. This would necessitate that some members of the team survey the runways for weeks or months in advance, most likely from an area where they could do so undetected.

Fourth, the red team assumed that the terrorists would use a MAN-PADS to shoot a plane as it took off, rather than as it began to land. The reason for this is that a plane taking off is loaded with tens of thousands of gallons of highly flammable jet fuel, which burdens the plane with a higher wing loading. This, in turn, reduces the climb rate, but also significantly limits its maneuverability, which would make it difficult for a pilot to turn around an airliner to land at the same airport if it were struck. Alternatively, for heat-seeking MANPADS, if a plane was hit as it was landing, the missile would most likely strike near an engine, which the pilot could potentially adjust to and still land the plane with relative safety. Moreover, for such heat-seeking missiles, a plane gives off a much larger heat signature from its exhaust trail as it takes off than from its engines as it lands.

These four assumptions about how terrorists would likely think and behave limited the areas of focus because the shooting zones were assumed to require ingress, concealment, and egress, and be within range of the missile performance for a plane taking off. It turned out that among the best and most likely MANPADS shooting zones for JFK International Airport were the many cemeteries in the borough of Queens, which tend to occupy high ground and have few visual obstructions between them and the runways. For LaGuardia, a high-performance speedboat sitting in the open waters of Flushing Bay might be an attractive option, as would be the Donald Trump golf course then under construction at Ferry Point in the Bronx. All of these locations, and many more, were visited and mapped with GPS coordinates by the four-person team, and studied from above by helicopter. They were then ranked for their attractiveness to terrorists, again based upon how the terrorists would most likely think and behave. There was always the possibility that savvy terrorist operatives would think further outside the box and launch a missile from a more densely populated area. But even in those instances, the assessment team knew what evidence would reveal that it had been a shooting location: a scorched black mark left by a missile, a telltale chemical residue, and a disposable battery coolant unit—which starts the boost motor that propels the missile out of the launch tube. The less densely populated areas the team had identified would be the most rational choices, and thus should receive the most attention.

As the FAA case and earlier examples demonstrate, the findings of any red team are only useful if they are listened to and inform future policies and plans. Unlike the FAA red team, the MANPADS-vulnerability assessments were effectively utilized to inform and refine the continuously updated aviation security Crisis Response Plan (CRP) that would be activated—if intelligence reporting indicated an active terrorist plot—by the New York area Joint Terrorism Task Force (JTTF). The JTTF is an FBI-led task force comprised of more than fifty federal, state, and local special agents and detectives tasked with collecting and analyzing counterterrorism intelligence, and uncovering and acting on threats of terrorism.

The CRP for aviation threats helped to identify and mitigate jurisdictional issues of which agency would be responsible for preventing or responding to an attack. For example, if the missile were fired from Jamaica Bay, the Coast Guard would respond, while the Port Authority of New York and New Jersey owned other potential shooting locations. Meanwhile, private security firms patrol cemeteries and golf courses, with local police precincts acting as law enforcement first responders. The presumption was that the air traffic controllers in the airport's control tower would be able to roughly identify the origin of a missile launch from the smoke trail it left behind. The responding law enforcement officers would then know, based upon the initial work of the assessment team, where exactly, within the estimated missile's origin, a shooting team would be located. Moreover, given that they would likely be well armed and trying to get the shooter out of the area, the responding officers would also expect to receive gunfire and would focus on the previously identified getaway routes.

After the initial two MANPADS-vulnerability assessments for the New York City airports in the mid-2000s, the assessments have been reviewed annually, but remain consistent—the geography and physics of shooting a missile at a plane taking off have remained the same. Moreover, the ownership and law enforcement jurisdiction for the most likely shooting locations and escape routes have not changed much. If intelligence warnings of MANPADS threats to New York City airports emerge, the vulnerability assessments' findings will immediately guide the additional preventive measures to be implemented by facility and security management at the likely launch sites, and the response procedures of local law enforcement. The CRP also covers other similar threats, such as blinding lasers. In the absence of these red team simulations done in the mid-2000s, the FBI, FAA, and NYPD would be starting from zero and operating by intuition rather than based upon realistic contingency planning. The benefit of the red-teaming simulation is an enduring one in that it has informed all successive MANPADS defense planning. The much greater concern today would be a MANPADS attack against a flight that originated overseas. In the past ten years, TSA has led efforts to conduct similar vulnerability assessments at the roughly 275 foreign airports that are the last point of departure for nonstop flights into the United States.

Needless to say, there is more that a comprehensive red team engagement might uncover. According to FBI and NYPD officials, the New York City airport scenarios have never been fully evaluated with a rigorous tabletop exercise or field training exercise. This type of red team activity, involving all of the relevant stakeholders, would most likely identify additional gaps or shortcomings in the security patrols and post-launch responses to the shooting zones. Moreover, since airport security and local law enforcement personnel turn over regularly, it would raise awareness of persistent security issues. However, given that the commitment of time and resources to various threats is finite and should be continuously reprioritized based upon those threats that pose the greatest harm, the perception of MANPADS being used against civilian airliners in the United States has diminished since the 2002 near-downing of an Israeli civilian aircraft that initially heightened US concern, and, subsequently, the attention has diminished correspondingly over time.

Even so, the potential for such an attack on US airports remains as real as it was in 2002 because thousands of such missile systems remain in the hands of non-state actors.[59] Moreover, MANPADS shoot-downs of helicopters and transportation planes by non-state actors or terrorist groups have increased in recent years, though, so far, only in overseas conflict zones—such as Iraq, Somalia, Syria, and Egypt. During one four-month period in 2014, separatist rebels in Eastern Ukraine shot down twelve Ukrainian military aircraft with surface-to-air missiles even before the July 17 downing of Malaysia Airlines 17, which killed 298 passengers and crew. Those lethal missiles were fired mostly from sophisticated, radar-guided, self-propelled missile systems that have a large logistical footprint, which probably could not be smuggled into the United States undetected.[60]

In October 2014, the Islamic State of Iraq and the Levant (ISIL) released an online guide providing instructions for using shoulder-fired missiles to shoot down Apache helicopters: "Choosing the launching spot: Preferably somewhere high. . . . The roof of a building or a hill with a solid surface to prevent the appearance of dust following launching."[61] Nevertheless, the growth in threats to military and civilian transportation aircraft compelled homeland security officials, in July 2014, to highlight their earlier red team efforts to identify and mitigate the risk of MANPADS attacks to domestic airports.[62] An important red-teaming best practice is to not do it too infrequently, lest the targeted institution become hidebound and complacent. Given the continued threats and evolving lethal technologies, this is an issue that is once again in need of repeated and up-to-date realistic simulations.

NYPD Tabletop Exercises: "Never Let the People Believe That They've Solved the Problem"

The three-day terrorist attack in Mumbai, India, that began on November 26, 2008, killed 174 people and injured some six hundred more. The complex, coordinated operation conducted by ten operatives of Lashkar-e-Taiba (LeT), a Pakistan-based Islamic terrorist organization, struck a train station, two luxury hotels, a café frequented by foreigners, and a Jewish community center. Due to the confusion and misinformation, it took twenty-eight hours for Indian security forces to confront and trade fire with the terrorists, and thirty more before all the terrorists were captured or killed.[63] A few hours after the shooting stopped, three senior officers from the New York Police Department (NYPD) were collecting information from the crime scenes. The NYPD investigators met with security services, monitored news reports, and took photos of the attack sites. Within days, the NYPD Intelligence Division compiled a forty-nine page "Mumbai Attack Analysis," consisting of a detailed timeline, the weapons and tactics used, the terrorists' modus operandi, and up-to-date information on the attackers and the casualties that they caused.[64]

New York Police Commissioner Ray Kelly instantly recognized that this brazen commando-style assault represented a new type of terrorist threat to New York City for which the NYPD would be inadequately prepared.[65] For him, the telltale sign that the Mumbai attackers were exceptionally proficient and patient was the absence of any bullet holes in the ceiling. An excited or untrained gunman shooting an automatic weapon fires too high and too often. Kelly recalled that his investigators instead found tight three-bullet clusters fired at head-level repeatedly throughout the course of the attack, which meant that the terrorists had been well trained to demonstrate such fire discipline. The day after the attacks started it had already been decided that a red team table-top exercise—modeled upon the Mumbai analysis—would be prepared as quickly as possible to test the responses and decision-making of the NYPD's senior commanders.

Fortunately, there was an already established small group of people within the NYPD's Counterterrorism Bureau that was responsible for developing and conducting such exercises. This group is charged with preparing tabletop exercises at the commissioner's direction in advance of prominent events (the Thanksgiving Day parade and the New York City Marathon, in light of the Boston Marathon bombings), in response to complex threats (missing highly radioactive material), or to prepare for new potential perpetrators (lone wolf attackers). On average, between four and eight of these tabletop exercises are held every year. The first one held under Commissioner William Bratton, who was appointed in December 2013, considered active shooters, backpack bombs, and a radiological event during Super Bowl XLVIII that was held at the Meadowlands Sports Complex in New Jersey on February 2, 2014. The second, in October 2014, focused on unidentified drones, a suspicious traffic accident that struck runners, and a bomb going off in Central Park during the New York City Marathon. For both exercises, Mayor Bill de Blasio attended and actively participated in the exercises. Mayor

Michael Bloomberg, by contrast, chose not to attend any during his time in office.

The NYPD's tabletop exercises are a classic example of red teaming as a preventive stand-alone activity based on a hypothetical set of facts. The exercises are written out as scenarios by "Bob," a thirty-three-year veteran of the department, under the oversight of the chief of the Counterterrorism Bureau, and often with input from a senior official from the NYPD's Intelligence Division.[66] A few days before an exercise is held, the scenario is provided to the commissioner. To ensure that the simulation is authentic and that participants cannot prepare themselves beforehand, only those three or four officials know in advance what the topic or scenario will look like. Moreover, "Bob" and the Bureau chief gather information about each participant's areas of responsibility and force levels when the hypothetical scenario is planned to occur, so they can determine if any participants "cheat" by claiming to have resources available that they would not have in an unplanned crisis. The participants include NYPD senior officials and commanders (approximately ten three-star chiefs and a handful of two-stars), relevant officials from outside of the department (from fire, emergency response, and transportation departments), and some from the private sector (for example, Goldman Sachs security officials and the New York Road Runners [NYRR] have participated in the tabletop exercises). Each participant is simply told on a Monday or Tuesday that a tabletop will be held a few days later in the late afternoon. The participants often try to inquire about or guess what the simulation will entail, but they never actually know what to expect in advance.

The exercises are usually held in a conference room—known as the Executive Command Center—on the fourteenth floor of One Police Plaza, the NYPD headquarters in lower Manhattan. Though each tabletop exercise lasts roughly two hours, Kelly personally attended them all during his time in office: "I thought it was important to demonstrate that they mattered to my people." Since he and his commanders lived "a total-immersion, 24/7 profession," Kelly found them invaluable because it was "the only time that we really stretched our imaginations."[67]

The participants sit at one of a few dozen assigned seats around the main table based upon a seating chart prepared by the chief of the Counterterrorism Bureau, strategically placing those who will be most involved in the simulation closest to the commissioner. Because the scenario will be a surprise to the NYPD commanders and government agency officials, and to avoid being unprepared or embarrassed in front of their colleagues, they review all of their respective contingency response plans in advance and bring the requisite briefing books into the conference rooms. These books include all of their personnel data for uniformed and plainclothes officers, including their rank, as well as how many patrol cars or tow trucks they would realistically have available. As the Bureau's chief James Waters described the setting: "There is a palpable tension that builds up just before we start. It's a helmets-on, mouth-guards-in sort of atmosphere."[68]

Over the years, the tabletop exercises have generally followed a consistent pattern. They begin with the commissioner (and the mayor, under de Blasio) welcoming everyone and briefly describing the strategic objectives of that day's simulation. Next, the narrator steps in and sets the scene for the upcoming event or fact-based scenario based closely upon current news or plausible threat assessments, and finally kicks things off by announcing, for example, that there are reports of a shooting at JFK International Airport. Prior to 2010, this was done by an outside consultant—a retired US Marine infantry officer and homeland security expert—who read aloud the scenario provided to him by the Counterterrorism Bureau. Since then, someone from the Bureau has served as the in-house narrator for all of the exercises, primarily as a cost-saving measure.

The simulations are highlighted by unexpected challenges—or injects—of varying complexity or lethality that are introduced by the narrator, often with incomplete or limited information. The injects are presented in clusters of two to four, allowing issues either to be partially resolved or to escalate. For example, during the October 2014 New York City Marathon exercise an unidentified drone with a three-foot wingspan was spotted loitering above the elite runners at the starting line near the Verrazano Narrows Bridge. (In 2014, there were more than forty such incidents involving drones that the NYPD investigated.) Helicopters were immediately dispatched to try to identify it. The next inject described it flying away, but it was soon replaced by a second unidentified drone. The assistant chiefs decided to direct their patrol officers to look for non-runners who might be controlling the drone with a phone and binoculars. In the final inject, two men were spotted on Staten Island placing a drone in the back of a van. They were held for questioning, but their responses are incomplete and did not address the primary concern of everyone around the table, which is whether the drones should have been perceived as hobbyists taking aerial photographs or as a potential threat to public safety. Indeed, how the commanders and officials from the NYPD and other New York City agencies responded to any given inject was strongly influenced by how had they perceived the previous ones. What looks like an everyday car accident to one official might appear to be a motivated act of terrorism to another.

NYPD officials describe this tension as resembling the Kobayashi Maru test that is given to Starfleet Academy cadets in the world of *Star Trek*, which are purposefully designed so that they can never truly be "solved."[69] Rather, they are intended to force commanders and government officials to make difficult and time-constrained choices about how to respond and allocate their resources given what they have heard, while never knowing what the next inject might entail. A well-crafted scenario should engage with just about everybody in the room at least once, clarifying who exactly would be "in the huddle" when making an important decision and who has the final authority. Nobody is punished for giving wrong answers, though the participants admit they feel immense competitive peer pressure to find the "right" solution when everyone's eyes are on them. Most commanders and officials give quick and confident responses, though others will often interrupt to critique or raise a challenge that they believe is being overlooked.

As Chief Waters noted: "Our motto is to never let the people believe that they have solved the problem. We want them to leave frustrated, unnerved, and questioning themselves." For example, one inject evaluated how the participants would respond if suddenly everyone lost walkie-talkie and cell-phone access (in response, they formed an ad hoc messenger system with cops on scooters). Another might feature a fictitious CNN news report, which would then require the department's communications head to quickly craft a simple and consistent message for everyone to use as a response. At the far more drastic end of the spectrum, the 2013 New York City Marathon simulation ended with an inject that would have overwhelmed the city's emergency response system: midway through the race, investigators determined that the water being handed out to the tens of thousands of runners had been tainted. During the Marathon simulation the following year, in October 2014, which included the race organizers from the NYRR, participants learned how difficult it would be to actually taint the water and about the multiple back-up hydration plans in place should such an event occur. Moreover, the NYRR has contingency plans to stop the race at any point, divert the course, and even set up an alternative finish line west of Central Park if need be. Most of these contingencies were news to many senior NYPD officials who participated in the exercise, highlighting the uniquely collaborative and information-sharing elements of such red team simulations.

Throughout the scenario process, "Bob" takes copious notes of all the recommendations and ideas that have emerged. At the end of each tabletop exercise, he reads back a summary of what happened and lists all the to-dos that are then tasked to each relevant department or agency. Those to-dos are put into a spreadsheet, and the Bureau continues to monitor and follow up on progress toward implementing the necessary changes. If the Bureau finds there are outstanding concerns before the next exercise, the commissioner is provided with a cheat sheet of outstanding to-dos from which he will inquire whether specific recommendations have been implemented. For example, at the conclusion of the 2014 Marathon exercise, Commissioner Bratton directed his senior commanders to make sure that the patrol officers lining the race course would be briefed ahead of time on what steps the NYRR would be likely to implement in case of an emergency.

This was the tabletop process used immediately following the 2008 attacks in Mumbai. On Friday, December 4, just one week after the attacks ended, more than five hundred NYPD officials and officers gathered at 10:00 A.M. for a two-hour briefing led by the three senior investigators still in Mumbai. Three hours later, forty commanders, deputy commissioners, intelligence officials, and backbench staffers gathered in the Executive Command Center to simulate a comparable event unfolding across Manhattan. One immediately apparent similarity between the two metropolises was the geography and transportation modes. Mitchell Silber, head of the NYPD's Intelligence Division's analytical unit, recalled: "Mumbai looked like a mirror-image of the island of Manhattan."[70] In the exercise, the terrorists came to shore around the South Street Seaport, dispersed throughout the city in multiple teams on foot and by taxi, and then took hostages in Macy's Herald Square department store, while simultaneously detonating bombs and shooting civilians inside the expansive lobby at Grand Central Station.

While the moderator read these incidents aloud as they were "reported" by patrol officers or the media, members of the NYPD's SWAT team, known as the Emergency Service Unit (ESU), engaged in a field exercise, which consisted of a stand-off with the hostage-takers in a mock Macy's constructed at the Rodman's Neck training facility in the Bronx. The commanders in the Executive Command Center watched the simulated stand-off on large video screens, while a few senior patrol officers were called up unannounced from the eighth-floor command and control center to be questioned as to how many police officers were actually available at that moment in case of a real event. What became clear to the participants was that the terrorists were not interested in negotiating away the hostages, but rather were using them to buy time for other terror teams to kill people in luxury hotels dozens of blocks away. Moreover, given the multiple, highly disciplined commando-style teams operating throughout Manhattan, it was also readily apparent that the available ESU teams were both outgunned and outmanned.[71] The narrator's inject of simultaneous, multisite attacks was intended to force the Special Operations Division chief first to allocate his heavy-weapons-proficient forces, and then to acknowledge that he had nobody left. Glancing down at a sheet of paper with the Division's available personnel numbers, Kelly declared bluntly. "Unless I am reading this wrong, you ran out of people twenty minutes ago."

The tabletop exercise's findings led Kelly to authorize two significant changes to enhance the capability of NYPD forces to respond to Mumbai-style terror attacks. First, just as the local police in Mumbai were outgunned, the tabletop exercise showed that the NYPD would be as well. While the four hundred members of the ESU were equipped to fire heavy weapons, these would be insufficient for multisite, multiple-day attacks requiring personnel to relieve the initial responders. Subsequently, 250 narcotics officers from the Organized Crime Control Bureau were trained over the following weeks to fire M4 and Mini-14 automatic rifles, and to guard a stairwell or elevator bank when called upon. Depots to store heavy weapons were also created within NYPD facilities throughout New York City. Finally, an automated phone system was established to recall specific off-duty officers back to work if such a terrorist attack occurred.[72]

Second, most ESU members would have had limited awareness of the locations and layouts of luxury hotels or airport terminals before responding during the confusion of a terrorist attack. Subsequently, they visited the major midtown hotels, and blueprints and video libraries were compiled for each, so that ESU responders would have basic knowledge of the layouts of the lobbies and where the computer servers and power rooms were located.[73] NYPD officials acknowledged that several of these changes probably would have eventually been made, but it was the vivid impact of the Mumbai tabletop exercise among senior commanders that drove home the immediate need for them.

The core recommendations that emerged from the Mumbai tabletop exercise were closely and quickly integrated into how the NYPD prepared to respond to commando-style terror attacks.[74] Moreover, it was considered such a potentially catastrophic scenario that additional exercises modeled on Mumbai were conducted in the following two years.[75] One of them ended with a bomb going off in a Bellevue Hospital Center emergency room while Kelly and the Chief of Department Joseph Esposito were visiting "wounded" officers. "Sirs, you're not dead, you're just among the missing," the narrator told the two.

The Bureau's monitoring and evaluation methodology has not always been adequate in ensuring that all the recommendations that emerge from the exercises are implemented, according to Kelly and his senior aides. Nevertheless, most current and former officials repeatedly emphasized the importance of tabletop exercises in familiarizing and socializing them, if nothing else, around the importance of an issue or threat, and remaining vigilant in preparing a range of responses. The NYPD tabletop exercises probe senior leaders' responses to high-consequence events through rigorous real-life simulations. However, like all red teaming, its enduring impact on the targeted institution is dependent on how faithfully its findings and recommendations are listened to and acted upon.

Information Design Assurance Red Team (IDART): Making Red Teaming a Commodity Tool

Raymond Parks announces on his LinkedIn profile: "I'm not a bad guy, but I play one while red teaming."[76] Though he lists his current occupation as "Consilient Heuristician," Parks is by reputation and experience one of the US government's foremost red teamers. He hacked his first government computer when he was in high school using an old teletype interface, well before there were laws prohibiting this: "I got tired of playing *Star Trek* on it, and wanted to see what else I could do."[77] After graduating from the US Air Force Academy, he conducted unauthorized launch analysis for nuclear-armed intercontinental ballistic missiles, to identify flaws and vulnerabilities in the procedural and design protections intended to reduce the potential of an unauthorized launch.[78] Parks found that a side-benefit of this was that the Air Force will not assign someone who has done unauthorized launch analysis to become a launch officer working underground for three- or four-day shifts in a ballistic missile silo. "After you had studied every way to corrupt the system, I guess the Air Force didn't want you to be responsible for its use," he said. After leaving active duty he worked as a reservist at the Air Force Weapons Laboratory at Kirkland Air Force Base with a focus on nuclear-surety issues. "What we were trying to do is figure out how some bad guy might be able to get at or use nuclear weapons, and trying to make sure it could never happen."[79]

Parks was also later one of the founding members of the Information Design Assurance Red Team, or IDART, which is a small special projects unit within the Sandia National Laboratories at Albuquerque, New Mexico. Unlike other homeland security red teams that are mandated and imposed upon targeted institutions, such as the FAA red team was with the commercial airline industry, IDART is more generally embraced and listened to because its services are sought out and highly valued. The roots of Sandia date back to the Manhattan Project, which designed and built the world's first nuclear bombs, including the only two used in warfare to date. Seven decades later, its primary mission remains assuring the safety, security, and effectiveness of the nonnuclear components— including command-and-control systems—and subsystems of nuclear warheads. Sandia's ten-thousand-foot rocket sled track slams warheads into walls at speeds of up to a few thousand miles per hour to model and simulate the acceleration, velocity, and impact angles that a bomb would encounter if used in a nuclear attack. Sandia's wind tunnels evaluate the expected performance of the tail-kit assemblies on the B-61 12 warhead, which is scheduled to replace all the other nuclear warheads in the US atomic arsenal by 2024.[80] While Sandia always pursued a range of missions related to national security, homeland security, and energy uses, its core responsibility is to make certain that nuclear weapons would be available if a president decided to authorize their deployment. However, as important as making certain that nuclear weapons are available is ensuring that they cannot be damaged, stolen, or misused when not authorized. This includes environmental stresses for lightning or hurricane-force winds, and, more worrisome, the potential threats of foreign military, terrorist, or criminal adversaries—just what Parks researched while at Kirkland Air Force Base.

It was within the context of Sandia's mission of preventing the unauthorized use of nuclear weapons that IDART was born. In the early-1990s, IDART founder Michael Skroch (pronounced "skraw") noted that he "started seeing more people at Sandia thinking about adversarial perspectives, to better defend against threats, but there was no structure, process, or way to define it so they could improve. It was all ad hoc."[81] Skroch pulled together a multidisciplinary core team that initially consisted of five to six people to compile the different adversarial and risk-assessment techniques that had accumulated within Sandia over the decades. He selected a mix of scientists and engineers with diverse skill sets and approaches, including technical experts that were immersed in their domain, specialists in analytical and modeling tools, and generally out-of-the-box thinkers. Skroch had determined that red teaming was simply being approached "based upon the inspiration or brilliance of someone who happened to be around." His long-term vision was "to make red teaming more like a commodity tool, which could be used even by people with varying degrees of skills." The way to accomplish this was to develop red-teaming techniques that could be defined, and would be repeatable and flexible enough to be improved over time.

Therefore, in 1996, under the direction of Samuel Varnado, then-head of the Information Operations Center, and with a small amount of laboratory-directed research and development money—meaning they had to pay out of the lab's own pocket—Skroch formed IDART. Varnado recalled that "the genesis of IDART was that we had people who worked with a high dedication to ensure nuclear weapons would not go off, and who also were cleared at the SCI (sensitive compartmented information) level."[82] He directed Skroch to bring coherence to the disparate red-teaming expertise at Sandia, and to take on the most challenging adversarial threats facing the United States—particularly to information systems and critical infrastructure, of which 85 percent were owned by private industry. "We had a ready-made capability at Sandia," Varnado noted: "It just needed to be redirected from nuclear weapons to the industrial sector, to help industry protect itself." The scope of IDART's activities would be centered on three domains: cyber, physical (including radio frequency), and humans. Their definition for red teaming reflected the intellectual capacity and skills that had been nurtured at Sandia: "an authorized, adversary-based assessment for defensive purposes."

From the start, three rules have guided IDART's red-teaming projects. First, Sandia employees describe their home institution as being "coin-operated" for all of its nonnuclear weapons work. Thus, all red team projects had to be fully funded by an external source. Second, IDART was prohibited, by law, from competing with comparable private-sector red-teaming firms. So, if a potential client requested a relatively straightforward penetration test of its computer network, they would decline the opportunity because many cyber-security firms have the requisite capabilities to do this. Therefore, IDART has accepted only red-teaming projects that could capitalize on the unique expertise found primarily at Sandia. These have been vulnerability probes and independent alternative analyses of highly complex systems related to national and homeland security, and would have significant consequences if they failed.[83] Third, Sandia's government administrator is the National Nuclear Security Administration (NNSA), and therefore Sandia's nonnuclear activities must be approved by NNSA.[84] Though approval was largely reserved for government programs—like the Defense Advanced Research Project Agency (DARPA), which has been a big customer—IDART has also red teamed systems and products for private-sector firms, but only if they had a government sponsor, which was usually interested in buying a particular product.

The first IDART assignment came from the Joint Command and Control Warfare Center in San Antonio, Texas. That command had been tasked by the deputy under secretary of defense (advanced technology) to perform what is called an Advanced Concept Technology Demonstration (ACTD) of an information system in order to determine all of the ways that an adversary could defeat it. The command found that the IDART security assessment was far superior to those done by other government red teams. Word spread quickly, and, as Skroch recalled, "Other government red teams started sending us their overflow work that they couldn't get done." The prospective workload soon became greater than the initial eight- to ten-person IDART core team itself could oversee. In response, IDART was forced to grow its core team, since Skroch found that "the population of red teamers is small, and you don't have a large number of people who can do this. You whittle down that resource quickly." Subsequently, he noted that they most commonly looked for three traits: "domain knowledge, out-of-the-box thinkers, and an ability to be ruthless and act in a way that is morally corruptible." Parks added that it was especially difficult to find people with that last trait: "We could always find people with new areas of expertise, but the hacker mindset is much more important and elusive." The IDART core team referred to their best and most reliable red teamers, comprised of Sandia and non-Sandia subject-matter experts, as the "Impossible Missions Force," a reference to the fictional elite team of part-time operatives from the television show *Mission Impossible* of the late-1960s and early-1970s.

One area in which IDART has become particularly well known within government and industry is evaluating the security of supervisory control and data acquisition (SCADA) software, which allows for the remote sensing and operation of critical infrastructure systems.[85] SCADA systems facilitate the interface between humans and critical infrastructure—allowing someone to remotely turn off a motor, close an exhaust vent, or turn on a heater—and thus have always made for attractive targets for criminal or terrorist hackers.

Varnado found that while the threat to SCADA systems had increased throughout the mid-1990s, owners and operators in the private sector did not want to hear about those threats or their potential consequences. "We would go down to Houston and speak with big oil companies to point out the vulnerabilities that existed in their refineries. The CEO would reply, 'but we have password-protected computers!'" Varnado added that these executives "just didn't see cyber attacks as a threat, because it wasn't obvious like eighteen militiamen coming over a hill with AK-47s."[86] Thus, he helped to establish a number of test-bed facilities and supercomputer simulations at Sandia to evaluate critical infrastructure for the Department of Energy (DOE) and the Nuclear Regulatory Commission. These security assessments were utilized collaboratively by IDART in order to develop risk-assessment methodologies that helped private industry understand the vulnerabilities that it faced and how it should spend money smartly to defend against them. During a 2003 broadcast of the PBS series *Frontline*—titled "Cyberwar!"—Skroch was asked, "Could your team, if you wanted to, take down the entire grid in the United States?" He politely replied: "I won't answer that question."[87]

IDART also conducted vulnerability probes on behalf of multinational financial institutions, foreign utility companies, the Singapore Mass Rapid Transit system, domestic nuclear power plants, and Internet-security firms. One of the latter was conducted on behalf of Invicta Systems, for which IDART—shortly before 9/11—did an assessment of a patented software purporting to have the capability to "hack back" against a malicious cyber attack.[88] For the US government, IDART has conducted vulnerability probes for container-security systems as part of the multiyear DHS's Container Security Test and Evaluation effort, as well as for the DARPA-sponsored Ultralog program, a net-based logistics architecture system built to withstand or repair damage from asymmetric cyber attacks on information systems, and effectively function during chaotic wartime environments.[89]

More broadly, between 1998 and 2000, IDART was able to successfully penetrate thirty-five out of thirty-five computer networks and information systems at various sites for both governmental and commercial clients. This was easily achieved despite having given every client advanced notice in order for them to prepare their defenses, and, at times, even having explained precisely how IDART would break in.[90] Moreover, each unauthorized intrusion was conducted exclusively with publicly available tools that any semi-competent malicious actor could use. Dino Dai Zovi, who was a twenty-one-year-old, technically sophisticated hacker when he joined IDART, recalled, "They always made a point to use low-sophistication, open-source hacking tools to make it believable. I was young and always wanted to escalate the exploitation, but now I see the value of their approach."[91] Skroch correctly highlights that the value of the thirty-five out of thirty-five measurement is hard to determine because each engagement is different, the level of effort required varies, it is only a snapshot assessment while long-term maintenance is dynamic, and it does not indicate the cost or effort required to implement a fix.[92]

Beyond these specific projects, IDART has played a leading role in teaching other national security and homeland security agencies how to use red teaming and spreading its awareness within government. In the mid-2000s, the Sandia unit conducted a vulnerability probe of a computer system that a DARPA-sponsored customer was proposing to install. The customer was so paranoid about the ability of the IDART hackers to break in that they constrained the scope of the engagement so narrowly that the hackers would only be permitted to evaluate a small portion of the system. Nevertheless, they still quickly found a zero-day exploit for that narrow portion and were able to obtain access to the entire system. Skroch and his colleagues realized that punching holes in defensive systems was easy, but that this would be pointless unless the targeted institution allowed IDART to scope the engagement in a manner that took into account the realistic threats posed by an adversary. Rather than merely breaking into information systems, the IDART core team believed that they had a responsibility and obligation to teach government and private sector program managers exactly what the red-teaming process was, and how it should and should not be used.

Therefore, in 2006, using funds that remained from a separate DARPA project, IDART developed the "Red Teaming for Program Managers" pamphlet. This four-step approach provided simple guidance for determining when red teaming should be used, specifying what should be red teamed (which includes identifying the type of red teaming—design assurance red teaming, behavioral red teaming, or penetration testing, for example), identifying who should be on the red team, and producing practical deliverables based upon the findings.[93] They mailed copies to government program managers, and IDART still requests that they follow its guidance before commissioning it to evaluate information systems on their behalf. To this day, IDART has a reputation for its clarity and ease of use among program managers who procure highly classified systems for their government agencies. Concurrent with this effort, IDART also hosted three critical conferences where it taught red-teaming approaches and methodologies to government experts from 2005 to 2007. As Skroch recalled, these were the very first times that scientists, engineers, and program managers from different reaches of government assembled to share red-teaming approaches and methods, and to inform the uninitiated about what the concept had to offer.[94] These products, methodologies, and instructions helped to cohere and spread red teaming within the US government as much as any other organization had before or has since.[95]

However, IDART has always remained focused on red teaming computer networks and information systems for national security and homeland security agencies. Although information is difficult to come by, given that most of IDART's work is classified, there are two notable available examples of instances where its red team efforts were impactful. The first involved a private vendor that, around 2004, was proposing to sell government agencies a write-once compact disc (CD) for securely transmitting highly classified information. The vendor claimed that information maintained on computer networks connected to the Internet—even if on a shared-network drive behind firewalls—would be susceptible to unauthorized theft. The proposed solution for safeguarding especially sensitive classified information was for government agencies to use air-gapped computers to write onto the CD, and then mail it to an intended recipient who alone could exclusively retrieve the information. Since the CD purportedly contained unbreakable encryption standards, the vendor contended that even if an unintended party obtained access to it they would never be capable of reading it.[96]

Thus, the program managers at the Air Force Information Warfare Battlelab (AFIWB)—who had determined that the proposed CDs were compatible with defense and intelligence agency computers—requested that IDART conduct a vulnerability probe of the CDs. Almost immediately, a two-person IDART work group was able to find the cryptographic key allowing them to break the encryption code and read the CDs' contents. The AFIWB managers were alerted, and government agencies were spared from buying a supposedly wholly encrypted communications system that was in fact insecure. The recommended security patch could have been integrated into the CD easily enough, but the vendor apparently did not try to resell it to government agencies. Parks recalled

instances where IDART found vulnerabilities in communications systems and years later that very same system—having been purchased by
a different defense contractor—was still being sold to the government,
but without the recommended patches ever having been implemented.

The second big IDART red-teaming success occurred in 2011 after
the Department of Labor's (DOL's) Bureau of Labor Statistics (BLS)
became suspicious that somebody was stealing its economic data before
it was formally released. BLS data—particularly the quarterly employment and wages summary, or "jobs report"—is highly anticipated and
devoured by the business media and investors for clues about future
market trends. If an algorithmic-based trader was able to illegally obtain this information beforehand, they could use it to make investment decisions in anticipation of the expected market reaction to the
information. Numerous regulatory authorities, including the Securities
and Exchange Commission and Federal Bureau of Investigation, had
repeatedly expressed concerns about the possibility of unauthorized
data leakage since 2007. Subsequently, DOL officials requested that
IDART perform an assessment of the facility where the jobs report is
released—a secure room in the basement of the Department's Frances
Perkins Building. Between 8:00 A.M. and 8:30 A.M., select journalists
from major media outlets were locked in the room with the data so
that they could prepare stories and background information. Then, at
exactly 8:30 A.M., a BLS official lifted the embargo by flipping a master control switch—that the journalists' personal computers were all
required to be plugged into—to "on," so that they could all transmit
their stories simultaneously.[97]

On several occasions the IDART team turned down BLS officials on
the grounds that it was not a national security concern. As Parks recalled:
"They kept asking if something bad could happen, but we kept telling
our bosses [in Sandia] that this was not what we do." However, because
BLS and the other regulatory agencies were so persistent, the red teamers
came to appreciate the significant economic value of that information
and agreed to do the assessment. Also, IDART had previously done a
comparable security assessment of the information maintained by the

Social Security Administration, because it was responsible for dispersing one-quarter of the federal budget every year.

The BLS red team assessment, titled CleanSweep, was intended to identify vulnerabilities within the secure basement room and the procedures surrounding the release of data, provide suggestions to mitigate these vulnerabilities, and assist with implementation if necessary. In line with IDART red team methodology, the assessment began with a planning phase. First, Han Lin, IDART project manager, and Scott Maruoka, project lead, collaborated with DOL to create a statement of work outlining the perceived threat, worst-case scenarios, goals and deliverables, and the scope of and constraints on the red team. During the second phase, data collection, the red team reviewed all relevant documentation and open-source material, conducted interviews with DOL and BLS officials, performed a physical inspection of the facility and surrounding areas, and observed a live BLS press event. The IDART red team, comprised of five members with technical expertise in cyber security, adversary modeling, physical security design, and electronic surveillance, was granted necessary access and given support by the DOL to conduct the assessment. Due to a constrained budget and schedule, the scope of the assessment was limited to "how an adversary might exfiltrate embargoed economic data from the press lockup facility during a press release event," and therefore did not consider BLS IT systems that produced the targeted economic data or the personnel security controls to consider potential insider threats. IDART concluded that these two sources were "the most likely vectors for data leakage," and participants believed the scope was too narrow to realistically identify all of the threats that the basement of the Frances Perkins Building faced.[98]

The red team determined that the likely non-BLS adversaries were "profit-driven, technically sophisticated individuals or organizations who may have considerable resources at their disposal," and that a "nightmare scenario" would involve a compromise or misuse of information or systems, resulting in negative press and a loss of reputation.[99] What they found most troubling was how the rules regulating media access had evolved from journalists using mechanical typewriters, to news outlets running communications lines into the room and using their own computers, monitors, and routers that had not been screened for transmission devices. Moreover, employees and contractors working for the news outlets were permitted to enter the communications closets to conduct maintenance and repairs. "A lax security culture had sort of evolved over time," as Parks described it. The red team determined that the most likely scenarios by which an adversary could obtain information was through hidden radio frequency transmitters or compromised communication infrastructure.

Once the assessment was complete, the red team conducted a preliminary analysis at DOL, the findings of which were presented to representatives from DOL Operations and the BLS. In the final report, and its supplemental technical details, both published in August 2011, the red team not only presented the findings, but listed mitigation options. These included simple and inexpensive recommendations such as prohibiting outside computers and IT equipment in the room, and shielding the room from emitting radio frequency communications. Also, several media outlets—including *Bond Buyer* newspaper, Nasdaq OMX, and RTT News—were kicked out of the secure room because their primary mission was to deliver data to high-speed traders, not to produce original news content.[100] One year later, IDART returned to the facility to assess the DOL's mitigation measures undertaken since the original red team and found that it had "made significant strides in improving the security posture of the press release facility."[101] As Parks described it, "some of the recommendations were strenuously implemented, and others were not." For example, the credentialed news outlets could still use their own computers, but supply-chain safeguards were implemented to keep them locked in the basement room when not being used during the half-hour prior to the release of the jobs report.

While the CD and BLS stories are relative successes, IDART, like all red teams, struggles to quantify the measurable dollars and personnel costs that its efforts save the targeted institution. Moreover, IDART only red teams at the request of program managers for specific projects to emulate the likely adversarial threats and potential costs and consequences.

Skroch has found that it is always difficult to demonstrate the value of any preventive security policy, but believes that IDART red teaming has proven its worth for program managers at targeted institutions in three ways. First, it can generate the "a-ha! holy shit insight" that uncovers some new thinking about a domain that had been previously ignored, which decreases the level of risk to adversarial challenges within that domain. Second, the vulnerability probe proves a point about inadequate security, which is used to trigger larger conversations that lead to a more comprehensive and systematic approach to defending some domain. Third, there is always the simple "cover your ass selling point" that humans are attracted to. The IDART findings report provides evidence that a program manager made a conscious choice to employ the best people and approaches to evaluate some system. "If you are questioned by Congress or the press, you will have this document as a shield to waive and say 'I did my best'." Of course, the true value is only derived when the findings are implemented, and IDART members acknowledge that they are powerless to compel their clients to do so.

After a career of attempting to prove the utility of preventive security and information assurance, Parks has found that the methodologies are flawed and impossible to draw broader conclusions from. When vulnerabilities of a system or domain are obvious and easily repaired, that is a clear success. But it is harder to know when your time was misapplied by focusing on relatively secure or low-consequence systems, which could have been better spent finding more glaring vulnerabilities on a different system that motivated adversaries want to exploit. Red teamers are always limited to the scope of activities agreed to with the targeted institution, and it is difficult to prove after the fact that the scope was not appropriate. However, Parks recalled reading a newspaper story soon after the terrorist attacks on September 11, 2001, which mentioned a biological sensor system that had been deployed throughout Washington, DC, to detect the presence of biological agents. Three years earlier, IDART had conducted an ACTD red team of that system—which was then called Portal Shield—for the Joint Program Office for Biological Defense.[102] As Parks noted: "We made some recommendations for how to improve the system's configuration by adding some additional sensors, and the government's program managers had taken them to heart. When you know that you did something, and that they fixed it because of your work, you get a great deal of satisfaction from that."

Conclusion

From its earliest days under trailblazers like Stephen Sloan, red teaming within the homeland security field has struggled to convince others of its usefulness and necessity in preventing terrorist attacks and criminal breaches before they occur. The FAA red team was easily the most tragic case assessed for this book because it undertook realistic vulnerability probes of the security procedures in place at airports to protect planes and passengers from terrorists, like those responsible for the 1988 Lockerbie bombing—the motivating impulse for the red team itself—but saw its warnings go almost entirely unheeded. The impact of the FAA red team was weak because the FAA—constrained by its Congressional overseers—was itself weak. The FAA senior managers who received the red team's reports were either unable or unwilling to use its shocking findings to sanction and pressure domestic airlines to make vital improvements. Unfortunately, they were engaged in red teaming without an ultimate purpose, which is the worst possible situation, rendering the red team and its targeted institution incapable of utilizing the findings.

The other red teams reviewed in this chapter were able to get better traction largely because they were mandated by Congress, demanded by a boss, or had fulfilled what was widely accepted as an urgent need. The MANPADS-vulnerability assessment occurred only because of a well-publicized threat to an Israeli airliner in 2002. This attempted shootdown elevated the importance of protecting US airports, which was best done by internalizing the likely motivations, tactics, and techniques that it was believed terrorists would employ. The NYPD commissioner's tabletop exercises occurred with the highest level of buy-in, given Ray Kelly's belief that they were the best means to evaluate the contingency plans and decisions that his commanders would be forced to make in a real-life incident. The tabletop exercises have endured over the past decade because the template is flexible enough to red team the reactions to new, emerging terror threats, and also the response plans if something went wrong at an upcoming event. Similarly, IDART persists because of its historical focus on nuclear weapons and critical infrastructure systems, and because the unique body of expertise found at Sandia Labs has been repurposed to red team an array of threats facing government and industry. As in the private sector (institutions that are detailed in the next chapter), IDART has always struggled to justify its relevancy. And as the person who authorized IDART's creation, Sam Varnado, stated, "Making a business case for why you need to do red teaming involves demonstrating the likely vulnerabilities, threats, and consequences of inaction."[103]

FIVE

COMPETITORS: PRIVATE-SECTOR RED TEAMING

The best way to get management excited about a disaster plan is to burn down the building across the street.

—Dan Erwin, Security Officer at Dow Chemical, 2000[1]

Previous chapters have shown how red teaming emerged in response to the national security needs of the federal government, but its techniques have also been adopted by the private sector, albeit in a more limited manner. Most common and widely used are vulnerability probes designed to test the security of a system or facility, and simulations that evaluate the potential outcomes of corporate strategic decisions. Yet, of all the fields researched for this book, the private sector is by far the least open to scrutiny and examination. This is because both external red teams and the targeted corporations they evaluate have every reason to be secretive, and even misleading, about the weaknesses they uncover. Outside red teams are most often consultants, armed with well-rehearsed stories of successful cases in which they conclusively enhanced their clients' performances. Consultants rarely share instances where they failed to improve a business. If they do, the fault for the failure inevitably lies with the client. Additionally, they largely denigrate competing consultants, even when acknowledging that they lack direct insights into how they differ from themselves. Moreover, external red teams sign nondisclosure agreements that greatly restrict the extent to which they can describe their actions, in turn making it difficult to validate their claims of effectiveness.

Given that corporations hire external red teams in the hopes of realizing relative advantages and subsequent profits based on information that others do not possess, it is unsurprising that most firms and their employees are unwilling to share this kind of information, even anonymously.[2] Corporate cultures generally reinforce the need for absolute secrecy lest their competitors gain an edge by obtaining direct insights into current or future plans. And, understandably, corporations also seek to hide or downplay their shortcomings either in order to not scare away investors or to deter suspicion from government regulators. Even more so than the classified, top-secret worlds of the US intelligence community and military, outside consultants and corporations are intentionally opaque and will actively disseminate misleading information about what they do and how well they do it.

Besides making it difficult to describe and analyze private-sector red teaming, this mindset can blind corporations to the real need for red teaming. When there is no spare nearby building to burn down, as Dan Erwin called for in this chapter's opening quote, it is difficult to get senior management to consider worst-case scenarios. Ultimately, based on corporations' abilities to grow and remain viable, the marketplace decides whether corporate strategies and plans have succeeded or failed. If corporations take the wrong path, or do not confront threats from criminal hackers or competitor firms, the market will "correct" their behavior with losses in profitability, market share, and reputation. If uncorrected, sooner or later they will fail and go out of business. According to the latest US Census Bureau statistics, the average exit rate—the rate at which all existing firms leave the business marketplace—is 10 percent.[3] However, measuring only availably known outcomes is itself often also misleading because a firm can implement the best conceivable strategy or defenses possible and still experience massive losses or outright failure for reasons outside its control. Totally unforeseen events—such as catastrophic weather, intense pressure from regulators, sudden shifts in consumer appetites, or technological breakthroughs making offensive attacks easier—can cause the best-laid plans to fail disastrously. Alternatively, the best strategy or security measures might not be the cause of value creation for a company and might not be the reason that an adversary did not attack it.

Nevertheless, companies take steps to lessen the magnitude of impact from both unforeseen events and normal market corrections. This includes the use of red teaming in all its forms—alternative analyses, vulnerability probes, and simulations. There is a growing list of consultancies that focus primarily on selling these services, usually tailored to particular industries. For instance, Lex Machina is a Silicon Valley–based legal consultancy that models and predicts the outcomes of litigation and settlement options for technology clients facing intellectual property lawsuits.[4] Chicago-based Sieben Energy Associates identifies weaknesses in its clients' energy management practices by using energy audits—usually identifying potential savings of 5 to 10 percent—or energy modeling, which involves alternative analyses of a building's energy consumption to optimize design and savings.[5] UK multinational company BAE Systems Applied Intelligence conducts both remote and on-site penetration testing to determine how well client networks are defended against adversaries.[6] In early 2014, it partnered with the Malaysian Ministry of Science, Technology and Innovation to conduct joint penetration tests and undertake assessments of the country's cyber networks.[7] Information security firm 360 Advanced, based in Tampa, Florida, conducts cyber penetration tests—which include assessing vulnerabilities and providing guidance on how to address them. Its goal is not just to ensure that companies are complying with regulations, such as PCI DSS (Payment Card Industry Data Security Standard) or HIPAA (Health Insurance Portability and Accountability Act), but rather to do more than "just check the boxes" and ensure that they truly protect themselves from malicious hackers.[8] While these four companies may not necessarily conceive of their activities as red teaming—perhaps because their practitioners did not cut their teeth on the kind of red teaming codified in US military doctrine—nevertheless, red teaming is exactly what they are doing. Moreover, many consulting firms that work in these areas would stand to benefit from reorienting their services around a red team framework, similar to the three current examples of red teaming within the private sector detailed below.

First is the practice of business war gaming by external consultants to help corporations facing unexpected challenges or a pressing strategic decision think through and simulate the most likely reactions of their competitors, and determine whether a new strategy is sound. Second is the evolving and expanding world of cyber vulnerabilities, where white-hat hackers assume the role of malicious hackers to conduct vulnerability probes of a company's computer networks or software programs. A case study of the white-hat hack of a Verizon femtocell is featured to illustrate how "responsible disclosure" hacking identifies and provides remedial solutions for defensive weaknesses that malicious hackers could exploit. Third, just as hackers uncover and fix shortcomings in the cyber realm, security professionals conduct physical penetration tests of supposedly highly secure facilities in the real world. By manipulating the trust of unsuspecting employees, or simply outsmarting a defensive system, these tests demonstrate how lax the security is at most buildings, almost certainly including the one you work at every day. The picture that emerges is of a vibrant strain of red-teaming practices, sometimes weakened by the inherent shortcomings of the private sector's hierarchies and biases, but otherwise innovative and colorful, as we will see from its practitioners.

Simulating Strategic Decision-Making: Business War-Gaming

In the business world, the most prominent use of red teaming is to help executives who are facing highly consequential strategic decisions. Strategic decisions are those that significantly alter the degree of a corporation's commitment (such as investments, disinvestments, or public proclamations) or scope (such as products, activities, or markets).[9] For executives, the inherent difficulty is how to analyze all of the conflicting information and balance the interests of various internal and external stakeholders in the face of unpredictability—where potential outcomes cannot be known or estimated by a subjective probability. "The world is non-linear, so the ability to cut through complexity relies on processing a large amount of information quickly and extracting nuggets to make quick decisions," according to Julian Segal, managing director and CEO of Caltex Australia.[10] Businesses recognize the challenges associated with such decision uncertainty and attempt to overcome or mitigate it by using a variety of internal frameworks and approaches—in other words, by red teaming themselves. Over the decades, hundreds of these methods, such as benchmarking, customer-relations management, or balanced scorecards, have been published and promoted, each contending that it provides a superior approach for senior executives. Broadly speaking, three frameworks or approaches are commonly used for internal decision support, each of which is insufficient and problematic on its own.

First is scenario (or strategic) planning—the process of envisioning desired objectives, and identifying steps to achieve them. This can be extremely difficult, especially given the tasks that senior executives face daily that require immediate attention, and it is often confused with simply listing objectives.[11] In 1958, sociologists James March and Herbert Simon labeled this phenomenon, "Gresham's Law of Planning: Daily routine drives out planning."[12] Much like the dilemma faced by military officers who serve on command staffs, which was featured in chapter 2, executives become absorbed and captured by completing what is necessary in the immediate future, at the expense of carving out the time to reassess and plan for tomorrow. Generally, strategic planning ascertains how to achieve objectives, while red teaming more often is used to determine what is wrong with a plan or to reevaluate what those objectives should be.

Second, to supplement strategic planning, lower-level managers might use "liberating structures," a concept first articulated in 1991 by William Torbert, and also taught at the University of Foreign Military and Cultural Studies mentioned in chapter 2. Liberating structures are experimental interactions that facilitate uninhibited discussions and creativity in an effort to solve problems or explore new opportunities.[13] Numerous versions apply different facilitation methods to group discussions to elicit an unexpected or inspired exchange of ideas. One example is the Four Ways of Seeing methodology, whereby employees assume multiple roles, including those of potential adversaries, to organize their culture, social system, power balances, historical narrative, and economies into a four-by-four grid. Another example is the String of Pearls (or premortem) analysis, which identifies gaps and weaknesses in plans by analyzing the assumptions upon which each component of the plan is based. This helps to identify measures that could mitigate secondary and tertiary risks associated with each vulnerability. These liberating structures—also known as "directed creativity"—are taught at business schools, and vice presidents or section heads in large firms tend to be well versed in their purpose and process. There are entire industries of researchers who develop or analyze templates or principles for how businesses can purportedly and suddenly identify their blind spots, self-diagnose shortcomings in an ongoing business plan, and think self-critically. Subsequently, many businesses believe that their in-house corporate intelligence professionals or strategy analysts can employ these frameworks to review current plans and upcoming strategic decisions—again, thereby attempting to red team themselves. While liberating structures are useful in many ways, institutional biases and internal cultural barriers limit their impact. Because insiders lack objectivity, they cannot simply employ a red-teaming trick or two and believe their institution has, in fact, been red teamed.

Third, beneath strategic planning and liberating structures is the assumption that businesses can foment and promote corporate cultures in which all their employees can be directed to identify strategic flaws or performance shortcomings, and be empowered to report them to their bosses. This administrative style, stemming from management theory literature, is purported to absolve executives of their direct responsibility for decision-making by flattening hierarchical structures in order to continuously elicit good ideas from within, which are then subsequently applied to refine a strategy. However, employees infrequently voice their honest opinions to their bosses either because they perceive it as pointless or, worse, fear that it will elicit retaliation. Such fears are justified. As one anonymous executive put it: "Devil's advocates, if occasionally right, will get hunted down and killed by the antibodies in a company. Remember, they just won an argument. That means someone else lost."[14]

The problem with all three of these approaches to processing information and making strategic decisions is that they face the same organizational biases that typically emerge within hierarchies. These biases make it less likely that employees will relay information upward that their bosses need to hear, or will openly and honestly challenge the strategies or initiatives that are overtly promoted by senior management. Business executives express tremendous faith in their abilities to either red team themselves or to overhaul a corporate culture by making every employee a red teamer. However, according to executives, strategy consultants, and business school professors, realistic internal red teaming either does not occur, or is so curtailed that it is simply ineffectual. Jami Miscik, who formed the CIA Red Cell while serving as the number two official in the Agency, described in chapter 3, has worked in senior risk-management positions since 2005. As she noted with regard to corporate red teaming: "In the private sector it is very hard for any corporation to do that to itself internally."[15]

Most bosses do not consciously surround themselves with "yes men and women" on their staffs. They do not have to. Most people learn over time to just say "yes," remain quiet, or qualify dissent to the extent that its impact is diminished or negligible. Survey data demonstrates that most employees are unwilling to speak up, and that formal mechanisms meant to encourage this—such as hotlines, complaint boxes, or ombudsmen—are generally pointless.[16] Ethan Burris, professor at the McCombs School of Business, notes, "If you have an anonymous suggestion box, it just reminds people that they work somewhere where it is not safe to speak up. It reinforces the feelings a company is hoping to address."[17] The 2009 Cornell National Social Survey of one thousand adults found that 53 percent of all respondents never spoke up to their manager about an idea or a problem—41 percent believed that it was a waste of their time, and 31 percent were concerned about the personal consequences of doing so.[18] Moreover, dissenting opinions are perceived of as especially problematic because managers will categorize employees who offer a "challenging voice" as poorer performers and less loyal than those who offer a "supportive voice."[19] Unsurprisingly, while employees usually openly discuss their company's shortcomings with coworkers—in an effort to get validation or buy-in for their concerns—they routinely refrain from "going up" with a problem.[20] As Burris and his colleagues have found: "When voice flows to the leader, it leads to increased performance. But, when voice leads sideways, it results in worse performance."[21]

In the real world, both survey data and people's everyday experiences demonstrate how and why employees' voices rarely flow upward. To comprehend this, you need only consider whether you feel comfortable speaking up within your own workplace, or if you refrain from doing so under the impression that it is unsafe or futile. Whether it is to warn of a blind spot in either a strategic plan or an internal process, odds are that you will openly discuss this matter with your colleagues, but not with a more senior person—even though that person is empowered to actually do something about it, or at least to inform their own bosses. Just as you learn over time how to perform your job based upon formal directives and guidance, you also informally learn, through the tone of and interactions with senior management and interpretation of unspoken rules, whether to address the hitherto unaddressed problems. And, if you are being honest with yourself, you have probably learned, like most employees at most jobs, that silence is the safest, least stressful, and most logical course of action.

Consider one multinational high-technology corporation that discovered through an internal survey of its fifty thousand employees that roughly half believed it was not safe to speak up or challenge the way the company operated. Business school professors James Detert and Amy Edmondson then randomly selected 190 employees from five different divisions of that corporation, representing all levels, to understand why they were afraid to express their opinions.[22] Examining only instances in which employees refrained from offering improvement recommendations, Detert and Edmondson found that the most prominent reasons for not speaking up, regardless of situation and context, were fear of being fired, lack of communication skills, and collectively held myths of leaders reacting negatively to such feedback. Those in higher-level positions also muzzled themselves, believing that speaking up would not make much difference and that they had more to lose at that point in their careers. Finally, employees reported that "ideas were valued based on where they came from rather than on their merit," with the best validation being that a competitor firm was already pursuing the same idea. The corporation's director of global finance admitted, "People don't go to management with the options because they are afraid—they try to second-guess what management wants instead of what management really needs to know, and so the problems build up."[23]

The consequences of problems going unaddressed in any firm can be tremendous, and are magnified when a firm faces an unexpected challenge that requires making a consequential strategic decision. This is the point at which slight adjustments or refinements to a strategic plan, based upon incomplete information at hand, are no longer sufficient. A major decision-forcing point requires senior executives to choose a new or alternative strategy. However, for all the reasons detailed above, they frequently fail, and often unnecessarily so. A detailed study of major business failures experienced by 750 publicly traded US companies between 1981 and 2006 estimated that 46 percent could have been avoided if the companies had been more aware of the potential pitfalls, and a significant percentage of the others could have been mitigated.[24] As the authors of the study emphasized: "We found the failures often don't stem from lack of execution. Nor are they due to timing or luck. What we found, instead, is that many of the really big failures stemmed from bad strategies."[25] Even after a strategic decision is made, there is widespread acknowledgment that it was unsatisfactory. A 2009 McKinsey survey of 2,200 executives from a range of industries and functional specialties found that they were dissatisfied by not having fully explored the "contrary evidence" or not having paid sufficient attention to "dissenting viewpoints" when making a strategic decision.[26]

This is where external red teams can play a highly consequential role in improving near-term performance through the use of business war games.[27] A business war game is a series of structured, moderated discussions in which small teams of managers or employees assume the role of competitors—primarily other firms, but also government regulators, insurers, or potential customers. The primary objective is to simulate the potential costs and consequences of various strategic decisions. What makes a war game uniquely beneficial for the participating business unit is that the exercise is done collectively, with the guidance of an outside facilitator who does not have allegiances to any group or a vested interest in the outcome. Executives and employees who faithfully participate in business war games overwhelmingly describe them as uncomfortable at first, but ultimately useful, as they cultivate solutions to emerging problems that employees simply would not have conceived of on their own. Moreover, because all participants—from the CEO to junior staffers—are required to play the role of someone from outside their institution, cognitive biases and institutional pathologies are limited. War games tend to significantly reduce the barriers to creative thinking and aversion to new ideas inherent to hierarchical institutions steeped in bureaucratic cultures and pathologies—essentially every modern corporation.

The two most critical elements for successful business war gaming are facilitators with a strong personality to prevent executives and employees from retreating to previously held positions, and senior executives who have accepted the logic in opening up their institution to the experience. According to Ken Sawka, president of the war-gaming firm Fuld and Company, the best facilitators do extensive homework in the form of internal interviews to identify a client's long-standing biases and prejudices, and they undertake research to become well versed in the terminology and lingo specific to that client's market, competitors, and regulatory structures. Facilitators also require personality skills enabling them to think on their feet, work the room to elicit ideas from otherwise tightlipped employees, and capture the concepts and strategies that emerge and present them in a short, actionable template that the company can then implement. Sawka noted: "Success is when a client comes up with four or five strategies that they hadn't thought of already, and they came up with on their own during the course of the war game."[28]

Consistent with other red-teaming techniques, buy-in from a senior executive—and ideally the CEO personally—is a mandatory first step for a business war game to be commissioned and have a meaningful impact. Buy-in is often challenging for two reasons: recognition and cost. Most CEOs are insiders, promoted only after having been immersed in their corporation's culture and values for decades.[29] For the reasons presented above, they are the least likely to recognize the underlying necessity for change, be informed by junior staffers of what needs to change, or accept viewpoints from external consultants that could upset their authority or harm morale. Realistic and impactful red teaming requires ceding some control over the outcome of the red team engagement. CEOs are often unwilling to concede this degree of influence. Worse, they tend to blame others for their company's shortcomings once aware of them.[30] Moreover, the costs of these war games are not trivial. They vary from as little as $20,000 for a tightly scripted, one-time engagement, to more than a half-million dollars for a highly elaborate war game taking months to research and construct. As one financial-services executive who has participated in dozens of them explained: "Unfortunately, it is precisely when a company's back is against the wall and could benefit from red teaming, that senior management will not find the money to do it."[31]

Corporations solicit and commission a war game for one of four reasons. First, war games are frequently deployed to support a new product launch. A business war game helps determine critical components to a new product's success, such as its timing, marketing, pricing, differentiation, and competitor responses. This is especially true for major pharmaceutical companies that might spend more than one billion dollars and a dozen years developing and testing a new drug. The ability of that new drug to find untapped users and compete in an already saturated marketplace can be a make-or-break outcome for senior executives—and they need to know all the ways that its launch might go wrong. Second, war games might be used if the firm has experienced a sudden or near-catastrophic disaster—be it reputational, financial, a harmful court decision, or a shift in a regulatory regime—that has shaken up the senior executives to the extent that they finally concede to the need for outside help to develop and test alternative future strategies. Third, a new vice-president or business-unit head might conduct a war game to differentiate themselves from their predecessors by establishing a new concept or point of emphasis for the corporation. As part of their hiring package, some incoming executives will even require that they be provided the necessary funding to commission their own war game once they have been hired. Fourth, though utilized for this reason less frequently, the board of executives might mandate that senior management experience some sort of business war game, not so much to attempt to improve performance, but to put the executives on notice that they are being closely monitored and might be on the precipice of being fired.

The two types of business war games that are most widely used are those that rely primarily upon statistical models, and those that rely upon moderated discussions. Mark Chussil is an established business war-gamer who conducts scenarios of the statistical variety. He has found that some executives remain "inherently suspicious of using numbers. They believe that somehow the computer will miss something that they feel in their gut." Many executives cling to the belief that their business is unlike any other, is also uniquely complex, and is therefore wholly incomprehensible to outsiders. Yet, as Chussil has found, "It's generally all the same: a customer makes a purchase decision, you have a cost structure, and there are various choices that you can make." Since most companies face such similar types of issues, their competitive environments and future choices can be modeled with complex simulations that take Chussil and his team only a few months to build. Chussil contends that those who refuse to use the right data—put in the proper context—place themselves at a distinct disadvantage. He has also discovered that an added benefit of quantification is that it makes it "very hard to sleepwalk through one of my war games."[32]

Though Chussil likes to remind people that "nobody has data about the future," he believes that quantifying simulated outcomes through war games resolves disputes between business units regarding the future direction of a product line, for example. The data both sharpen differences and, at times, serve as a neutral, third-party broker. Chussil described a war game that he ran for a major telecommunications firm that faced a new competitor about to enter its market, and in which the firm's senior executives were split between two different strategies to respond. They were unable to reach agreement by using their own conventional strategy tools—mainly trend lines, benchmarks, and spreadsheets—since they do not take into account competitive dynamics. So, instead, Chussil built and ran a simulation that estimated the likely consequences from each scenario, including the actions and reactions of the competitors. Either way, the telecommunications firm was going to lose some market share, which is inevitable when a credible new competitor enters a market. However, the simulations revealed that "the potential revenue differences between the two options were enormous, but they just couldn't identify this on their own."[33]

For a typical war game, Chussil likes to run through the entire decision-making process and time horizon at least twice. In the first round, the participants inevitably try to micromanage the outcome by merely tweaking the strategy just enough so that the company cannot fail. He noted: "That's not because they're stupid, narrow, or complacent; it's because they think that'll be enough . . . and because it's what everyone has always done in their company." The simulation reveals that doing so either makes very little difference in achieving the company's goals or even causes the company to lose ground relative to its competitors.

In the second round, participants usually stop trying to manage the outcomes because they have just experienced how small steps have too limited an impact and should be avoided. Then, during the subsequent rounds of the war game, the participants will actually strategize and compete. According to Chussil, "They invariably get one really big surprise, an 'oh my God, I never thought of it that way!' moment, which they have to willfully tune out in order to miss." This willful ignorance rarely happens because the types of clients that come to him are generally open to and expecting new ideas. Chussil adds, "It is not simply that some idea was new, but that it was generated collectively."[34]

Benjamin Gilad takes a different approach, one that avoids basing the war games on numbers. He has run hundreds of war games, including many for Proctor & Gamble, Mars, Pratt & Whitney, and other Fortune 500 companies, and he wrote one of the more accessible books on the topic.[35] He is a strong proponent of conducting business war games through moderated discussions, facilitated with a no-nonsense approach that one might expect from the former Israeli police intelligence officer. His reluctance to employ data-driven simulations stems not from a discomfort with numbers, but rather from a disbelief that they provide an accurate or complete picture for executive decision-makers: "The second you put numbers into a computer, you move from reality to fantasy."[36] Gilad finds that it is difficult for businesses to apply liberating structures to themselves for two reasons. First, senior vice presidents often suffer from myopia, believing that their company is the center of the universe and that the actions and reactions of other companies do not matter. The second challenge is overconfidence in the strategy that an executive already has in mind. Thereafter, the self-imposed war game becomes, in practice, simply a "confirmatory game."

Prospective clients often find out about him via word of mouth or because they have experienced a war game before, and they usually approach him at a time when their firm is at a difficult crossroads. It is exactly when a company is most under stress that it becomes receptive to the often-unpleasant experience of a war game, and is therefore willing to change based upon the outcomes. Though, as a self-described "mercenary," Gilad recognizes that some floundering companies might have difficulty affording to commission a war game, it is at that moment that "you can have a revolution."[37]

Gilad conducts various types of war games, but the one used most routinely is a competitor-response simulation. For this, he relies upon Harvard Business School professor Michael Porter's Four Corners Model—a liberating structure intended to predict a competitor's reactions to a business strategy.[38] Gilad requires participants to assume the role of their competitors in order to stress-test how they will likely respond to a strategic choice. Since most executives and managers think of themselves as intrinsically better than their rivals, they generally find it extremely difficult to understand or empathize with those rivals. In order to push them to assume the role, Gilad uses tricks like having them dress in a shirt with the competitor's logo and bringing in the competitor's products. This model also requires a small commitment to learn the competitor's position in the market, the types of hot buttons that drive their executives, and the blind spots that the competitor appears to ignore. By going through the steps of Porter's liberating structure, participants are able to see things from their competitor's point of view, and new insights emerge about likely responses to a strategic decision. Having immersed himself in the industry in preparation for the exercise, Gilad's primary role as the facilitator, as he describes it with a brutal frankness, is "to call bullshit on everybody in the room, especially the executives." When they do not play their part, he likes to remind the participants, "I am the market and I want to save your jobs. You don't want to be faithful in doing this, you'll be out of a job." He tells them, "This is the only safe environment you will have to put the elephant in the room on the table and discuss."[39]

The second half of Gilad's war games involves developing a new strategy utilizing the findings of competitor responses. This step is also challenging, and most companies that Gilad works for have difficulty clearly articulating such a new strategy. Firms and institutions in any field tend to mistake objectives (which most everybody can identify) with strategy (the guiding principles and courses of action to achieve those objectives). Once they grow accustomed to the terminology and approach, this is the point in the war game that people finally speak freely, and propose new ideas and initiatives. Gilad describes success as when "somebody proposes a really good, concise idea and the room suddenly goes quiet. Everybody knows that they've nailed it. In every game that I oversee, I am struggling for one of those 'a-ha! moments'."[40]

Occasionally, Gilad runs into cases where executives' egos prevent open discussion and the emergence of such moments. To minimize this, he requires that the senior executives sponsoring the war game attend as observers, and then, at the conclusion, he has them vote on the best proposed strategy. "I force them to be concrete, to propose the outline of what are the best steps that should flow from that strategy."[41] Ideally, those senior executives will later require that a management team expand that outline to develop an operational plan, which is then presented to a management review committee. Gilad also writes up a two-page after-action review of the war game pointing out obvious blind spots that the targeted company still faces, but which senior executives do not want to confront. According to Gilad, in the absence of a scheduled event or unexpected external shock, a large business need only perform a war game once every five years. If any business is commissioning an annual war game to review its strategy, then that probably means it is simply war gaming in place of having one.

Ultimately, war games help executives and employees to collectively generate insights that they could not come up with on their own. These insights lead to information gathering and research, further clarification of new business initiatives, specific tasking and work plans, and, ultimately, an updated strategy. Most business war-gamers aspire to ultimately transform a targeted institution's corporate culture so that everybody is able to think like a mini-strategist. Indeed, after having participated in a truncated version of one of these war games, it is evident that they do make you think more strategically, if only for a limited time. This is no small feat because most people either do not consciously, or cannot practically, think in a truly strategic manner. Even so, while the effect on those exposed to business war games is powerful, it is ultimately ephemeral. Employees return to their daily jobs, which are shaped by the same set of accepted behaviors, hierarchical pressures, and carefully prescribed tasks. Like other external red teams, consultants who run business war games cannot make the targeted institution that hired them do anything differently based upon the experience. Whether quantitative or qualitative, business war games tend to fail for the same reasons that red teams have trouble making an impact on targeted institutions in other fields.

Most often, a senior executive attempts to restrict the scope of the war game so that internal processes or personnel issues—at times the critical weakness of the business—are off the table. Once the war game is under way, an executive might also try to use their influence to restrict or direct what is supposed to be an open-ended conversation toward one strategic outcome. Facilitators of war games can recite instances where the process was a total wasted effort, which, they claim soon afterward resulted in executives losing their jobs. Chussil, Gilad, and other business war-gamers can all relate to stories where an executive at some level commissioned their services simply to obtain external validation for a decision that had already been reached within the CEO's suite. One of the critical skills that good business war-gamers develop to prevent such pointless or fraudulent simulations is to sniff out a corporation's intentions during the initial scoping conversations. Most business war games fail because an executive simply does not want to hear bad news.

Whether steps are taken based on the bad news that the red team finds depends wholly upon the executive—or group of executives—with the authority to execute them. Chief executives claim above all other traits to value creativity as the most important leadership competency, even over effectiveness and influence.[42] Yet, virtually all of the research that has been conducted on business decision-making finds that executives are distinctly uncreative, deeply myopic, and overconfident both in themselves personally, and also in their company's ability to beat its competitors. Or, at least, not to fail. For those rare executives who possess the self-awareness to recognize their personal limitations and inflated confidences, business war games provide a meaningful and impactful solution to information overload, increasing complexity and velocity, and cutthroat competition. However, there are other types of red teaming that corporations employ as well—in particular, vulnerability probes to test the viability assuredness of their defensive systems and the security of something they value.

White-Hat Hackers and Hamster Wheels: Cyber Penetration Tests

Red teaming is a natural fit for the private-sector cyber domain, especially given the potentially enormous costs and consequences of cybersecurity breaches. Though corporations go a long way to conceal the breaches they suffer regularly, the frequency and gravity of such attacks are undoubtedly increasing. According to anonymous surveys of cyber-security officials, the costs of not conducting faithful penetration tests are significant, and rising, in terms of both money and time. A 2014 survey of 3,900 IT professionals by Kaspersky Lab found that the average damage from a data-security incident was $49,000 for companies with less than 1,500 employees, and $720,000 for those with more than 1,500.[43] A similar 2014 survey of fifty-nine US companies conducted by the Ponemon Institute found that the average time to resolve a cyber attack was forty-five days, at an average cost of $1.6 million—an increase of 33 percent from the previous year's average cost of just over $1 million, with an average thirty-two-day resolution period.[44] The vast majority of these attacks are denials of service, malicious insiders, and web-based attacks—that together account for more than 55 percent of cyber costs—with approximately 86 percent of perpetrators residing outside of the firm and 12 percent inside, and 2 percent perpetrated by joint actors.[45] Whereas large corporations—those with more than 2,500 employees—were once the direct targets of the majority of cyber attacks, criminals are increasingly turning toward stealing data from smaller firms, or attacking third-party vendors as gateways to larger corporations.[46]

Consider three recent prominent examples. In 2013, Neiman Marcus was hacked when malware installed on its system collected and transmitted payment data from July 16, 2013 to October 30, 2013, potentially affecting 350,000 customers.[47] From this attack, the retailer incurred an initial estimated cost of $4.1 million during the second quarter of fiscal year 2014.[48] In another instance in May 2014, the Midwest grocery chain Schnunks Markets disclosed that a data breach caused by criminal hackers—which had remained undetected for more than four months—would cost approximately $80 million.[49] Most notably, in 2013, Target experienced a massive data breach that began on Black Friday, in which criminals obtained at least forty million customers' credit card numbers. In that attack, the hackers gained access by first stealing the network credentials Target provided to Fazio Mechanical Services, a heating, ventilation, and air-conditioning contractor hired to monitor energy-use levels in stores, and then breaching Target's internal network. While the initial price tag for the intrusion was estimated to be $61 million in direct financial costs, not to mention the firing of the CEO and chief information officer (CIO), costs reached $148 million less than eight months after the intrusion.[50]

With the increase in breaches such as these, and senior-executive awareness of it, spending on cyber security in the United States has exploded in recent years. The US government spent $12.7 billion on cyber security in fiscal year 2014, with $14 billion requested for fiscal year 2016, and an estimated growth of more than 6 percent expected through 2020.[51] Meanwhile, private-sector cyber-security spending reached $71.1 billion in 2014, and is projected to increase to approximately $86 billion by 2016.[52] These costs will only continue to escalate given two trends facing the cyber domain. The first is the "Internet of Things"—the growing number of Internet-connected devices, which will provide ever more openings for hackers to exploit. By one estimate, the number of these devices is projected to leap from thirteen billion in 2013 to more than fifty billion by 2020.[53] The near-ubiquity of chips, sensors, and implants placed into almost all conceivably Internet-connected devices will provide not only unprecedented conveniences for users, but countless publicly accessible portals for hackers. This expanded "attack surface" is not limited to the personal conveniences in your home and car, but even includes medical devices that keep you alive. Security researchers have repeatedly demonstrated how easy it is to hack and control—at distances of up to three hundred feet—many wireless-implanted medical devices, including pacemakers, neurostimulators, and insulin pumps.[54]

The second trend is the commodification and diffusion of hacking. The cyber black market is growing larger and more complex, signified, in part, by the increasing introduction of malware and exploit kits— programs used to carry out automated malware attacks usually sold for between $25 and $2,000. Between 2006 and 2011, the number of new exploit kits entering the market each year increased from one to sixteen, but during the two years that followed, that number more than doubled.[55] Among the most well-known examples of off-the-shelf hacking was the aforementioned Target data breach, which was reportedly conducted with BlackPOS malware, developed by a seventeen-year-old hacker known as "ree4" in St. Petersburg, Russia. The boy reportedly sold the source code for either between $1,800 and $2,000 or a share of the profits generated from stolen credit card information. Hackers simply purchased the boy's malware and used it to penetrate the computer network of Target's third-party heating, ventilation, and air-conditioning contractor to get to Target itself. Even though BlackPOS was not a particularly advanced program, it went entirely undetected by the contractor and Target's antivirus programs, with Target ultimately only learning of the breach from federal investigators.[56]

Despite these troubling trends, most cyber intrusions plaguing the private sector can be prevented or at least mitigated by implementing a handful of best practices that require little additional time and money.[57] The problem is that these defensive measures are only capable of preventing or detecting older types of well-known and relatively unsophisticated cyber attacks. In the offense-defense dynamic characterizing the cyber domain, defensive best practices are eventually defeated or become irrelevant as attackers continually develop new offensive tactics to break into targeted networks. Moreover, as is true with every institution researched for this book, internal cyber-security improvements tend to become part of the normalized day-to-day routine of the senior management, employees, and IT staff. The institution comes to assume that their company's current network security configuration or procedures are the acceptable and expected way of doing things. Security becomes a given in the absence of a harmful attack. Needless to say, motivated and sophisticated criminal hackers have proven time and time again that private-sector cyber defenses are eminently vulnerable.

To address this gap, internal best-practice improvements are increasingly supplemented with red team vulnerability probes. These probes are called penetration tests, or "pen tests,"[58] and are conducted by "white-hat" hackers—a reference to the color of "good guys" cowboy hats in Hollywood westerns. "White hats" are distinguished from "black hats"—who also hack into computer networks and software code, but often do so with malicious intent and without a target's authorization. This distinction can be an oversimplification because all of the best and most proficient white hats started off doing some black-hat hacking before they began to hack lawfully as a profession. And even then, it is not uncommon for hackers to have a day job conducting penetration tests, but then in their personal life to also engage in unauthorized hacking for political or ideological purposes, or just as a hobby. Indeed, the fluidity of identity within the hacking community is one of its core defining features, and efforts to pigeonhole somebody into one category or the other is strongly resisted. In countless conversations with hackers, the motivating impulse, repeated in slightly differing forms, is an innate curiosity to discover what new authorized or unauthorized hacks they can accomplish. This generally tempers with age, as hackers eventually prefer a greater degree of stability and a reliable salary over open-ended exploration and comparatively little income.

The idea that computer hacking is glamorous or exciting could not be further from the truth. Essentially, it can be distilled down to an ability to sit and meticulously stare at a computer screen—while often fueled by copious energy drinks—and recognize patterns or vulnerabilities that can be exploited. Hackers describe what they do as comparable to a book editor trying to make sense of a partial manuscript in a foreign language or a medieval monk copying by hand a religious text onto parchment paper. There are increasingly powerful software programs that allow some of this to be done through automation, especially the mass scanning of network vulnerabilities and the line-by-line reviewing of source code. However, manual web hacking and source-code review by a human being still consistently finds a greater number of serious vulnerabilities than an automated assessment can by itself.[59] There is also a widely held perception within the community that the best hackers have some degree of autism, allowing a higher degree of focus and concentration than others (though this is not stated to trivialize the syndrome itself). Additionally, the field is almost 90-percent male, and, according to many women and men attached to it, hugely unwelcoming to women.[60] One cyber-security professional who has taught penetration testing—including courses exclusively for women—for several years observed, "Women are too smart to be pen testers. Once they made it through the rigorous training to be a computer engineer, they want to be part of an organization where their participation adds value. Breaking into things and pointing out flaws doesn't do this."[61]

Hacking is also more of an art than a science because the approaches and tactics utilized are highly dependent upon each individual's background and skillset. Veteran white hats estimate that if you told two hackers to identify as many security vulnerabilities as they could for one website, they would find only around 50 percent of the same vulnerabilities. For software source-code reviews, the amount of overlapping vulnerabilities is estimated to be even lower. With individuals coming into it from distinct paths and backgrounds, there is no universally embraced industry standard for penetration testers, other than the Certified Ethical Hacking (CEH) training and certification that one earns by simply taking a five-day course and passing a four-hour, 125-question exam. Among virtually all prominent penetration testers, CEH training is considered woefully formulaic, insufficient, and outdated—and most even suggest that it is a good idea to omit the qualification from one's résumé.[62] In February 2014, the website of the CEH-sponsoring institution, the International Council of E-Commerce Consultants, was hacked and a copy of Edward Snowden's passport and his application letter to become CEH certified was posted on its homepage.[63]

The state of hacking can be summarized, in part, by looking at the trends in its conferences. Once simply showcases where small numbers of hackers showed off their skills, built reputations, and developed some shared sense of community, the number of such conferences has grown significantly, as has the number of participants. According to one estimate, there were just five conferences in the United States dedicated exclusively to hacking in 2009. By 2014, there were thirty-seven, and an additional seventeen on cyber security.[64] Over that same period, attendance at the two largest conferences—the freewheeling DEF CON and the more professional Black Hat—grew from 10,000 to 16,000, and from 4,000 to 9,000, respectively.[65] However, according to many longtime participants, these gatherings have become increasingly dull and pedestrian, as presenters routinely describe their latest hacking stunt in the hopes of it getting picked up by the press, rather than out of a sincere effort to educate and inform others. Another reason is that the market for what are called zero-day exploits—essentially hacks that have not yet been disclosed, or of which the target is still unaware—has grown markedly.[66] While the best hacks were once bragged about at conferences, now they are kept quiet and sold on the black market to a vulnerable company, interested government, or criminal network. Though the zero-day exploit market is deeply opaque, it is estimated that the average price for potentially harmful hacks is between $40,000 and $250,000, with the US government believed to be the largest purchaser.[67]

Jeff Moss (a.k.a., The Dark Tangent) founded both the DEF CON and, later, Black Hat conferences.[68] At forty years old, he is considered both a grandfather and conscience of the field, and is the former chief security officer at the Internet Corporation for Assigned Names and Numbers (ICANN), the international body that sets Internet rules. Moss said of this black-market phenomenon: "In the early days there was no way to monetize exploits. Now they are worth huge amounts of money on the underground market, so they aren't being shared as much in public. Subsequently, the conferences have been going downhill a little bit because some of the most interesting exploits and ideas remain hidden." Moreover, because the size of the community has expanded so rapidly, with highly specialized subfields of expertise, there is less of a community feel at the conferences and of a shared sense of accepted and expected norms of behavior. Moss noted that "in the early days, you knew everybody important from the message boards or the conferences, but now it is impossible to keep track. I keep thinking this [cyber-security] world can't get any bigger and diversified, but it just does."[69]

Corporations generally commission a penetration test for one of three reasons: they experienced a costly breach to which they are reacting; they became security conscious after learning how well-reported breaches have impacted others; or they are mandated to commission them by regulatory agencies or insurers, an increasingly common circumstance. For example, the Commodity Futures Trading Commission requires financial institutions to hire "an independent party to test and monitor the safeguards' controls, systems, policies and procedures" at least once every two years.[70] The Health Insurance Portability and Accountability Act (HIPAA) requires health-care companies to "conduct an accurate and thorough assessment of the potential risks and vulnerabilities to the confidentiality, integrity, and availability of electronic protected health information," which has been interpreted by the National Institute of Standards and Technology to include "conduct[ing] penetration testing . . . if reasonable and appropriate."[71] In November 2013, the latest Payment Card Industry Data Security Standard (PCI DSS) requirement standards were released, which included new penetration-testing requirements.[72] There has also been an emergence and growth of cyber risk insurance—with spending on insurance nearly doubling from 2013 to 2014—that provides protection against the financial costs incurred from a data, network, or privacy compromise in the cyber domain.[73] These policies require maintaining an "effective and updated" level of security, which some corporations have interpreted to include the commissioning of a pen test.

The efficacy of a white-hat penetration test is inevitably influenced by a company's motivation for subjecting itself to one. When compelled by regulators or insurers, it is usually doomed to be a perfunctory, check-the-box exercise, scoped as narrowly as possible. One white hat even described being hired to conduct penetration tests for as little as one IP (Internet Protocol) address at a predetermined time, which is not a realistic adversarial assessment of any company's cyber defenses. However, when penetration tests are conducted soon after a harmful incident, or out of an awareness of cyber threats to an industry, the company will often be more open to a realistic and comprehensive assessment, and more willing to listen to findings. In advance of a software device or website launch, most Fortune 500 firms will commission an external pen test. Goldman Sachs, for example, will hire two white-hat firms to conduct separate independent pen tests for applications or websites that are deemed highly critical assets.[74] The cost of these tests varies from as little as $1,000 for a one-time test of a limited number of IP addresses, to over $150,000 for the open-ended and continuous testing of large corporations or nonprofit institutions.[75] Even as financial costs and reputational damage from cyber attacks grow, companies still must try to keep operating costs low. Subsequently, the overwhelming majority of companies do the minimum amount of preventive security possible, including the fewest possible number of mandated penetration tests.[76]

White-hat penetration tests come in many forms, but fall within three broad categories: black box tests, in which the pen testers have no knowledge of the target apart from a website or software name; white box tests, during which they have full knowledge of and access to a network configuration or some device; and grey box tests, which feature some degree of knowledge and access. The category of test selected by a company depends on what it is most concerned about protecting, what sorts of adversaries it is most worried about, and how much information it believes such an adversary could gather about it to use in a malicious cyber attack.

A typical external white-hat penetration test of a company's computer networks consists of four steps. First, it involves scoping the terms of the engagement with the targeted institution, through phone calls, in-person meetings, and surveys with the CIO or information security manager. The white hats learn why the targeted institution has commissioned the test, what resources and time it will commit to the engagement and to implement any recommended corrective actions, and what impacts of a cyber attack worry it the most—with financial and reputational costs always being the top two. At this point in the process, the rules of engagement for the test are established, including who and what will be tested, when it will occur, and who within the targeted institution will be informed in advance—ideally, the fewest people possible. The category and scope selected determine the composition of the white-hat team, which might include experts in networks, operating systems, databases, and mobile devices, and a manager who serves as the "conductor" and "muralist."

Second, white hats conduct reconnaissance of the targeted institution, and use widely available software programs to map the network, determine the operating system, and scan for publicly accessible portals. As a real-life example, white hats can quickly determine who the network administrators are for any company, gather granular personally identifiable information about them from LinkedIn profiles, social media websites, and publicly available datasets, use a software program to build a wordlist of their potential passwords, rank those passwords based upon likelihood, and then continually try to log in with them. If administrator access requires a second level of authentication—fingerprints, voice- or facial-recognition, or eye scans—white hats either preempt or bypass that requirement or design software that spoofs the fingerprint, voice, face, or digital retinal display of the administrator. They also gather the e-mail addresses and phone numbers of all employees, the locations of the server rooms, the type of operating system and version used at that time, information about vendors, and much more, depending how much time is allotted.

Third is the penetration test itself, when white hats will almost always obtain some degree of unauthorized access, usually through some glaring lack of human judgment. Veteran white hat David Kennedy has found that the two most common ways, in order, that he gets into a client's networks are through reusing default passwords that IT administrators simply do not change, and via spear phishing attacks on employees.[77] The latter consist of those misleading e-mails you receive that attempt to lure you into clicking a corrupted link; if you have gone through cyber awareness training at your job to try and prevent this, white hats are well aware of this too, and have long ago adjusted their tactics to take it into account. Brendan Conlon, a hacker formerly with the National Security Agency's (NSA) Tailored Access Operations group and founder of the pen-testing firm Vahna, described a spear phishing attack against one small company: "We sent an e-mail to one hundred people, disguised as a Fidelity retirement plan e-mail, and fifty of them opened it immediately, and entered all of their personal information."[78] Such stories are not uncommon.

Sometimes, the targeted institution has restrictive firewalls and responsive intrusion-detection mechanisms. In these cases, while it might take more thought and effort, and white hats might employ more advanced tactics, they will nevertheless find a way in.[79] For example, they might obtain access to the voice mailbox for the IT help desk, erase a recent voicemail left by a frustrated employee, immediately call that employee back impersonating a member of the IT team, and then ask them for their user ID and login information. Or, if you can e-mail PDF files to the copy machine at your office, white hats can use the copier as a Trojan horse to get access to your desktop computer. Similarly, when information-security company Trustwave's white hats could not find vulnerabilities or passwords at one targeted company, they obtained access to its security cameras and used them to zoom in on employees as they logged into their computers (known as shoulder surfing), eventually allowing them unfettered access to the company's network. That was back in 2010. Today, there are a vast number of more advanced methods and pathways available to breach computer networks. Moreover, if the white hats know about these tactics, there is no doubt that criminals and malicious hackers know them as well.[80]

Fourth, during the final stage, the white hats provide a report featuring an executive summary, documentation—through screenshots and scripts—of exactly what vulnerabilities they identified, and a list of corrective actions prioritized by immediate need and costs. According to most white hats, the CIO, or occasionally the CEO, rarely reads more than the executive summary, after which they thumb to the recommendation section and inquire: "So how much will all of this cost?" Though rare, senior management will, at times, even dismiss outright what white hats were able to achieve, on the mistaken belief that they were uniquely sophisticated, beyond what a black-hat hacker might be capable of. Moss said, "Executives will try to dismiss what you have done. Say it is a one-point-in-time fluke, or that their network was just malfunctioning." There have been instances where the white hats activated a piece of malware on the CEO's desktop, essentially announcing that she or he has been hacked, just to drive the point home. White-hat firms offer follow-up pen tests as often as needed, with most recommending one at least annually for a Fortune 500 company. The shared opinion among many is that a targeted institution will fix the most severe vulnerabilities identified

roughly three-quarters of the time, but that for less consequential vulnerabilities, the requisite corrective actions are rarely implemented.[81]

White-hat red teaming is often a constant source of frustration for
everyone involved. The white hats always penetrate the targeted institution, deliberately doing so with a very low level of skill, by employing relatively crude and widely available tactics. In fact, most white-hat
hackers find their jobs to be so easy that they pursue more innovative,
and potentially illegal, hacking activities while off duty. After a penetration test, the IT staff members at the targeted institution are invariably
demoralized, not only because their fears have been confirmed, but also
because they know they still will not receive the level of support and
funding from higher management necessary to fully address the vulnerabilities. The most obvious weaknesses are addressed with a software
patch, alteration in network architecture, or minor changes to IT and
employee procedures, when a more comprehensive security overhaul is
probably required. "Cybersecurity on a hamster wheel," is how cyber-
security specialist (and former IDART member) Dino Dai Zovi describes this commonly experienced phenomenon. At the RVASEC Conference in June 2014, one speaker asked the three hundred information
security professionals in attendance two questions: "How many of you
have the resources you need to protect your networks? How many of
you have the personnel you need to protect your networks?" Zero hands
were raised.

Red teaming in the private-sector cyber realm is now widespread,
and, for most large corporations, mandatory for identifying a company's
most obvious and consequential vulnerabilities. The inherent challenge
for white hats is convincing senior management, by emulating adversarial hackers and easily breaching the company's cyber defenses, that
more spending on preventive measures—which subtract from short-term
profits—is necessary. "You have to demonstrate the business value of a
potential vulnerability, and the likelihood that someone could exploit
that vulnerability in order for a company to spend the money to change
its overall security posture," is how longtime security professional Ira
Winkler described it.[82] But just as important as obtaining more money

is making sure that it is redirected to more realistic threats. Bob Stasio, who was an NSA hacker and is now vice president of threat intelligence at the security firm CyberIQ Services, has found that "there is money in the C-suite, but the way that it is spent on cyber security is often totally irrelevant to the threats posed by adversaries."[83] Thus, red teaming in the private cyber sector, as in other fields and domains, is done for multiple reasons and on behalf of multiple audiences, but it's done most importantly to provide the justification for allotting or redirecting additional resources to the IT staff. For the foreseeable future, white-hat penetration tests will both remain sorely needed to protect institutions against the growing number and sophistication of cyber threats, and be continuously commissioned.

Of course, not all white-hat penetration testing is done at the request of a company. Sometimes, as we shall see, it is done to satisfy hackers' innate curiosity to explore whether supposedly secure computer networks and supporting infrastructure can be used to do something beyond their original intent.

I Can Hear You (and Everyone Else) Now: Hacking Verizon

In 2011, Sean Parker, cofounder of Napster and a founding president of Facebook, became convinced that somebody might be listening in on his cell-phone conversations. The previous year, Justin Timberlake had portrayed him as a cocky and über-paranoid entrepreneur in the movie *The Social Network*, adapted from Ben Mezrich's 2009 book *The Accidental Billionaires: The Founding of Facebook, A Tale of Sex, Money, Genius, and Betrayal*. Apparently, that portrayal of paranoia had some basis in reality. Parker relayed his concern to a friend who worked at iSEC Partners, a security firm specializing in penetration testing and software-design verification. Though his friend expressed skepticism given the normal encryption standards that are built into cellular communications, Parker wondered if someone could have gained unauthorized access to his Verizon cell phone through the femtocell in his apartment.

Femtocells are basically miniature cell-phone towers that look like normal Wi-Fi routers. They are used to prevent coverage "dead zones" in rural areas or office buildings, and are given away freely where reception is especially poor or can be purchased at a Verizon store for $250. If you are within approximately forty feet of a femtocell—depending on any obstructive objects—your cell phone will automatically associate with it, without your permission or knowledge. Your phone connects to the femtocell over cellular radio, either through the CDMA (for Verizon or Sprint) or GSM (for AT&T and T-Mobile) radio systems. The femtocell then uses a broadband Internet connection to create an Internet portal security tunnel back to your carrier's internal network. If you work in or even just walked through a large office building in any major metropolitan area, your cell phone will almost assuredly be connecting to multiple femtocells automatically.

Parker's friend had never heard of them, but came to Parker's apartment to retrieve the femtocell, intending to hack into it at some point. Parker did not explicitly hire iSEC to do anything—the project was to be a sort of pro bono white-hat penetration test. From there, until the summer of 2012, it sat on a shelf for about a year until iSEC Partners had the free time—and an intern, Andrew Rahimi, who had a solid grounding in Verizon products and CDMA—to begin trying to uncover its vulnerabilities. Dan Guido, who was a senior security consultant at iSEC at the time, recalled that it was an open-ended assessment: "We were asking 'wouldn't it be cool if we could get free Internet all the time?' as much as 'what sort of radio emanations could this sniff?'"[84] Like many cyber-security firms, iSEC builds in sponsored research time for such open-ended projects when its employees are not billing clients for their time. This is done in part to satisfy the natural curiosity of hackers, but is also a form of marketing, attracting future employees by giving them the opportunity to explore new areas—in this case, hardware reversing and embedded-device security. It also shows off the firm's skills to the public to hopefully attract future clients.

The initial necessary step of the penetration test was to get access to the targeted device. The Verizon femtocell had an HDMI port—normally used for televisions—so they had to build a special console cable by soldering one that contained an HDMI connector to another with a USB connector. (They took advantage of a helpful online video demonstrating how to do this.) With relative ease, they discovered that they could get persistent root access to the femtocell by simply exploiting a built-in delay in the boot-up process. The device ran a Monte Vista Linux operating system, and after a few months of working during their scheduled research time, and repeating it through trial-and-error, they were able to write a custom code that found and translated all of the data packets that passed through it.

Once they were in the femtocell, the level of access was astonishing. They were able to record calls made by phones that were connected to the femtocell by transcoding the captured data streams into playable audio waveforms. In doing this, they were shocked to find out that cell phones start to transmit a caller's voice into the carrier's network once the caller presses "send"—even before the phone starts ringing or connects with another phone. (To many mobile-device-security experts, hearing about this incidental discovery was as consequential as the femtocell hack itself: very few people knew that a phone transmits any audio it receives before a call is even connected.) Eventually, they were also able to get SMS text messages, and, easiest of all, capture smartphone data, including any websites visited, as well as the user names and passwords entered into an online banking portal. In essence, they were able to completely compromise a Verizon cell phone through the femtocell. Tom Ritter, a senior consultant at iSEC and member of the team, emphasized that what they achieved was not particularly difficult, although someone with no expertise could not have done it. Overall, approximately five people participated in the project, including at least one principal-level consultant. Nevertheless, Ritter estimated that perhaps the top 5 percent of college-age hackers could have pulled it off given enough time.

The iSEC Partners pen testers also identified three far more nefarious vulnerabilities that they could have exploited. First, since the mobile identification number and electronic serial numbers for nearby Verizon phones also transited the femtocell, they figured out how to capture those handset registration numbers. They could then enter those two number sets into a separate handset, thus cloning a smartphone without even having to touch it, and without alerting the owner. Using the cloned smartphone, the pen testers could have sent calls or text messages that would have appeared to come from the victim's phone.

Second, they could have proactively targeted specific individuals or anyone in a fixed area by simply placing a femtocell into a large handbag or backpack, powered by a small battery pack, and simply standing near anyone whose calls or data they wanted to intercept. Since they could identify each phone number as soon as it connected to the femtocell, they could have then quickly left the area once the target's phone was captured. Third, they believed that they could have used the femtocell to get into the internal Verizon network, and could even see specific servers that might have allowed this. (In fact, two years earlier, three cyber researchers demonstrated precisely how to do this with femtocells provided by the French mobile carrier SFR.[85]) The iSEC Partners white hats did not attempt the latter two exploitations, however, as their lawyers informed them that both were illegal.

Self-directed white-hat penetration testing of this sort entails an ethical dilemma. Once a group of hackers discovers a vulnerability, they must then decide how, to whom, or for how much money, they should uncover their findings. The hackers can gratuitously expose it either to gain quick publicity or to embarrass a company or government. They may also use it for highly malicious activities like spying or just sell it to the highest bidder on the black market. The growth in this black-market industry has led to an increasing number of social media and technology companies publicly offering a small "bug bounty" of a few hundred to a few thousand dollars for white hats disclosing vulnerabilities in their networks or software.[86] Finally, white hats engage in what is called "responsible disclosure," where the impacted stakeholders are given time to take an exposed system offline or distribute a security patch before the vulnerability is published or presented at a conference. The challenge for hackers who wish to practice responsible disclosure is that many software or web-based firms that may have critical security vulnerabilities do not have a system in place to receive and triage any reports of vulnerabilities.[87]

In this instance, iSEC Partners chose responsible disclosure, though it did not receive any payment for doing so. In early-December 2012, the iSEC Partners team contacted Verizon to detail the vulnerabilities it had found within the carrier's femtocells. (The team contacted Verizon informally through a friend who worked on the security team there. This is common practice because unknown hackers that report vulnerabilities can find themselves facing a lawsuit from the victimized company, which might perceive itself as facing a blackmail threat.) Though Verizon has internal security teams that are supposed to uncover such security short-comings before and after devices like femtocells are released, they were unaware of this specific vulnerability before iSEC Partners alerted them of it. Moreover, Verizon had earlier commissioned a penetration test of the femtocell by an external white-hat firm that specialized in mobile application device and security. Both that company and iSEC Partners were owned by the same British holding company, NCC Group, which has bought up more than a dozen small pen-testing firms in an effort to corner the market. Behind the scenes, Verizon would later express its frustration with NCC Group because one of its firms was hired to find vulnerabilities in the femtocell and failed, while another one of its firms, looking in its spare time, succeeded.

The team informed Verizon that it would go public with what they had accomplished, but only after Verizon had fixed the problem. Verizon issued an over-the-air patch in the form of a Linux software update in March. As the patch went out, the iSEC Partners team also informed the Computer Emergency Response Team (CERT) Coordi-nation Center, a federally funded research center serving as a repos-itory for reporting software vulnerabilities. The Vulnerability Note listed the security weaknesses, how the team was able to breach them, and five proposed corrective actions that would reduce the likelihood of Verizon femtocell exploitations in the future.[88] The pen testers were surprised that the script used in the hack, which they had provided to CERT, was published in its complete form, thus providing more detailed information than they, or certainly Verizon, would have chosen to be made public.

It was not until after working with Verizon and CERT that the white hats went public with their hack in July 2013. This was just one month after the initial disclosures of National Security Agency (NSA) surveillance collection of audio, video chats, photographs, and e-mails from most of the largest US Internet companies. Reporters were looking for new stories of how Americans' privacy and civil liberties were potentially being exploited by the government or telecommunications firms. Subsequently, when iSEC Partners contacted several media outlets, there was tremendous interest in what it had uncovered, with a particular fascination in each demonstration to reporters of how the white hats could intercept their calls and text messages. As Ritter told Reuters: "This is not about how the NSA would attack ordinary people. This is about how ordinary people would attack ordinary people."[89]

Months later, they presented their findings to a standing-room-only audience at the two biggest hacker conferences, DEF CON and Black Hat.[90] After warning attendees ahead of time, during the question-and-answer session they displayed real-time texts sent by audience members, whose phones had unknowingly linked to the femtocell. Most of the texts were juvenile, promoted personal websites, or had some political message, such as "'You talk, we listen'-#NSA." Finally, iSEC Partners released an app called FemtoCatcher—with its source code—for Verizon Android smartphones, which automatically switches a device into airplane mode when it detects that your phone has connected to a femtocell. Ultimately, it believed carriers should get rid of femtocells altogether, since they would always be vulnerable to anybody who could get access to one, and instead pursue the more costly and difficult gold standard of end-to-end encryption.

This responsibly disclosed pro bono red team vulnerability probe conducted by the iSEC Partners white hats turned out to be indispensable. At the time, Verizon had more than one hundred million American subscribers. And although Verizon claimed in a press release that no customers had complained about their phones being breached, other groups with less benign motives already knew of the security flaw. After the hacker conferences, a few hacker groups approached the iSEC Partners presenters and told them that, with slight variations, the hacker groups were also able to get persistent root access on femtocells. The iSEC Partners team determined that these sources were telling the truth, based upon the highly technical vernacular they used and process steps that they described.[91] In addition, no representatives from law enforcement ever informally spoke to them about the hack, which would normally be the case for such a consequential vulnerability, leading the iSEC Partners team to assume that law enforcement already knew about it as well. Thus, although others had identified the vulnerability in Verizon femtocells, iSEC Partners was the only group that brought it to the carrier's attention and publicized the results. Most critically, it did not do so in a "gotcha" fashion to humiliate the telecommunications giant, but rather did so to improve customer privacy. This was assuredly just one of many, still-unknown security weaknesses that cell phones face. But if the white hats had not taken the time and effort to uncover this particular vulnerability, it would have remained a potential threat to privacy and civil liberties. The femtocell hack illustrates the inherent challenge for even a security-conscious telecommunications firm like Verizon to find its own weaknesses. It was only through an external ad hoc red team that this dire vulnerability was uncovered and responsibly reported.

Why Your Secure Building Isn't: Physical Penetration Tests

In the course of conducting interviews for this book, I was fortunate to secure an interview with a very senior official in a government security position.[92] After initially having failed to obtain a meeting with him, I requested that a mutual acquaintance pass along a short e-mail, from a Gmail account, describing my research project and the sorts of questions that I hoped to ask. Weeks later, an administrative assistant to this senior official reached out to me and let me know that he had agreed to meet me in person. The administrative assistant and I spoke over the phone to arrange a time the following week, mid-morning at the senior official's office. The assistant then sent me a confirmation e-mail with information about the location, different transportation options to get there, and a reminder to bring along my government-issued ID.

The office building was a highly secure facility, set back more than a block from any traffic, and ringed with blast walls, a series of controlled-access points, armed guards, surveillance cameras, and metal-detection screening equipment. Once past the access points, visitors are required to show their IDs, have scheduled a meeting that appears in a shared internal database, get their photograph taken, receive a visitor's badge with their photograph that is always supposed to be stuck to one's chest, and, finally, have an employee escort them through the hallways.

Due to heavy traffic, I arrived at the facility already five minutes late. While waiting in a long line to pass through a metal detector, a security guard answered a phone call, and then she shouted out a close approx-imation of my name. When I stepped out of line to answer her, before I could say anything, she said, "Oh you can go ahead, they are waiting for you upstairs." I walked to the front of the line, thinking that I still needed to be screened, but she simply waved her arm and declared, "No, no, you can just go around and head on in." Next, I approached a front desk, which several armed guards stood behind, to show my passport in order to get my picture taken or receive my badge. Instead, before I got to the desk, a young man—almost certainly an intern—asked me, "Are you Zenko?" After I nodded in the affirmative, he replied, "Okay, let's go." Not only was I never asked to show my ID, checked against the internal database, nor provided a badge, but also, before the young man and I walked away, a guard behind the desk handed me a slip of paper that mysteriously read: "SCREENED." I placed it in my pocket. We then walked to a bank of elevators and took the next available one to the senior official's office. After a two-minute wait, he and I were sitting together in a small conference room. Nobody had ever verified who I was or even screened me for weapons or explosives.

Ironically, though I was barely aware of it at the time, I could have been conducting a red team vulnerability probe of the facility myself.

It would have required little effort combing through publicly available databases to determine who was the best candidate to serve as a trusted intermediary between the senior official and myself. The technical skills required to obtain unauthorized access to the mutual acquaintance's Gmail account, and then simply pretend to pass along an e-mail that purportedly came from me, are easily obtainable. By conducting simple reconnaissance of the allegedly highly secure facility, I might have recognized the vulnerabilities in processing visitors who arrived late for meetings with people who are pressed for time. Furthermore, I could have coerced or bribed the intern to vouch for me once inside, or even placed a trusted accomplice in the internship program ahead of time. I may have been able to obtain access to the shared internal database and create a "scheduled" meeting with the official. Finally, I could have determined that visitors received a "SCREENED" piece of paper and made several duplicates of it, in case someone had stopped me unescorted. What happened in this particular instance was that I broke in, but only by accident. And while I found it troubling how relatively easy this was, it should have been in no way surprising. Moreover, in the private sector, the level of security for most buildings is actually far worse.

When you walk into most modern office buildings—whether a corporate high-rise, hospital, or casino—you expect and recognize the prerequisites of security. These include surveillance cameras, doors requiring the swipe of an employee-access card, a magnetometer screening device you walk through, friendly greeters sitting behind the front desk to answer questions and process visitors, and somber security guards observing the environment. When you see these ubiquitous symbols of security you might be reassured that the building is adequately protected from criminals, terrorists, or disgruntled employees. However, you would be deeply mistaken because the outward appearance of security is rarely correlated with the actual protection of that building, or the people and contents within.

Most companies spend the minimum amount possible securing their facilities because this funding is pulled out of their immediate profit margins. The level of security rarely rises beyond the minimum insurance or government-regulated standards, as interpreted through industry-approved best practices. And much like in the cyber-security domain, physical-security best practices, while worth adopting, are wholly insufficient for dealing with truly motivated and adaptive adversaries. The security personnel that are hired and trained to protect any facility are fixtures of the environment, and they simply do not think like an enemy or conceive of all the ways they could cause damage or break in. The tactics and techniques that any motivated person could use to gather information about a facility and its employees, and then gain unauthorized access to it, are readily and freely available online.[93] These include entering through the loading dock or entrance to an employee smoking area; through a locked door with help from an insider or via rudimentary lock-picking techniques; by "tailgating" an employee with a proximity badge or swipe card (which themselves can be easily hacked) who is kind enough to hold the door open for the next person who happens to be struggling with several packages; by creating a backstory to stage an appointment with an executive who is out of the office in order to loiter and covertly photograph the security system; by scheduling an appointment somewhere in a multifloor, multitenant office building in order to wander off to surveil the targeted office; or even by impersonating a "contractor" who arrives to fix the air conditioner, which hackers might have shut down remotely ahead of time so that an uncomfortably warm security guard is already eagerly expecting someone to show up.

As the former Army Delta Force commando and physical penetration tester who goes by the pseudonym Dalton Fury describes it: "Anyone can assess a threat whose face is smeared with camouflage paint and is running with an automatic weapon in his hand. It becomes much tougher if that same threat is an attractive female, wearing a body bomb underneath a fleece, with a pistol in her purse."[94] Fury also relays stories of obtaining unauthorized access into secure buildings by dressing up as Santa Claus around the holidays, posing as the pizza delivery guy from a national chain, and even staging a horrific hunting accident just outside of the front gate in order to lure a security guard away from their assigned post.[95] Once you become conscious of typical building vulnerabilities, and how routinely such tried-and-true tactics are successful, you begin to see poor security awareness everywhere. Or, in the case of my unanticipated "break-in" to the government building described above, the elaborate construction of visual intimidation actually "feels" more like lax security, once you become aware of what that resembles.

Protecting buildings or facilities should be easier than protecting computer networks or software because they are tangible, and people experience and interact with them directly. A building's management and security team presumably is expected to conceive of and implement sufficient security policies. Indeed, most security professionals falsely believe that their organization has a sufficient and integrated defensive strategy to address security threats, including from insider leaks, stolen assets or data, or physical threats to staff. A 2012 survey by Health Facilities Management and the American Society for Healthcare Engineering found that more than 69 percent of hospital-security professionals reported that they had an "integrated security plan" that addressed "all critical access and controlled areas."[96] However, only 62 percent believed physical and cyber security were integrated—two areas now inseparable from one another. In general, employees tend to have a similar belief. The 2014 Federal Employee Viewpoint Survey found that 76 percent of employees thought their organization had adequately prepared employees for security threats.[97] The perceptions most likely do not reflect the truth of the situation.

Supposedly secure facilities are broken into all the time—by some combination of insiders, hackers, criminals, or competitors—with relative ease and with substantial reputational and financial consequences for the targeted corporations. For example, between 2009 and 2011, Amed Villa and other members of a Miami-based crime ring conducted a series of heists by cutting holes in the roofs of various warehouses or entering through roof-access doors. They then repelled to the floors, disabled the security systems, and used the facilities' forklifts to carry millions of dollars' worth of merchandise to trucks in the loading docks.[98] Most notably, Villa stole $90 million worth of pharmaceuticals from an Eli Lilly and Company warehouse in Connecticut—the largest heist in state history—just one month after the company's security provider, Tyco Integrated Security, had conducted a vulnerability assessment and outlined the findings in a "Confidential System Proposal."[99]

According to corporate security officers, when such breaches result in the capture of high-value assets or trade secrets, they are often never revealed to the public. Just as corporations hide or downplay cyber-security breaches, high-consequence larceny thefts occurring on a company's property are carefully hidden from the business press and even government regulators, insurers, or law enforcement agencies. The illusion of security can prove to be even more damaging than the trade secrets themselves. Conversely, the perception that senior management and its security team cannot protect the assets or trade secrets that generate revenue for a corporation is particularly damaging to that corporation's reputation and its attractiveness to investors. This perception can be far more detrimental than the actual theft itself. According to chief security officers at several corporations, even when a likely suspect has been identified, senior management most likely refrains from filing charges because the negative information that would emerge publicly from litigation makes it not worthwhile.

Hospitals and other health-care facilities are particularly vulnerable because of their high volume of personal information and high number of transient employees and third-party vendors. In June 2014, nearly 34,000 patient x-ray records were stolen from the outpatient radiology facility at St. Joseph Health of Sonoma County—formerly known as Redwood Regional Medical Group—in Santa Rosa, California, when a burglar gained undetected and unauthorized access to the hospital and stole a USB drive from an unlocked employee locker. The drive contained a backup of the patients' records—including the full name, gender, medical record number, date of birth, area of the body x-rayed, and other information—which were intended to be transferred to the Santa Rosa Memorial Hospital's electronic back-up records.[100] A few months prior, in March 2014, the personal information of nearly 342,000 patients in San Francisco was compromised when eight unencrypted HP Pro 3400 computer towers were stolen from Sutherland Healthcare Solutions office, which provides billing services to the San Francisco Department of Public Health.[101] Finally, also in March 2014, a Florida federal judge approved a landmark $3 million data breach class action settlement with the health-insurance provider AvMed. The judge ruled that even plaintiffs who suffered no ascertainable damages were entitled to claim part of the settlement. The data breach stemmed from the December 2009 theft of two AvMed laptop computers from a secure Gainesville facility. Because of the personal information in them, having two $700 laptop computers stolen cost a medium-sized business $3 million plus litigation fees.[102]

Physical security breaches are not limited to the health-care industry, and come in many forms. In March 2014, Justin Casquejo, a sixteen-year-old boy from New Jersey was able to squeeze through a one-foot opening in a fence and climb to the 104th floor of One World Trade Center, the building that replaced the two original World Trade Center towers. One World Trade Center is owned by The Port Authority of New York & New Jersey, which provides security for the outside, while the real estate firm the Durst Organization is responsible for maintaining security on the inside. Neither prevented Casquejo from gaining unauthorized access. "I walked around the construction site and figured out how to access the Freedom Tower rooftop. I found a way up through the scaffolding, climbed onto the sixth floor, and took the elevator up to the eighty-eighth floor. I then took the staircase up to the 104th floor," the boy recollected.[103] He spent two hours taking pictures before beginning his descent, during which time a construction worker stopped him and called the Port Authority police. While he did not cause any destruction or harm, he was freely able to move around undetected. Even after running into an elevator operator—who was later reassigned because he didn't ask questions or request an ID before taking him up to the eighty-eighth floor—and a sleeping Durst Organization security guard, who was later fired, he was able to ascend to the top of the iconic and allegedly highly secure building.[104]

To prevent people far more malicious than Casquejo from breaking in, security professionals hire red teamers to conduct physical penetration tests to assess a building's defenses from the perspective of the most likely adversaries, identify vulnerabilities, and offer corrective recommendations. As is the case for cyber pen tests by white-hat hackers, a physical pen test is most often commissioned because of government- or industry-mandated standards. Physical penetration testing helps to meet audit requirements under the Health Insurance Portability and Accountability Act (HIPAA), Sarbanes-Oxley Act, or Gramm-Leach-Bliley Act, for example, and also to meet industry standards. For instance, the Department of Health and Human Services' HIPAA Security Rule of 2003 proposed testing of physical security to ensure that patient records are not at risk of breach. The National Institute of Standards and Technology later examined the security rule to provide further guidance, and suggested that realistic penetration testing be conducted. Similarly, the latest Payment Card Industry Data Security Standard (PCI DSS) was released in November 2013, compliance of which includes new penetration testing requirements. While the previous version of PCI DSS provided a basic testing framework requiring internal and external pen tests annually, or after "any significant infrastructure or application upgrade or modification," the new version offers further clarification and a more robust guide for its users. Rather than grouping internal and external pen testing together, it gives specific clarification that external and internal pen tests should be conducted separately.[105]

Outside of legal requirements, there are also industry standards that strongly recommend pen testing. ASIS International is the leading organization for standardizing industry requirements and establishing best practices. ASIS published a "Facilities Physical Security Measures Guide" to provide guidance on standard physical security of buildings and facilities, which includes security strategies and measures, and recommends conducting a risk assessment to identify weaknesses before moving forward with a strategy. It also proposes a three-layer approach to security—including the outer layer (perimeter), middle layer (exterior), and inner layer—and a "security convergence" between physical, IT, and other security actors to adopt and apply a comprehensive strategy. Another industry leader, the Institute for Security and Open Methodologies

(ISECOM), publishes the *Open Source Security Testing Methodology Manual* (OSSTMM) for security professionals. Taking a more detailed approach than ASIS, the latest OSSTMM version provides a guideline that allows the user to "no longer have to rely on general best practices, anecdotal evidence, or superstitions because you will have verified information specific to your needs on which to base your security decision."[106] ISECOM suggests that physical pen testers use a variety of tools—both physical and interpersonal—and offers a range of tests for various aspects of security, such as a posture review, access verification, or property validation. Both organizations emphasize comprehensive approaches to physical pen testing—rather than merely "breaking and entering"—to include multiple layers of physical barriers, and access and controls.

Many of the same firms that perform cyber pen tests also offer physical pen tests, and increasingly utilize physical-pen-testing techniques, such as attempting to attain unauthorized access to a building or data storage center, to complement an external cyber penetration test.[107] Between 2011 and 2014, the number of cyber-security incidents attributed to physical-security shortcomings grew from 10 to 15 percent.[108] For example, an external black box penetration test (in which the tester has no knowledge of the internal structure, design, and implementation of a system) might be supplemented with an internal white box test (in which the tester has full knowledge) whereby the white hats are given some degree of administrative access to the network to assess potential insider threats by evaluating the detection mechanisms and incident-response controls in place. This can be as simple as a white hat walking into an employee's office, telling them they are from the IT staff, and informing them that they need to access their desktop computer. Most of the time, employees, including those with administrator privileges, will fall for this commonly employed trick, no questions asked.

Physical pen tests proceed by following the same four underlying steps as cyber pen testing—scoping the engagement with the targeted institution, information gathering and reconnaissance of the building or facility, the physical penetration test itself, and finally the presentation of findings and a prioritized list of recommended corrective actions. The frustrations felt by white-hat hackers and IT staffs in the cyber domain are similar to those experienced by physical-penetration testers and facility-management teams in the real world. Corporations that are required by regulations or insurers to commission a penetration test will often scope it as narrowly as possible (to just a few days and only for a limited number of entry points), or completely "cook" the test by stationing new security cameras, barriers, or security personnel around the perimeter of the targeted facility in advance of a test.

Nicholas Percoco of the security firm Rapid7 described one particularly corrupted penetration test encountered by a team from his old employer, Trustwave Holdings. The CIO at a multinational corporation hired Trustwave to do a comprehensive test of the company's cyber, physical, and human security systems. The Trustwave team determined that this corporation had a large distribution warehouse in the Midwest, which it would attempt to breach in order to gain access to the protected networks and servers. In preparation, it conducted reconnaissance of the warehouse both onsite and with Google maps, which revealed an attack pathway—an area without any perimeter security where trucks and vans drove toward the loading docks. The team told the CIO exclusively that it was going to do an assessment of the distribution warehouse and identified the date on which it would occur. It was clear that the information had leaked, however, because on the day of the prescheduled test the Trustwave team arrived to discover that, for the first time, a single security guard was standing at the entry point checking IDs and requesting information. Charles Henderson of Trustwave added that the team noticed employees staring out the windows awaiting whomever they believed to look like the expected security professionals. "Of course, we didn't come in through the way that we planned, but rather another entry point." Bordering the facility, but away from the front gate and loading docks, was a housing development with an eight-foot-high fence. One pen tester simply hopped the fence, walked into the facility through a café area used by truckers, and, soon after, plugged a remote access switch into a UBS portal. The entire test was compromised, but the CIO had the evidence he needed to demonstrate that his company had indeed commissioned a physical penetration test, which apparently was all that he was interested in.[109]

Breaking into "secure" buildings is often as easy as breaking into secure computer networks, but much less frequently publicly reported. Chris Nickerson became well known in the security community through the short-lived 2007–2008 cable television series, *Tiger Team*, in which he and two colleagues documented their penetration test endeavors. In the first episode, "The Car Dealership Takedown," Nickerson's team conducted a two-day, no-notice test of a luxury car dealership in Southern California, which purportedly had a state-of-the-art security system.[110] They found that one skylight could be partially opened and was not protected by a pressure plate alarm. (Rooftops are often the least-secure area of any building, according to many pen testers.) By dumpster diving, they unearthed a business card for the dealership's IT company, which allowed them to get into the server room by posing as tech support from that company. This in turn allowed them to erase the cars' vehicle identification numbers from the dealership's internal hard drive, which makes a stolen car significantly harder to track and detect. Finally, by posing as a potential customer, they conducted reconnaissance on the showroom floor of the layout of the security cameras and motion detectors—the latter of which were positioned too high to detect a human crawling on the ground, as they often are.

During the actual 2:30 A.M. test, they broke in undetected, picked all the locks of the internal doors and safes in under a minute, collected the social security numbers and financial records of the clients, erased the video from the security cameras, and drove a yellow Lotus out the front door and turned it around and parked it in the opposite direction, with a humorous note warning: "Hope this inspires you to turn your security around." The operations manager of the car dealership, who claimed before the test to have implemented an adequate level of security, acknowledged after reading the note: "Pretty much, they got everything that we didn't want them to get." Afterward, Nickerson and his team provided the operations manager with a detailed plan of how to fix the security vulnerabilities that they had found and exploited in less than two days.[111]

While that reality television series helped to establish his reputation—
and drum up some early business—Nickerson is now considered by many
within the security community to be both a leading voice and conscience
of the industry. He no longer finds routine security breaches, like the ones
used against the luxury car dealership, to be that challenging or cool.
Rather, he considers his role to be one of a mentor or therapist for potential clients seeking to hire him to assess their security posture. Because
he is well known and is an owner of his company, Lares Consulting, he
can turn down clients interested only in achieving some minimum level
of compliance—as determined by security auditors. He also denounces
"check book pen testers," who conduct rote by-the-book security assessments that allow the targeted institutions to falsely believe that they are
now secure. Finally, though Nickerson holds all of the requisite industry certifications—which he believes are generally pointless and "freely
available to anybody with Photoshop"—he judges the security industry
to be in a dismal state. "It is the only industry that grows bigger and
bigger every year, as our customers lose more and more money from poor
security every year." Nevertheless, he envisions that it is his responsibility
to the industry—through conference talks, podcasts, and a forthcoming
book—to inspire people to care about security and to change how they
think about it.[112] Ultimately, Nickerson believes that the importance of
"security awareness is greater than knowledge" because any product a
vendor sells or procedure a company implements will eventually be out
of date or easily bypassed.[113]

Nickerson has three overarching thoughts about how red teaming
should be done to improve the security of the targeted institution. First,
the initial conversations with senior management and its security teams
are the most consequential component of any red team engagement.
Nickerson asks for an explanation of basic goals and strategy: "Explain
to me what you are doing, and why you are doing it?" This encourages
everyone to agree upon exactly what assets should be valued above all
else, which then leads to a mutual understanding of how the corporation
should prioritize the protection of those assets. "When the attacker comes
in, what are they really going to go after?" Here, while the CEO—and

perhaps the CSO—can articulate exactly what these assets are, the security team often cannot because it is focused on implementing only those best-practice security procedures and processes that an outside security auditor will look for on their checklist.

However, in these initial conversations, both management and the security team will often voice disbelief that somebody can just walk into their building, an unwillingness to conceive of what nobody has done in the past, and a faith that the processes they have put in place will prevent this—"you need a badge to get in!" is a common refrain. Even the Fortune 100 corporations, for which Nickerson's company conducts penetration tests, simply cannot comprehend the patience, thoughtfulness, and "bad ass skillset" that a motivated adversary will assuredly possess. Nickerson will ask the senior managers, "You are the number one company in a multibillion-dollar field; what makes you think the number two company won't attempt to take what you value to beat you?"[114]

Second, Nickerson emphasizes that how the test is conducted directly affects the red team's impact. During the reconnaissance phase, Nickerson and his team quickly determine the robustness of the security system that is in place. Where a facility uses legacy security controls—like security cameras with visible and unarmored wires, glass-break sensors on windows that are clearly inactive, or wafer locks rather than more secure Medco locks—the team might simply bypass a penetration test altogether until the security is overhauled and upgraded.[115] During the actual break-in, Nickerson's pen testers sometimes wear cameras that broadcast video and audio directly to the mobile phone of a client: "When they actually see us get past the security guard and wander around their building in real time, it impacts them much more directly." Longer engagements—lasting up to a year or more—might require breaking in multiple times through multiple pathways, and assuming several different aliases to do so. One penetration test required nine months of reconnaissance and spear-phishing attacks, and a last-minute flight to South Korea to obtain several levels of credentials, so that Nickerson could make up a story that featured him posing as a credentialed employee in order to get close to a valued asset near Shenzhen, China. "It was one of the coolest things that I've done in a long time."[116]

Third, Nickerson has found that the presentation of the red team's findings ultimately determines whether the targeted institution does anything to resolve the newly uncovered vulnerabilities. "I have to show them where they are failing so that the money can fall from the sky." This requires being sensitive to a particular institution's corporate learning style, and, more specifically, to how the executive, who can authorize more money for security, learns. "I have found that the most successful thing in physical penetration testing is to take an executive with me and make them break in. I have them pick the locks, show them how to strip the posi-tap connectors to the alarm, and enter undetected." Suddenly, the executive has experienced firsthand how lax security is, because if they could get in with simply a few minutes of training, so could anyone else. Nickerson defines success as getting the boss to understand the threats and lapses, or getting the boss's buy-in, which then socializes awareness and induces conversations for security across all of the targeted institution's business units. "When the IT administrators are talking the same language with the facility management team, that's a really positive first step." However, overall, Nickerson remains disappointed with his field. "We don't have a Hippocratic oath, and you find most people are overly greedy and underperforming. Pen testing has improved slightly over the years so you can no longer just sell snake oil to clients. Now it is more like snake oil mixed with a child's aspirin."[117]

If Nickerson is thoughtful and conscientious, Jayson E. Street is admittedly impulsive and loud. Street's bio on LinkedIn lists him as "one of *Time*'s persons of the year for 2006." The actual person for that year was "You," so, hilariously, Street naturally assumed it meant him. However, he proudly proclaims himself to be a hacker, which includes his side job of conducting physical penetration tests—or what he calls "social engineering engagements"—to rigorously test and improve building security for his clients. (Street also maintains the self-explanatory website www.awkwardhugs.org, which displays the humorous hugs that he unleashes at cyber-security and hacker conferences to break down social barriers, including one with then-NSA Director General Keith Alexander at DEF CON 2012.) His presentations at hacking and security conferences are legendary for their humor, passion, and decidedly cheesy production values, which effectively convey Street's ultimate objective: educating red team pen testers and blue team security professionals about their shared responsibilities of uncovering and patching vulnerabilities in the cyber and physical worlds. In his words: "We made red teaming so rock star that everybody wants to be a red team ninja, but I'm here to help the blue team. So now I tell everyone I'm purple team."[118]

Whereas Nickerson and his teams conduct detailed surveillance and reconnaissance, Street consciously tries to make his penetration tests as unsophisticated and simple as possible. Street noted, "I limit myself to two hours on Google to gather intelligence on the client. The point is to show that anyone could do this to your institution."[119] Rather than develop an Ocean's Eleven-like meticulous plan to get inside a building, he walks in through the door used by a company's smokers like he belongs there—"just walking in through the door being my charming self." He does so under the guise of several roles, including the "outsider" who shows up for an interview only to wander the halls to conduct surveillance, the "authority figure" who shows up demanding access to inspect something while pretending to take notes on a computer tablet, or the "technician" who enters the premises under the pretext of fixing something—for which he wears a work shirt that reads: "Your company's COMPUTER GUY."[120] Like most physical-penetration testers, he has a 100-percent success rate in getting into secure facilities that clients hire him to assess. But rather than relying upon exhaustive research or well-honed skills, Street instead highlights that "my best assets are bad impulse control, and a total lack of shame."[121]

Unlike most other pen testers who employ more subtle methods, Street continues to escalate the engagement until he is eventually caught. Like all penetration testers, he carries an engagement letter and a business card with the CSO's phone number on it, which a security guard can call to verify. If he does not produce the "get out of jail free card" fast enough, he could be beaten up or tasered by an overzealous guard. He will often carry two engagement letters, one false and one real. Or, he might tell the security guard, "I am doing a security assessment," which will often prompt the guard to simply wave him past. Or, "If you let me go past, I won't write up all of your mistakes in my report." Finally, if a random employee asks him what he is doing in the building, he will tell them, "Congratulations, I am doing a security assessment and you caught me; here, have a Starbucks gift card" and simply continue on his way without the building's security being notified. All of these encounters are clear violations of the security procedures within the targeted institution. They all get recorded by the many hidden cameras that Street wears and are written up in his final report.

While on an engagement in Kingston, Jamaica, for a multinational financial firm, Street improvised a penetration test that he described as "the most evil thing I'd ever done." The very security-conscious firm challenged Street to get into its main headquarters building, which it claimed was as secure as Fort Knox. Reviewing e-mail addresses and then using a network-scanning tool, Street determined that the headquarters and its charity arm—which was located across the street—used the same computer network. Street contacted the firm's charity posing as an American television producer who was making a documentary about corporations doing charitable work in the community. Explaining that he was flying back to the United States the next morning, he was able to secure a meeting with an executive at the charity building without ever providing verification information. During the meeting, Street volunteered to show the executive and public relations staffer videos of his alleged documentaries, which required him to put a thumb drive in the executive's computer. The thumb drive was a "rubber ducky"—a USB processor that's a "keyboard human interface device" that allows it to be automatically detected and accepted by a computer. This allowed Street to later obtain access to the main headquarters building's computer network. Street later prepared an after-action report documenting how he had compromised the security protocols, listing what steps its managers should implement to prevent a similar attack (essentially segmenting the charity network from the corporate network), and detailing what the incurred costs would be for the financial firm.[122]

While Street revels in showing off what he has broken into at hacker conferences, he is quick to point out that his larger goal is to raise awareness of the security vulnerabilities within a client's defenses and recommend corrective actions. He finds that government or insurance-regulation levels of security compliance are necessary, but wholly insufficient for "actual evil dudes that just want to get in. They don't care how they do it, or how pretty it looks. They just want to get in, steal what you have, and not get caught." The inadequate standards must be complemented with realistic external physical penetration testing, because, as he says, "Humans do not want to think about negative things happening to them."[123] The most consistent problem he encounters is that firms' security teams still "build walls based upon how they have been taught walls should be built. But you really need to build walls based upon how a likely enemy will attack you." Street finds that one of the fastest ways to make clients care is to create a high-impact event, which can be as simple as sending executive clients a picture of themselves sitting in their office and surfing on their computer. Suddenly, the boss experiences their company's security shortcomings personally and is more likely to authorize the time, money, and training to improve things. "If you don't make it hit home with management, they probably won't do anything, or else they'll ask 'what's the least amount of money I have to spend to get you out of here?'"[124]

Finally, like Nickerson—who Street refers to as "the smartest guy that does this professionally"—Street believes that pen-testing firms and the security field more generally must do a better job of explaining themselves to the general public and improving their clients' security. While the publicity and profitability for security professionals has never been greater, there is also a growing and shared frustration that the field is increasingly misrepresented by the media and by unscrupulous and misleading practitioners. "This is not a great career choice if you just want to do your job. You have to have passion." Street's prescription is for security professionals to have greater transparency with journalists and government agencies about what hackers do, more collaboration on research projects, and more teachings among security professionals to understand what works and what does not, even more conferences, and definitely more hugs.[125]

Conclusion

Robust and realistic red teaming in the private sector faces an inherent challenge everywhere it is practiced: it does not provide the targeted company with an immediate return on its investment, nor can it be affirmatively demonstrated to have been necessary. External consultants conduct business war games to provide senior executives with a perspective on the potential outcomes of a strategic decision, including the reactions of their competitors. Corporations, on their own, face the inescapable realities of hierarchy and institutional pathologies that make honest self-assessment and unrestricted discussions on new strategic plans difficult. Unlike business war games, penetration tests usually fulfill an externally mandated requirement, whether for government regulators or insurers, or to meet expected industry best practices. Although virtually all large businesses experience harmful cyber-security incidents, few IT professionals believe that businesses are adequately prepared to deal with them.[126] Dino Dai Zovi, who was an IDART hacker before doing commercial pen testing, notes how executives struggle with knowing how much preventive security is enough: "If you do too much, it can hurt the development time, functionality, and profitability of a system. Do too little, and there can be a security event that threatens the profitability or even viability of the company."[127] White-hat pen testers balance these competing interests by identifying vulnerabilities but presenting them in a manner that sets out achievable goals for the targeted institution.

The pro bono vulnerability-probe red teaming done by iSEC Partners on the Verizon femtocell revealed that, given enough time and effort, even semiskilled hackers can break into just about anything. Moreover, as the team learned, after it announced its results, several other groups had already uncovered that specific vulnerability of the femtocell. The critical difference was the team's practice of responsible disclosure by alerting the vendor and the DHS's Computer Emergency Readiness Team to ensure that the security patches could be implemented before the vulnerabilities were breached. And though most believe that buildings, given their guards, cameras, and metal detectors, are more secure than digital packets traveling over cables or the air, they clearly are not. Jayson E. Street has found that while many companies now have no sense of security in the cyber realm, they maintain a false and misplaced sense of security in the tangible world.[128] Physical penetration tests are necessary to prove to the targeted institution's executives and security team that their procedures and protocols have shortcomings that can be bypassed by motivated and clever malicious actors. Whether executives act on the findings of a war game or cyber or physical penetration test depends on their perception of how critical the newly revealed shortcomings or vulnerabilities are to their core business. Indeed, red teaming is not a core business practice, but a mindset, approach, and set of specific techniques that can improve business performance by challenging untested assumptions, identifying strategic blind spots, simulating competitor responses, and uncovering security weaknesses.

SIX

MODESTY, MISIMPRESSIONS, AND THE FUTURE OF RED TEAMING

I have never learned anything from any man who agreed with me.

—Dudley Field Malone, defense attorney in *The State of Tennessee v. John Thomas Scopes*, 1925[1]

Poliomyelitis, or polio, is an acute, infectious virus that is highly contagious, attacks the body's nervous system, and has no known cure. The enduring consequence of polio varies widely: most victims have no, or very mild, symptoms. Paralysis results in less than 1 percent of cases, or, even more rarely, death if the paralysis strikes the respiratory muscles. While its most recognized victim, Franklin Delano Roosevelt, contracted polio at thirty-nine while swimming in the Bay of Fundy off Campobello Island in New Brunswick, Canada, it predominantly impacts children under five. Vaccines proved that it could be prevented, and by 1979 it was eliminated from the United States. However, polio has remained a scourge in developing countries where there is poor sanitation and hygiene because it can be spread through person-to-person contact.

In 1988, the World Health Assembly (WHA) unanimously endorsed the ambitious goal of "the global eradication of poliomyelitis by the year 2000."[2] At the time, more than 125 countries were considered endemic to the virus, with approximately 350,000 people, primarily children, stricken by it. Subsequently, the Global Polio Eradication Initiative (GPEI) was launched. It was led by a "cluster" of public health institutions: the World Health Organization (WHO), United Nations Children's Fund, the Center for Disease Control, and Rotary International. The GPEI catalyzed a multilateral strategy that included an expansion of funding, reaching more than $375 million in 2000 and increasing throughout the next decade to more than $700 million, better coordination among the cluster, and a more effective delivery of vaccines—thereby decreasing the number of polio-endemic countries from 125 in 1988 to 20 in 2000.[3] During that same time frame, the number of cases of polio declined 99 percent from 350,000 to 3,500, and as of 2014, the polio vaccine had saved the lives of approximately 650,000 people.[4] Nevertheless, the mission remained incomplete. After vastly reducing new incidences of polio relatively quickly, progress unexpectedly stalled in the first decade of the millennium: by 2009, the number of cases was down to 1,600, but the eradication of that stubborn final 1 percent seemed ever more distant.[5]

To confront this problem, it took a person who could see the challenge through a red teamer's eyes: Gregory Pirio, a renowned communications expert with a doctorate in African history from the University of California at Los Angeles, who was teaching at UFMCS, detailed in chapter 2. While there, he received hands-on training in red teaming, and co-taught a training seminar on how it could improve institutional performance for the US Customs and Border Protection, Kansas City Police Department, and the Kansas City Chiefs' coaching staff, among many others. In 2010, while researching the history of communication strategies used in polio eradication for a journal article, he noticed patterns of groupthink, stagnation, and unwillingness of key decision-makers to question their underlying assumptions regarding polio eradication.[6] The officials within the cluster were operating under the belief that whatever had successfully reduced new cases of polio by 99 percent should simply be continued and implemented more rigorously to eliminate the final 1 percent. As Pirio described the operating environment: "Everyone was cheerleading the orthodoxy. Nobody was questioning the strategy or the tactics." Moreover, in-country experts and skeptical cluster officials were hesitant to challenge the conventional wisdom because they believed that doing so would put their annual funding streams at risk.[7]

Pirio relayed his concerns to his colleague Ellyn Ogden, the longtime worldwide polio-eradication coordinator at the US Agency for International Development, telling her, "I see tunnel vision." It was only because Pirio was steeped in the red-teaming approaches and techniques taught at UFMCS that he quickly identified polio eradication as a quintessential case that should be subjected to alternative analysis. Ogden was initially somewhat reluctant because the public health field is hesitant to embrace concepts developed by, and associated with, the military. However, after meeting with UFMCS Director Gregory Fontenot and his colleagues to understand how liberating structures could be employed to challenge the stagnation and confirmation bias found within GPEI, Ogden embraced the concept. Shortly thereafter, three UFMCS instructors convened a two-day red-teaming session in Seattle at the Bill & Melinda Gates Foundation headquarters—a primary funder for global public health initiatives—where they challenged every assumption and goal of the polio eradication campaign through the Four Ways of Seeing and String of Pearls liberating structures described in chapter 5. The following day, the Gates Foundation held its annual meeting with the WHO to review funding proposals for the upcoming fiscal year. The Gates Foundation staffers had adopted the language and perspective of the red teamers, and "shook everything up with the WHO proposals by asking the sort of hard questions that they hadn't in the past," Ogden recalled.[8]

This is exemplary of how red teaming most frequently tends to spread: by happenstance. Pirio was exposed to red teaming only because he was teaching African and Islamic history at UFMCS at the time. He began investigating polio eradication solely because he was asked to coauthor an article on the subject. Finally, he brought his red teamer's perspective on the topic to Ogden only because they were longtime professional colleagues. Ogden, in turn, found a receptive audience at the Gates Foundation for the UFMCS instructors to employ their liberating structures, in part because of the Gates staffers' frustration with the lack of measurable progress toward eliminating the remaining 1 percent of new cases of polio.

Though the path to incorporating red teaming at the Gates Foundation was random, it has had a positive impact on operations. According to Ogden and Gates Foundation participants, the annual strategies and work plans that the cluster had once adopted by rubber-stamp consensus are now more rigorously questioned and challenged. In addition, in late 2010, the Independent Monitoring Board (IMB) was created at the request of the WHA and WHO Executive Board as a mechanism to independently evaluate progress toward the major milestones of the GPEI's Strategic Plan. Members are experts from a variety of fields who are nominated by GPEI core partners, and appointed by the director-general of WHO.[9] It is impossible to directly connect either the cluster's enhanced skepticism regarding polio-eradication strategies or the formation of the IMB to the two-day red team engagement at the Gates Foundation headquarters, but it is credited as playing a major factor. There was no independent review of the plans conducted between 1999 and 2011 to identify weaknesses in assumptions, internal barriers to eradication, or alternative methods of delivery. The remaining few hundred new annual polio cases are no longer because the GPEI is not questioning assumptions, but rather are due to a lack of political commitment in unstable regions such as Pakistan, which prevents administering vaccines, or an unwillingness of parents to vaccinate their children in Afghanistan.[10] That there was any impact on this complex challenge was by chance, and only a result of Gregory Pirio's exposure to red teaming.

Realistic Outcomes of Red Teaming

The polio-eradication story shows how red team engagements can rarely be classified as outright successes or failures in achieving their ultimate goals. However, red teaming always achieves one of two outcomes. First, it delivers some new finding or insight that otherwise could not have been self-generated within the walls of the targeted institution. The institutions surveyed for this book all faced varying degrees of structural or cultural limitations, which effective red teaming can overcome. Almost every leader claims to value openness and creativity in order to bring into existence new ideas and concepts that add value to their institution. Yet, the same processes that are required to make an institution function smoothly—such as hierarchy, formal rules, unit cohesion, and behavioral norms—are precisely those that make differentiation and varietal thinking extremely difficult to achieve.[11] This is not a criticism of anyone who works diligently at their job, but rather it is a consequence of the normal structural, interpersonal, and cultural dynamics that we all experience and cannot avoid.

The case studies detailed in this book show how properly resourced, situated, and empowered red teams overcome these inevitable limitations to produce revealing "a-ha!" insights or independent assessments that could not otherwise have come about. This may be done to simulate the likely reactions of an unnamed—but clearly Saddam Hussein-like—adversary to the military transformation concepts evaluated during the Millennium Challenge exercise in the summer of 2002; to independently estimate the probability of whether Osama bin Laden was living inside a high-walled compound in Abbottabad, Pakistan, in April 2011; or to examine the security of the Verizon femtocell by the iSEC Partners white hats in the summer and fall of 2012. In each instance, without utilizing a red team, senior decision-makers at the White House, Pentagon, and Verizon would have been far less informed about the probability of bin Laden's whereabouts, the dependability of future military concepts and technologies, and the reliability and security of customers' cell phones.

As for the second outcome, even when red teaming fails to have a demonstrable impact on a targeted institution, it reveals something about the thought processes and values of that institution. A primary cause of red-teaming failure lies in bosses' belief that it is either unnecessary or irrelevant for their particular institution or, if the boss authorized the red team engagement, that its findings are unimportant. When pressed for an explanation as to why they believe this, bosses'—whether government officials, military commanders, or business executives—answers cluster around two theories: if something of consequence was going wrong they would either already know about it, or somebody working for them would have already told them. This first claim assumes a degree of awareness and omniscience that is simply unrealistic for any large institution. The second claim assumes that employees have the time or ability to identify shortcomings or blind spots and a willingness to present them to management. Bosses cannot take it for granted that they or their employees can grade their own homework, or envision what paths their competitors might take. And successful red teaming requires that senior leaders and middle managers be transparent and cede some degree of authority to the red team, which is not easy because they are often overconfident and have domineering personalities.

It is also mandatory that leaders value the red team's findings. And if those findings are somehow truly irrelevant then the red team was most likely improperly scoped at the outset. In 1976, the Team B competitive-intelligence estimate of the CIA's National Intelligence Estimate of Soviet Union nuclear weapons capabilities was disregarded by then-Director of Central Intelligence George H. W. Bush. Why? Because the Presidential Foreign Intelligence Advisory Board so wanted to roll back détente with the Soviet Union, that it pressed for the creation of a Team B that it assured was composed of biased red teamers. The result was a product that Bush would not even authorize for publication. Similarly, the pre-9/11 FAA red team was established without clear guidance as to how its findings would be used—such as through letters of correction or punitive fines—to pressure domestic airlines and airports to improve their security. The FAA red team uncovered and documented troubling vulnerabilities that any semiskilled and motivated adversary could have capitalized on to take over an airplane and kill its passengers and crew. However, the red team members believed they were unduly constrained and generally ignored by the associate administrator for Civil Aviation Security—the manager responsible for overseeing the red team's operations.

Red-Teaming Misimpressions and Misuses

Mark Mateski has engaged in and thought deeply about red teaming for far longer than most people in the field. Of those few others who actively study or practice the concept, he is also the most respected reference point for articulating the current state of red teaming. Mateski became aware of the utility of red teams while running war-gaming exercises, leading him in 1997 to found the online *Red Team Journal*, which still serves as the best open-source repository for helpful hints and emerging practices in the field.[12] Mateski later worked at the Information Defense Assurance Red Teaming, featured in chapter 4. As head of the Watermark Institute, he teaches military officials, information security professionals, and business executives how they should think about, structure, and utilize red teams. Classroom instruction and exercises on red teaming are critical because, as he describes it, "The best red teamers are intuitive systems thinkers. You're in the flatlands while they operate in another dimension, and those people are just hard to find."[13]

In becoming a distinguished instructor and philosopher of red teaming, Mateski has come to discover that the concept has developed a cachet and mystique among many who nevertheless lack direct experience in its application. "Red teaming has become both oversold and under-appreciated at the same time," he says. This contradiction is often a consequence of how the problem that the red team is commissioned to investigate is framed upfront. Here, most red teams lack the self-awareness or humility to make explicit their "negative space"—meaning to know and articulate those areas or topics that they cannot plausibly assess or evaluate. If the red team is not conscious of its own blind spots and aware of its inherent limitations, it may diligently pursue its work, but do so while heading in the wrong direction. Alternatively, Mateski believes that red teaming's "most interesting methods give you a competitive advantage that you don't want to share with people. It is usually sensitive or proprietary, and that tends to stay hidden."[14]

Since red teaming best practices often stay hidden, and because there is no comprehensive account of the concept, people understandably have a poor grasp of what those best practices are. Moreover, there is undeniably a fascination surrounding the term, which some practitioners capitalize upon to promote their services. Chris Nickerson, the security professional featured in chapter 5, relayed his concerns about how firms in his industry are increasingly using the term to cover virtually all their security assessments. "They say, 'pen testing is kind of 2000, and red teaming is now,' and then they can charge more money because they call it red teaming." Although he is among the more prominent and respected red teamers, he says that, "my company doesn't use the term much in public anymore because it has become so co-opted by so many people."[15]

Even where the term itself is not specifically used, the notion is often deeply misunderstood, blindly embraced, or dangerously misapplied. As important as understanding what red teaming is able to do is the ability to acknowledge what it cannot, and should never be intended to, accomplish. Thus, it is worth taking the time to counter and correct five notable public misimpressions and worst-uses of red teaming: ad hoc approaches, mistaking red team findings for policy, freelance red teaming, shooting the messenger, and using red teams to decide rather than to inform.

1. Ad hoc devil's advocate

Midway through the cinematic thriller *World War Z*, based upon Max Brooks's novel of the same name, Brad Pitt's character Gerry Lane meets Jurgen Warmbrunn, a fictitious high-ranking official in the Mossad, Israel's national intelligence agency. Lane asks him how he anticipated the zombie pandemic spreading worldwide, and Warmbrunn tells him they received a communiqué from India saying they were fighting the *rakshasa* ("zombies"), an evil mythological spirit in Hinduism, which Warmbrunn translates to mean "undead." Lane then asks, "You build a wall because you read a communiqué that mentions the word 'zombie'?" Warmbrunn responds by explaining Israel's "Tenth Man Theory," created after the horrors of the Holocaust, the 1972 Olympics' massacre in Munich, and the 1973 intelligence failure preceding the Yom Kippur War. "If nine of us look at the same information and arrive at the exact same conclusion, it's the duty of the tenth man to disagree. No matter how improbable they seem, the tenth man has to start thinking with the assumption that the other nine were wrong."[16]

There is a romantic appeal to this concept—that dissent can be assigned to just one person who will then be able to uncover hidden truths that others, collectively, simply cannot see. And based upon singular abilities found within that person, a country, organization, or even all of humanity itself will be saved—at least in the zombie apocalypse world of *World War Z*.

The problem with this story is that it is just that—a story. In reality, there is no Tenth Man Theory used within the Mossad itself, according to former and current Israeli officials. (How the Israel Defense Forces have actually employed the lessons they learned from the 1973 Yom Kippur War to institute red teaming is described in chapter 2.) Perhaps this notion evolved from a passage in the Babylonian Talmud, which suggests that in a capital case, if the Sanhedrin, or judges, unanimously find the accused to be guilty, then they should be acquitted.[17] This concept has also been attempted in real life in the United States. In his memoir, Robert Kennedy described witnessing a cabinet officer "vigorously and fervently" change his own opinion while briefing President John F. Kennedy as the cabinet officer "quite accurately learned would be more sympathetically received by the President. . . . Thereafter, I suggested there be a devil's advocate to give an opposite opinion if none was presented." Robert Kennedy's recognition for the vital need for dissenting viewpoints stemmed from the near unanimity that President Kennedy's cabinet expressed while it reviewed and endorsed the wholly implausible and far-fetched Bay of Pigs invasion scheme launched in April 1961. Robert Kennedy went on to note that a designated devil's advocate "was obviously not needed" during the Cuban missile crisis in October 1962 because, having learned from the Bay of Pigs fiasco, there was rigorous, auththentic dissent and disagreement expressed throughout the thirteen-day crisis.[18]

The notion that institutions arrive at better decisions by directing one person to produce a dissenting viewpoint and serve as a check against groupthink is deeply flawed. It assumes that the person selected, who is "the tenth" person only because he or she has refrained from offering an opinion yet, has the freethinking personality type needed to truly challenge the underlying assumptions or facts supporting the opinions of everyone else. It also assumes that the person is capable of identifying the typical flaws characterizing group decision-making processes, or has served as a devil's advocate frequently enough to possess the sensitivity and finesse required for an opposing viewpoint to be heard and valued. Of course, it also assumes that this person can temporarily escape their immersion in the institutional pathologies experienced daily, and will re-experience, probably punitively, soon after having given a one-time authorized dissent. Finally, this notion presupposes that red teaming requires no training or guidance in its approaches or techniques, which is a dangerously misleading understanding of how true dissent actually improves institutional performance.[19] Indeed, even the Vatican's Devil's Advocate (highlighted in this book's introduction) was not a role assigned to just any Church official. Rather, the person was required to receive several years of instruction in Church law, undertake the equivalent of a two-year apprenticeship at the curia (the Catholic Church's administrative body) and finally pass a special examination before being admitted to the position of Devil's Advocate.[20]

Alternatively, leaders might dismiss authentic opposition by claiming that a dissenter was only acting like a devil's advocate out of stubbornness rather than principle. In conversations with government and military officials, several disparagingly pointed to Under Secretary of State George Ball's internal dissent to the Vietnam policies of the Lyndon B. Johnson administration. These officials remarked that a valuable red teamer should not become "just another George Ball," meaning someone taking a contrarian viewpoint just for the sake of doing so. In one notable example, in 1965, President Johnson told his senior advisors that Ball was merely engaging in a "devil's advocate" exercise when Ball wrote a memo proposing a negotiated withdrawal from Vietnam rather than further deepening US military engagement, an opinion that ran counter to the administration's long-standing strategy.[21] Johnson's contention, however, was intentionally false. Ball claimed in his memoir that Johnson assigned the label to him only to sustain the appearance of consensus within the administration in case Ball's memos leaked to the press:

> To negate any impression of dissent among the top hierarchy, President Johnson announced that he would refer to me as the 'devil's advocate,' thus providing an explanation for anyone outside the government who might hear that I was opposing our Vietnam policy. Though that ruse protected me, I was irked when some academic writers later implied that my long-sustained effort to extricate us from Vietnam was merely a stylized exercise by an in-house 'devil's advocate.' Thus are myths made.[22]

President Johnson consistently used red teaming as a convenient cover to describe away what were authentically dissenting opinions. Johnson's press secretary, George Reedy, later described how during White House debates "[devil's advocate] objections and cautions are discounted before they are delivered. They are actually welcomed because they prove for the record that decision was preceded by controversy."[23] Ball was never actually directed to red team US strategy in Vietnam, though in 1965 this would likely have been a potentially consequential and beneficial undertaking. After he left his position in the fall of 1966, Johnson's senior aide Bill Moyers temporarily assumed the sham role of White House contrarian. Yet President Johnson would infamously greet Moyers before meetings about Vietnam by saying: "Well, here comes Mr. Stop-the-Bombing."[24] Needless to say, Moyers was never actually empowered to provide a meaningful, dissenting viewpoint, and the bombing of Vietnam never stopped during the Johnson administration.[25] The lesson is: be cautious of someone randomly designated as a devil's advocate because their contrived dissent will have little impact counteracting group biases throughout the decision-making process.[26]

2. Mistaking red team findings for policy

Many of the biggest misimpressions about red teams are amplified by news reports lacking all context, and, by doing so, oversubscribe the significance of their findings. Over the past decade, enterprising journalists have frequently been able to obtain a classified alternative analysis produced by a military or intelligence community red team.[27] However, the journalists' reporting based upon the documents is often misleading and misinterprets an out-of-the-box analysis as being representative of mainline analysis, emblematic of senior officials' thinking, or a precursor to a forthcoming policy change. By their very design, alternative analyses are not supposed to be any of these things, nor, obviously, are they usually intended for external release. But once leaked to reporters, they find their way into public debates via irresponsibly or necessarily one-sided reporting, and they elicit confusion and misunderstandings.

For example, in 2010, veteran defense journalist Mark Perry reported on a US Central Command (CENTCOM) "Red Team" report titled "Managing Hizballah and Hamas." According to Perry, the CENTCOM red team had gone against US policy and suggested strategies to engage Hamas and Hezbollah politically and attempt to integrate them into the domestic politics and security services in Palestine and Lebanon. Perry wrote, "There's little question the report reflects the thinking among a significant number of senior officers at CENTCOM headquarters." In this case, Perry missed the entire point of the red teaming, which was commissioned for the sole purpose of questioning US foreign policy and proposing out-of-the-box ideas contrary to mainstream ideas.[28] In response, Middle East scholar Bilal Saab, based upon his own meetings and discussions with the CENTCOM red team, provided helpful and relevant vital context about the process by which the red team had operated. Saab did not dispute Perry's characterization of the report, but rather pointed out that Perry "was more or less accurate about the content of the Red Team report, but not about its purpose." As an advocate of negotiating with radical Islamist groups, the report's analysis supported Perry's ideas and made him believe that "his ideas have achieved credibility at high levels within the US policymaking community." Rather, in fact, the report simply stemmed from an idea voiced by one analyst that it did not trigger follow-up, debate, or analysis.[29]

Red teaming is quite common in regional US military commands. From 2008 to 2010, when General David Petraeus was the commander of CENTCOM, he employed a number of "initiatives groups" that conducted alternative analyses that benefited from receiving total access to the command while also being independent from the command staff structure. These initiative groups provided their findings exclusively to Petraeus in the form of five- or six-page papers, including a range of worst-case scenarios that could occur after the 2007 surge of US combat forces or the surge anticipated to take place four years later.[30] A lengthy August 2005 CENTCOM red team report for Petraeus's predecessor, General George Casey, was described by journalist Michael Gordon as "one of the most important—and until now, unknown missed opportunities of the war."[31] Casey, in turn, called Gordon's claim "a contrivance that is not supported by the facts on the ground," pointing out that the red team was supposed to offer alternative views, which were just one of many sources that US civilian and military officials used to refine policies in Iraq.[32] Similarly, for many years, analysts in the intelligence—or "2"—section of US Pacific Command (PACOM) based in Honolulu, Hawaii, produced a regular series of alternative-analytical reports under the theme, "From the Diary of Kim Jong-il."[33] These were intended to help PACOM officials and staffers imagine how the reclusive former North Korean leader might be perceiving his sheltered world, which could provide clues for his unpredictable behavior.

None of these aforementioned red team reports reflected what the military commanders or civilian officials necessarily believed, nor were they indicative of any forthcoming changes in policy. Indeed, truly out-of-the-box analysis should by its nature be vastly different from what commanders and officials believe, given their immersion in the mainline analytical products they read daily, which are intended to chronicle and interpret reality. Moreover, alternative analysis almost never directly results in a concrete policy change the likes of which requires extensive meetings among various stakeholders to develop new plans and then to coordinate and ensure their implementation.

So the next time that a red team report from the military, government, or private sector—as in the cases of the 1976 Team B report or the 2002 Millennium Challenge exercise—finds its way into the press, be skeptical about any importance assigned to it by journalists and uninformed commentators. They almost assuredly do not know what the red team's structure, scope, or purpose was, nor what its written products were intended to accomplish for the targeted institution.

3. Freelance red teaming

In January 2014, news station KSDK in St. Louis, Missouri, conducted an undercover investigation to assess safety protocols at five schools in five local districts. At Kirkwood High School, a KSDK staff photographer entered through an unlocked door and roamed unimpeded through hallways and past classrooms for several minutes before asking a teacher for directions to the main office. Upon arrival at the main office, the photographer asked to speak to the school resource office, but the secretary notified him that no one was available. He left a business card with his name and work cell phone number, and then, to determine whether he would be escorted, asked where the restroom was located. After merely receiving verbal directions, the photographer exited the building the same way he had entered. Shortly thereafter, the school called his work cell phone number on the card, only to receive a voicemail, prompting the school's communications director, Ginger Cayce, to call KSDK directly. Inexplicably, however, the news channel refused to confirm or deny the man's affiliation with KSDK. "I told them, 'I'm going to have to go into lockdown if you can't confirm that this was a test'," Cayce said. "When we couldn't confirm or deny it, we had no choice."[34] This triggered a forty-minute lockdown of the school, and, unsurprisingly, sparked a lively debate about media ethics.

Parents, teachers, and students panicked when the photographer's identity could not be confirmed, and those inside the school were forced to huddle against the walls with the doors locked and lights off while police searched the building. An angry parent, after learning of KSDK's involvement, vented, "If someone else did this, they'd be arrested. It's just not smart, with all the things that have happened in our country."[35] In its news report that evening, KSDK admitted that it was one of its reporters who had conducted the test, asserting that this investigation was based on one premise: "Are the security systems set up by school districts in St. Louis really working to keep our students safe?" The anchors acknowledged the angry calls they had received, and apologized for any "emotional distress" caused by the lockdown. They went on, however, to state that they "will continue to be vigilant when it comes to the safety of our schools and our children."[36]

Although this test revealed apparent gaps in the school's security measures, it also exposed glaring problems with the station's ad hoc red teaming. The photographer's business card was meant to serve as a means of contacting KSDK to discuss the findings of the test, but a lack of responsiveness immediately afterward only induced panic and disrupted school functions. "We learned some things from this, but we are still dismayed that a call was not given after to let us know this was a test," Cayce said. "We could have prevented the alarm to our parents, students and staff."[37] Although the district reviewed all its safety protocols after the incident, the lack of basic communication between the school and news station, coupled with the immediate publicizing of the security test, only served to leave the school's leadership embarrassed and unreceptive to any of KSDK's relevant findings.

Freelance red teaming such as this—conducted without the knowledge of the targeted institution or without appropriate mechanisms in place to prevent panic—is generally a poor idea. The news station did not conduct any research or reconnaissance to learn the security systems in place, nor did it even disclose what the photographer was doing when requested. For a few thousand dollars, KSDK could have hired a professional physical penetration tester with extensive experience in conducting security assessments. It would have alerted relevant district officials beforehand, and been prepared to address any situations or questions that emerged. Indeed, news organizations commission out-side experts to assist them with vulnerability probes all the time. For example, in 2012, NBC hired Jim Stickley, a security expert, to test the vulnerability of Onity electronic locks—then used on four million hotel doors worldwide. Using a small screwdriver-like electronic device hidden in a magic marker, Stickley simply plugged it into a port found on the bottom of the lock and opened the door. The device is built using open-source hardware and following instructions posted on YouTube. Although Onity had known about the problem for months and stated that "1.4 million locks and all customer requests for this solution have been fulfilled or are in the process of being fulfilled," Stickley found that most hotels remained wholly vulnerable. Moreover, Stickley easily picked the door locks in front of several hotel managers so that they could see precisely how unprotected their customers were.[38] Compared to KSDK's embarrassment of Kirkwood High School, and itself, NBC showed how a responsible news organization can red team to serve the public without needlessly causing panic and confusion. It is crucial that red teaming, especially unauthorized vulnerability probes like the one detailed above, be conducted in a manner that does not cause collateral damage or unnecessary panic.

4. Shooting the messenger

In 2009, a Marine Corps colonel with an infantry background and two Army majors—both graduates of the elite School of Advanced Military Studies—were brought to Afghanistan to serve as a small red team, known as the "effects cell."[39] The three officers operated independently from the chain of command and traveled into the field to assess the robustness of partnerships between NATO's International Security Assistance Force (ISAF) units and those of the Afghan National Army (ANA). At the time, "partnering" in the field was the primary approach toward building a professional Afghan military, which would presumably then begin to take the lead in independently securing areas where they operated. In 2009, Secretary of Defense Robert Gates said during a House Committee hearing, "Making this transition possible requires accelerating the development of a significantly larger and more capable Afghan army and police through intensive partnering with ISAF forces, especially in combat."[40] If the partnering mission was not working on the ground, then the overall campaign strategy would not be either.

The effects-cell officers were deeply disturbed by what they witnessed—with little variation—at more than a dozen combat outposts. They found that ISAF troops were living completely separately from the ANA forces that they were supposed to be training. This was even before the outbreak of so-called green-on-blue attacks that began in 2012—violent attacks by actual or disguised Afghan security forces against ISAF personnel.[41] The effects cell noticed, in particular, that ISAF perimeter machine-gun nests were perched high above their Afghanistan counterparts, with the heavy weapons pointed directly toward where their Afghan colleagues slept and ate. Moreover, the daily security patrols conducted by both forces were poorly coordinated and integrated. Also, on some days, literally no training or advising events took place. The Marine colonel recalled how the company and platoon leaders had developed a "FOB mentality"—a derogatory reference to ISAF forces hunkering down in their forward operating bases—and were "just counting the days until the next guys came in to replace them."

The Marine colonel briefed the effects cell's findings, first to senior ISAF staffers and eventually in front of General Stanley McChrystal, the commander of all US and international forces in Afghanistan. The Marine colonel was, and is, a gruff and brutally honest person, which an ISAF staff officer contended "couldn't have been more different than how the general [McChrystal] liked to run things."[42] The colonel described in detail instances where the effects cell found that ISAF units were not implementing the commander's strategic guidance. To drive his point home, the colonel graphically stated, "Sir, if they aren't shitting together, they aren't partnering together." Aides to McChrystal contend that the commander objected to both the tone and content of what he was being told, and, at one point, he berated the colonel, saying, "It sounds like you're telling me how to run my war."

The briefing ended soon after, and the impact of McChrystal's vo-
calized opposition was soon echoing throughout other staff sections.
Ultimately, the ISAF's plans and operations staffs did not accept what the
Marine colonel had revealed, nor did they adjust their campaign plans
to reflect the findings. Moreover, the effects cell had difficulty getting
traction in the remaining few months that it operated in Afghanistan.
This 2009 effects cell study exemplifies an instance when red teaming
was rigorously conducted to independently evaluate a plan, but then was
ignored by senior leaders and their staffs. It was pointless red teaming,
and its assessment was disregarded in part because it conflicted with how
the ISAF command hoped things would be going. But, unfortunately,
the blunt manner in which the Marine colonel delivered the effects cell's
recommendations undoubtedly made the ISAF command's senior leadership even less receptive to the bad news. Shooting the messenger accom-
plishes nothing other than signaling to the entire staff that dissenting
viewpoints are neither wanted nor welcomed. The red team is there for a
reason, to help improve the targeted institution's performance, and the
boss, general, or leader, whoever they are, should be open-minded toward
the red team's purpose and message.

5. Red teams should inform, not decide

Related to public misimpressions of red teams is the tendency of government or business officials to knowingly misuse them. An adept red
team will inform decision-makers by challenging conventional wisdom,
identifying blind spots, revealing vulnerabilities, presenting alternative
futures, and considering worst-case scenarios. Throughout this book,
leaders have described how red teaming helped them "envision failures,"
"stretch our imaginations," or "ask 'what if?', and challenge assumptions
and facts." However, what red teams should not be authorized to do is
to go far beyond this supporting role, and actually be expected to make
final decisions on its own.

It is understandable that it may be tempting to pass the buck where
partisan gridlock and executive clashes prevent a necessary and timely

decision. But this would be a mistake, and, thankfully, there are no prominent examples of red teams directing the decision-making process, even though they have been portrayed as needing such influence. A 2014 *TechCrunch* article describes the role of devil's advocate as someone who should point out all the reasons a strategy will fail and who has "the power to kill or postpone a [product] launch."[43] While a devil's advocate, or any form of red team, should be tasked to point out vulnerabilities, it must not be empowered to decide strategies on policies.

Along with assuring everyone that red teamers will not be making decisions, leaders should be reasonable and realistic in what they call upon red teams to do. Over the past fifteen years there has been a proliferation of Congressional members requesting that some federal agency activity or defensive system be subjected to a red team assessment. In part, this reflects the exponential overall growth in Congressional reporting requirements for federal agencies. While Congress required only 470 reports in 1960, that number multiplied by nearly five times to 2,300 by 1980, and has since doubled, reaching 4,637 expected reports in 2014—few of which will ever be read.[44] However, it also reflects the relatively recent awareness and appeal of the concept. There were zero legislative requests for government red teaming before September 11, 2001. Since then, there have been thirteen legislative requirements for red teams within federal agencies, three of which were passed into law.

For example, the 2003 defense bill mandated that Department of Energy labs establish red teams to challenge intra-laboratory assessments and perform inter-laboratory peer reviews. This was removed before the final version was passed because the annual reviews already taking place were considered to be sufficient.[45] In 2004, during debates over the landmark Intelligence Reform and Terrorism Prevention Act (IRTPA), senators introduced a provision that would have mandated the creation of an Office of Alternative Analysis in the not-yet established Office of the Director of National Intelligence (DNI).[46] The Office of Alternative Analysis would have been required to red team each National Intelligence Estimate, and any intelligence document, at the request of the director of the DNI.[47] When Senate and House leaders met behind closed doors to reconcile competing versions of the IRTPA, this proposed language was removed and replaced with a watered-down requirement for the DNI to assign the responsibility for alternative analysis of intelligence products to just one individual or entity.[48] Between 2005 and 2009, there were no fewer than eight attempts to mandate that the Department of Homeland Security (DHS) conduct a red team vulnerability probe of the defenses of some critical infrastructure system. Of these, only one was signed into law.[49] Most of these mandated red teams were removed at the request of DHS officials, who contended that they were a strain on agency resources and duplicative of security assessments and reviews already in place.

For a more revealing instance of congressionally mandated red teaming, in May 2013, Senator Angus King and Senator Marco Rubio cosponsored the Targeted Strike Oversight Reform Act of 2013. This legislation would add an additional level of review to US drone strikes against US citizens "knowingly engaged in acts of international terrorism against the United States." The DNI, fifteen days after receiving notification of a citizen having been targeted, would have to "complete an independent alternative analysis (commonly referred to as 'red-team analysis') of the information." Senator King claimed that the bill would "ensure that an independent group—or 'red team'—reviews the facts and that the details of that review are shared with the Congressional Intelligence Committees."[50] The provision was placed into the classified annex of the Intelligence Authorization Act and was signed into law in July 2014.[51] The two senators asserted that this red teaming would "provide an additional layer of accountability within the decision-making process."[52] Yet this required alternative analysis would almost assuredly not have a demonstrable impact on whether or how a US citizen suspected of terrorism is killed or not. According to congressional Intelligence Committee staffers, committee members already could, and routinely do, receive the same amount and granularity of information that they would receive from any red team. Moreover, these staffers acknowledge that they will never know what individuals, methods, and rigor were used in the DNI's internal review, nor will they see the complete findings.[53] For these reasons, this red team's effectiveness will be limited.

Recommendations for Government Red Teams

The strengths and weaknesses of red teaming have been explored over the past few chapters, as well as several of its most enduring lessons in the previous pages. But there are even more specific recommendations about how it can be applied. These takeaways focus primarily on the US government since it remains the setting and inspiration for most red teaming. However, the following five recommendations could definitely be tailored to the private sector too. They include the following:

1. Red team the biggest decisions

Before intervening militarily in a new country, White House officials bring in analysts and journalists for an off-the-record discussion, to share their thinking and offer strategic guidelines for an upcoming decision. But such events are mainly about socializing with and charming them in an attempt to influence how they write or speak about the upcoming intervention. Similarly, when asked about subjecting a big decision to rigorous and critical assessments, senior administration officials recount long debates where everybody was "free" to voice their opinions. However, having the same officials and staffers who developed the strategy over many weeks and who are deeply vested in it, then reverse course and poke holes in it does not count as a valid critical assessment.

Instead, the White House should establish a temporary red team of former officials, academics, and experts with the requisite security clearances to receive the latest intelligence, task it with asking one-on-one questions of the relevant civilian officials and military planners, and have it evaluate and critique the proposed strategy. This would take only one or two weeks, with the results presented directly to the president and whomever else the president decides should read it. For example, in the rushed decision to initiate airstrikes against ISIL in the summer of 2014, a red team could have evaluated the strategy at any time between the conclusive National Security Council Principals Committee meeting on

August 28 and President Obama's strategy speech on September 10. Obviously, as the commander-in-chief, presidents are free to incorporate or reject the alternative analysis as they see fit. However, given that initiating wars is among the most costly and consequential decisions ever made by presidents, an independent review of the information and proposed strategy by a red team deserve strong consideration.[54]

2. Compile US government red team efforts

In interviews with government employees who either currently or have previously served on red teams, a re-occurring issue raised was their lack of awareness of other government red-teaming efforts, and a genuine curiosity about what they could learn from them. Indeed, for all of its uses and misuses within the military, intelligence community, and homeland security agencies, there has never been a comprehensive governmental study and evaluation of what this management tool is, how to create a red team, or how it should best be employed. There was a single 2003 Defense Science Board red-teaming report, but it was narrowly scoped to examine only the use of red teams in the Department of Defense at the time.[55] Government red teams occasionally share best practices informally through chance encounters, e-mails, and ad hoc video teleconferences, but these insights have not been captured, catalogued, or disseminated.

It is crucial to get this information out. The existing Defense Science Board report needs to be expanded and updated to assess all permanent or semi-regular US government red teams. Given that many red teams work on classified programs there would likely need to be a classified internal version of this as well as an unclassified "for official use only" or public one. This study should be conducted by the Government Accountability Office, or perhaps one of the Congressional committees on Government and Oversight Reform. With an up-to-date repository of active red-teaming efforts, and what tends to work and what does not, government employees would be better able to learn from their colleagues when forming their own red teams. Ideally, such a study might be supplemented with a wiki-sharing platform that can be continuously updated and utilized by as many government agencies as possible.

3. Expand red team instruction

Red team training and educational opportunities should be made broadly available for nonmilitary government agencies. Given that all agencies have training and education elements, this will not require establishing new offices or spending much in the way of additional money. Based upon interviews with officials and staffers in the State Department and USAID, to give just two examples, there would be tremendous demand if this professional development opportunity was offered. The current educational offerings for government employees tend to be centered narrowly on acquiring incrementally updated technical or administrative certifications. These are useful for bureaucrats, but they do not improve upon or broaden the critical thinking skills of those midlevel officials who actually make the micro decisions that allow the federal government to function. Senior personnel and management officials should make two-week red-teaming courses available to meet this overwhelming demand and need. Just as important as offering red team instruction for staffers, brief, two-hour training sessions for their bosses—whether they are program managers or more senior officials—should be mandated in order for them to best understand what red teams can offer and how they should be used.

4. Review military red team instruction efforts

Despite more than eight years of red team instruction at UFMCS and Marine Corps University (MCU), there is no study that has measured its impact on the students, their professional careers, or their future positions when they become red-teaming practitioners. Surveys conducted after Army and Marine students graduate overwhelmingly demonstrate a strong satisfaction with the red-teaming approaches and techniques that they learned and a willingness for others to take similar courses. What is needed to complement these individual impressions is a comprehensive survey of how impactful the classroom instruction and practiced techniques learned have been at later appointments in their career. In particular, this survey would need to evaluate whether, how, and how often the graduates applied approaches and techniques later in their careers as part of a red team. The feedback provided could be applied to fine-tune and revise the courses taught at UFMCS and MCU, and allow the Army and Marines to recalibrate what they should expect from military red teaming.[56]

5. Make red teaming meaningful, not a rubber stamp

The structure, conduct, and composition of government red teams should include truly divergent and creative thinkers, and not just former officials who most likely reflect the accepted thinking of the targeted institution. This notably occurred in the case of the National Defense Panel (NDP). Since 1996, the secretary of defense has commissioned a comprehensive examination of national defense strategy, force structure plans, and budget proposals in order to determine future defense programs. This Quadrennial Defense Review, or QDR, absorbs a great deal of senior Pentagon officials' time since it provides broad strategic guidance for the armed services and various Department of Defense elements. Subsequently, for both 2010 and 2014, Congress mandated an additional independent review of the QDR in the form of an NDP. The panel received clear legislative guidance about the structure and scope of its activities—"conduct an assessment of the assumptions, strategy, findings, and risks of the [QDR]."[57] The NDP's shortcoming, however, was in its composition. The secretary of defense appointed the chair and vice chair, which in 2014 consisted of retired Secretary of Defense William Perry and retired Army General John Abizaid, while congressional oversight committees appointed the other members, which included all former military officers or Pentagon officials, and one former senator—all of whom had ties to defense or aerospace industries.[58] Moreover, the NDP consulted almost exclusively with serving military and civilian officials, or their retired counterparts.[59]

Unsurprisingly, the 2014 NDP's findings did not directly challenge any core assumptions of US military strategy. Its primary recommendation was simply to vastly increase defense spending without providing a roadmap for how this could be achieved given the largely bipartisan support for flat or declining defense budgets. Subsequently, the 2014 NDP had little impact upon the targeted institution—the Pentagon—since it re-endorsed the continuation of what the US military was already doing. That the NDP's findings and recommendations would closely reflect the conventional wisdom was to be expected. Future NDPs must be composed of fewer political strategy- and force-planning experts who are professionally or financially tied to the Pentagon or the defense industry.[60]

The Future of Red Teaming

After spending five rewarding and fascinating years meeting with and learning from more than two hundred red teamers operating in a wide variety of fields, the most difficult challenge is to remain as skeptical and honest as possible in evaluating their utility—that is, to maintain the distance and open-mindedness of a red teamer, while also becoming intimately acquainted with their fascinating work. This book opened with a warning to readers about the inherent difficulty that institutions face in identifying their own shortcomings, and in realistically understanding how competitors or adversaries might behave; in short, their inability to grade their own homework. This caution applies equally to the author, who has been immersed in the personalities, experiences, and confidences of a group of people who, by nature, tend to be divergent thinkers, somewhat proprietorial of their well-honed tradecraft, and skeptical of outsiders pigeonholing their profession. In relaying their stories and assessing their value, this book has attempted to remain as honest and analytical as possible. Yet the overall conclusion is that red teamers are so interesting and engaging that there is no need to hype or mythologize them. Indeed, almost everybody in the field rejects the over-exaggeration of their unique skills or influence. As retired Brigadier Tom Longland, head of the UK's

Development, Concepts and Doctrine Centre red team, declared, "The misconception is that red teaming is magic, secrecy, or wonderful. Most of the time, when we are briefing people, I tell them, 'This is just the application of common sense from a different perspective'."[61]

Nevertheless, red teams do make a demonstrable difference on their targeted institutions—especially when they are correctly scoped, adequately structured, and sufficiently empowered to carry out their objectives without undue influence. To reiterate: red teaming is a structured process to better understand the interests, intentions, and capabilities of an institution—or those of a potential competitor—through simulations, vulnerability probes, and alternative analyses. Senior government officials, admirals and generals, and business executives acknowledge that they are increasingly unable to process the complexity of the information before them, in a limited time frame, to make consequential decisions. There are simply too many factors informing each decision and too many actors to account for, whether they are foreign militaries, industry competitors, or malicious hackers.

Red teaming has its limits and there are times when it should be avoided. Red teams cannot—and should not—supplant an institution's embedded planning and operational components. Yet, they can provide a valuable check on those constraints that—in a red team's absence—would make well-informed strategic decisions and properly configured defensive systems less likely to be developed or to succeed.

Like any management tool, red teaming is only effective when it is embraced, resourced, and tailored to the needs of the targeted institution. This requires being cognizant of its strengths and weaknesses. When red teams are empowered to select their engagements, they should reject those where the problem set is undefined—and cannot be clarified in successive scoping conversations with the targeted institution—or when the intended objectives are simply unachievable. Red teaming is not a cure-all for every problem, but rather is a conceptual approach combined with specific tactics to prevent, mitigate, and respond to specific challenges.[62]

There is no single blueprint for how leaders and program managers can accomplish this because red teaming's very nature makes it impossible to devise rigid instructions that would be practical. Nevertheless, the research conducted for this book shows that a red team's success generally depends on the extent to which the following six best practices are adopted.

1. The boss must buy in

Leadership must value, provide adequate resources for, and want red teaming, and make this clear to the rest of the institution. Otherwise, the entire process will likely be unsupported and the findings will be ignored.

2. Outside and objective, while inside and aware

Red teamers need to be at least semi-independent to effectively conduct assessments, and the targeted institution's structure, processes, and culture must be taken into consideration when constructing the team.

3. Fearless skeptics with finesse

Red teaming requires a distinct personality type—open-minded, creative, confident, and a little odd, while maintaining the ability to relate to and communicate with the targeted institution without coming across as antagonistic.

4. Have a big bag of tricks

Variety is inherently the lifeblood of red teaming. Methods cannot become predictable or institutionally ingrained—this requires practitioners to be able to think on their feet and always have new tactics and techniques up their sleeves.

5. Be willing to hear bad news and act on it

Targeted institutions that are genuinely unable to hear and integrate a red team's findings as faithfully as possible should not bother doing it in the first place.

6. Red team just enough, but no more

Red teaming should not be a one-off event because undetected vulner-abilities will likely go unaddressed and blind spots will inevitably arise. However, red teaming too often is disruptive to the targeted institution and its employees and does not allow adequate time to make adjustments based on previous red team findings.

As business war-gamer Mark Chussil observed in chapter 5: "Nobody has data about the future." Yet, ideas about where red teaming is heading have already begun to emerge. Like many other human-intensive en-deavors, this will include replacing people—who are expensive and have physical limits—with sensors, communication links, algorithms, and automation, which are increasingly becoming cheaper and ubiquitous. Cyber penetration testers have touted the ability and eventuality of being able to conduct lower-cost and largely autonomous pen tests. Automated red teaming has been pursued by university and private-sector researchers for more than a decade and involves the integration of computational intelligence, evolutionary algorithms, and multiagent systems to better understand competition. In support of decision-making and planning, computer models and methodologies are used to carry out red-teaming exercises in order to help explore alternative strategies, identify cyber and physical vulnerabilities, uncover the evolving tactics of a competitor or adversary, and reveal biases.[63] Of course, there are certain limits to making automation the default approach to cyber vulnerability probes.[64] Former NSA official and current cyber-security executive Samuel Visner believes that stand-alone penetration tests cannot uncover the vulnera-bilities built into larger, more integrated, and increasingly complex digi-tal environments. Therefore, the future of cyber-vulnerability probes are trending toward more continuous and automated testing and analysis, while recognizing that only humans will determine what those models and algorithms will look like and judge whether they work.[65]

Similarly, Raphael Mudge led the development of "Cortana," a script-ing language allowing penetration testers to create automated bots (i.e., web robots) to simulate virtual red teamers. Funded through DARPA's Cyber Fast Track program, Cortana extends "Armitage," an exploit-management program used to set up a central server for a team of pen testers, to breach a network through one access point and then share its data.[66] In another example, information systems professor Philip Polstra has even written a detailed guide on how to conduct cyber and radio frequency penetration tests at a distance, using only cheap, small, low-powered devices.[67]

Researchers at several security firms are also spending their set-aside research and development time to more precisely calculate the "adversary work factor"—a measurement of the time and effort that a red team requires to breach different configurations of a defensive system.[68] If security managers could better quantify what it takes for a plausible adversary to break into a system, they could much better inform what personnel and resources should be preventively committed to defend that system. Moreover, it would allow red teams to better tailor each of their vulnerability probes for defensive systems over time, and to facilitate comparing similar defensive systems in different fields and industries.

The intelligence community's research arm, the Intelligence Advanced Research Projects Activity, has funded projects measuring cognitive bias and attempts to reduce that bias through gamification.[69] In 2012, this resulted in a video-game platform—"Macbeth" (or Mitigating Analyst Cognitive Bias by Eliminating Task Heuristics)—that trains participants to recognize and mitigate cognitive biases and measure their progress over time. Modeled after the board game "Clue," Macbeth presents a series of suspects and provides information to help players determine who committed the crime. Players must then decide whether that information was affected by cognitive biases—such as anchoring, projection, or representativeness.[70] According to a senior intelligence official, the project can demonstrably reduce analysts' cognitive biases and measure how much of that reduction is sustained over time with subsequent testing.[71] Permanently mitigating the impact of bias in the work of intelligence analysts should make the need for alternative analysis less pressing, because their products—memos, reports, and briefings—would be less bound by the anchoring effect of mainline analysis.

There will always be barriers to eliminating human beings from the red team process. While computers might pass the Turing test to mimic human behavior, they will likely never be able to fully contend with the skills, out-of-the-box thinking, and instant agility required to interpret tense situations and adjust courses of action on the fly any time soon. Only Marine majors have the necessary intuitive feel, understanding of the stresses that an operational planning team faces, and internalized doctrinal terminology and slang that will make criticisms of an evolving operational plan be listened to; only skilled white-hat hackers are able to sense, based upon their reconnaissance and scanning of a network, where and how to prioritize time and effort in order to make an engagement the most beneficial for a client; and only human physical penetration testers are able to embody a human adversary and behave outside of the constraints and limits of industry regulations and best practices.

Finally, much of what makes red teaming effective and causes its results to be acted upon is its practitioners' ability to explain findings in the form of stories that resonate with senior leaders. Across all fields, red teamers emphasized how storytelling and personal vignettes, tailored to spark and hold the interest of their intended audience, are critical. As longtime security professional Nicholas Percoco described it, you have to "make it personal" in order for a red team's findings to be heard and acted upon. Rather than presenting the technical details of a critical vulnerability in a mobile device, Percoco would show his clients, "Here's exactly how I could steal your personal photos or download your calendar off your phone." Cyber penetration test findings told by way of personally relatable anecdotes free of technical arcana are simply much more likely to be listened to and acted upon than pages of screenshots and malware script.[72]

Where red teaming is heading will ultimately depend upon the perceived value among government, military, and business leaders that it delivers to their targeted institutions. As the number of red team practitioners grows, as awareness is disseminated, and as those who have been exposed to it ascend to senior positions, its utilization as a management tool will undoubtedly become more prevalent and widespread.

The preceding pages have shown how simulations, vulnerability probes, and alternative analyses, when used correctly and heeded by superiors, are increasingly relevant to helping leaders confront and mitigate the challenges and threats that characterize all competitive environments. Red teaming is not a silver bullet that can solve every problem, but then again, nothing is. Embracing a red teamer's mindset can help almost anyone think more critically and divergently about the complications they face in their jobs and everyday lives.

As the astronomer Carl Sagan eloquently put it: "People in power have a vested interest to oppose critical thinking. . . . If we don't improve our understanding of critical thinking and develop it as kind of a second nature, then we're just suckers ready to be taken by the next charlatan who ambles along."[73] Likewise, red teaming is similarly beneficial, and even empowering, for those of us who are willing to learn from and appreciate all that it has to offer.

ACKNOWLEDGMENTS

This book project received the support of more people than I can adequately thank or remember. I am tremendously appreciative of the opportunities and assistance provided by the Council on Foreign Relations (CFR), under the leadership of President Richard Haass and Director of Studies James Lindsay, who both gave insightful feedback throughout the proposal and drafting processes. Paul Stares, director of the Center for Preventive Action, and Stewart Patrick, director of the International Institutions and Global Governance Program, also lent their encouragement and vast expertise. Additionally, I am grateful to my CFR colleagues who were invaluable sounding boards and champions, including Elizabeth Economy, Adam Segal, Shannon O'Neil, Michael Levi, Isobel Coleman, Steven Cook, Gayle Tzemach Lemmon, Laurie Garrett, Robert Danin, Julia Sweig, John Campbell, Sheila Smith, Matthew Waxman, Max Boot, and Richard Betts. I was also honored to have received invaluable perspectives from six years' worth of CFR military and intelligence fellows, and five years' worth of Stanton nuclear security fellows.

The book also benefited from contributions from the CFR David Rockefeller Studies Program staff, particularly Amy Baker, and Patricia Dorff and Eli Dvorkin in the publications department. I would also like to thank the Global Communications and Media Relations team, especially Lisa Shields, Kendra Davidson, and Jake Meth, and National Program and Outreach Vice President Irina Faskianos, for their book-promotion efforts. The Smith Richardson Foundation was instrumental in funding the research and writing phase of the book.

This project could not have even been started without the dedicated efforts of my agent Geri Thoma. Obviously, my tremendous thanks goes to Basic Books, especially Vice President and Publisher Lara Heimert and my initial editor, Alex Littlefield. In addition, editor Brandon Proia and copyeditor John Wilcockson greatly improved the work during its later editing phase. I would also like to recognize the other Basic Books team members, including Elizabeth Dana, Sandra Beris, Betsy DeJesu, Rachel King, and Leah Stecher.

The source material for this book originated from more than two hundred interviewees who were generous with their time, brutal candidness, and encouragement. Special acknowledgment belongs to: Gregory Fontenot, Steve Rotkoff, Mark Monroe, and my friend Kevin Benson at the University of Foreign Military and Cultural Studies; countless Marine Corps officers; the United Kingdom Ministry of Defence's Development, Concepts and Doctrine Centre red team; innumerable current and former Intelligence Community officials; Stephen Sloan; Bogdan Dzakovic; many NYPD and FBI officials; the Information Design Assurance Red Team, particularly Raymond Parks and Michael Skroch; business war-gamers Mark Chussil and Benjamin Gilad; hackers and security researchers, including Dan Guido, Jeff Moss, Chris Nickerson, Catherine Pearce, Nicholas Percoco, Jayson Street, and Dino Dai Zovi; Ellyn Ogden at the US Agency for International Development; and finally Mark Mateski, who has done more to honestly evaluate and responsibly promote red teaming than anyone.

I am forever indebted to the love and support of my friends and family, most practically in the form of the thoughtful editing and advice provided time and again by my brother, Adam Zenko.

I am also deeply appreciative of the CFR staff members who helped to research, edit, draft, and improve this book, particularly the amazing interns Julia Trehu, Priscilla Kim, Julie Anderson, Sara Kassir, Elena Vann, Sean Li, Aliza Litchman, Eugene Steinberg, and Samantha Andrews.

Finally, I dedicate this book to the three brilliant research associates with whom I am fortunate to have worked—and learned from—every day: Rebecca Friedman Lissner, Emma Welch, and Amelia Mae Wolf. Without them, the book would never have been started, finished, or been nearly as much fun to write.

NOTES

INTRODUCTION

1. André Vauchez, *Sainthood in the Later Middle Ages*, trans. Jean Birrell (Cambridge, UK: Cambridge University Press, 1997); and Robert Bartlett, *Why Can the Dead Do Such Great Things?: Saints and Worshippers from the Martyrs to the Reformation* (Princeton, NJ: Princeton University Press, 2013), pp. 3–56.

2. Eric W. Kemp, *Canonization and Authority in the Western Church* (Oxford, UK: Oxford University Press, 1948), p. 35.

3. Nicholas Hilling, *Procedure at the Roman Curia: A Concise and Practical Handbook*, second ed. (New York: John F. Wagner, 1909).

4. John Moore, *A View of Society and Manners in Italy*, vol. 1 (London, UK: W. Strahan and T. Cadell in the Strand, 1781), pp. 454–455.

5. Matthew Bunson, *2009 Catholic Almanac* (Huntington, IN: Our Sunday Visitor Publishing, 2008).

6. Alan Riding, "Vatican 'Saint Factory': Is It Working Too Hard?" *New York Times*, April 15, 1989, p. A4.

7. Melinda Henneberger, "Ideas & Trends: The Saints Just Keep Marching In," *New York Times*, March 3, 2002, p. C6.

8. George W. Bush, *Decision Points* (New York: Random House, 2010), p. 421.

9. *Ibid.*, pp. 420–421; Dick Cheney, *In My Time: A Personal and Political Memoir* (New York: Simon and Shuster, 2011), pp. 465–472; Robert M. Gates, *Duty: Memoirs of a Secretary at War* (New York: Knopf Doubleday, 2014), pp. 171–177; and David Makovsy, "The Silent Strike: How Israel Bombed a Syrian Nuclear Installation and Kept it Secret," *New Yorker*, September 17, 2012, pp. 34–40.

10. Interview with Stephen Hadley, June 12, 2014.

11. Interview with Gen. Michael Hayden, January 21, 2014.

12. *Ibid.*

13. Interview with a former senior CIA official, May 2014.

14. Interview with Gen. Michael Hayden, January 21, 2014.

15. Interview with Stephen Hadley, June 12, 2014.

16. Interview with Robert Gates, June 24, 2014.

17. Bob Woodward, "In Cheney's Memoir, It's Clear Iraq's Lessons Didn't Sink In," *Washington Post*, September 11, 2011, p. A25; and Gen. Michael Hayden, "The Intel System Got It Right on Syria," *Washington Post*, September 22, 2011, p. A17.

18. Bush, *Decision Points*, p. 421.

19. Interview with a former senior Central Intelligence Agency (CIA) official, May 2014.

20. Central Intelligence Agency, "CIA Comments on the Senate Select Committee on Intelligence Report on the Rendition, Detention, and Interrogation Program," Memorandum from the director of the CIA to Dianne Feinstein and Saxby Chambliss, June 2013, p. 25.

21. *Ibid.,* p. 24.

22. David Dunning, *Self-Insight: Roadblocks and Detours on the Path to Knowing Thyself* (New York: Psychology Press, 2005).

23. Thorstein Veblen, "The Instinct of Workmanship and the Irksomeness of Labor," *American Journal of Sociology,* 4(2), 1898, p. 195.

24. Adam Bryant, "Bob Pittman of Clear Channel on the Value of Dissent," *New York Times,* November 16, 2013, p. BU2.

25. Interview with Amy Edmondson, June 3, 2014.

26. Mike Spector, "Death Toll Tied to GM Faulty Ignition Hits 100," *Wall Street Journal,* May 11, 2015 [www.wsj.com/articles/BT-CO-20150511–710130]; and GM Ignition Compensation Claims Resolution Facility, "Detailed Overall Program Statistics," updated June 26, 2015, accessed June 30, 2015 [www.gmignitioncompensation.com/docs/programStatistics.pdf].

27. Michael Wayland, "Deaths Tied to GM Traced to 'Catastrophic' Decision: Report Finds Automaker Lacked Accountability," MLive.com, June 6, 2014.

28. Anton Valukas, "Report to Board of Directors of General Motors Company Regarding Ignition Switch Recalls" (Jenner and Block, May 29, 2014).

29. Massimo Calabresi, "A Revival in Langley," *Time,* May 20, 2011.

30. Warren Fishbein and Gregory Treverton, "Rethinking 'Alternative Analysis' to Address Transnational Threats," Sherman Kent Center for Intelligence Analysis, Occasional Paper 3(2), October 2004; and CIA, "A Tradecraft Primer: Structured Analytic Techniques for Improving Intelligence Analysis," March 2009, publicly released May 4, 2009.

31. The CIA Red Cell, which has an unprecedented remit to do alternative analyses, should not be confused with military red cells that only take an adversary's perspective. As Marine Corps doctrine declares: "The purpose of a red cell is to assist the commander in assessing [courses of action] against a thinking enemy. Depending on the size of the organization, a red cell can range in size from an intelligence officer to a task-organized group of subject matter experts (SMEs). While a red cell's principal duties center on course-of-action (COA) development and the COA war game, it participates in the analysis of the [center of gravities] and also supports the commander's understanding of the problem during the initial stages of design." See, US Marine Corps, "MCWP 5–1: Marine Corps Planning Process," 2010, pp. 2–6.

32. McKinsey & Company, "Red Team: Discussion Document," presentation to the Center for Medicaid and Medicare Service, undated, p. 2.

33. Hearing of the House Committee on Energy and Commerce, Subcommittee on Oversight and Investigations, "Security of HealthCare.gov," November 19, 2013; and Sharon LaFraniere and Eric Lipton, "Officials Were Warned About Health Site Woes," *New York Times,* November 18, 2013, p. A17.

34. Interview with Gregory Pirio, July 18, 2013.

CHAPTER ONE

1. Gregory Fontenot and Ellyn Ogden, "Red Teaming: The Art of Challenging Assumption," presentation at PopTech Annual Ideas Conference, Camden, ME, October 21, 2011.

2. Interview with Lt. Gen. Paul Van Riper, May 31, 2013.

3. Interview with Ben Gilad, December 20, 2013.

4. Interview with Mark Chussil, April 9, 2014.

5. Interview with Gen. David Petraeus, February 19, 2014.

6. Interview with Jami Miscik, May 21, 2012.

7. Interview with Gen. David Petraeus, February 19, 2014.

8. Interview with Lt. Gen. H. R. McMaster, December 4, 2014.

9. Interview with an Army colonel, June 13, 2013.

10. Interview with Ken Sawka, May 9, 2014.

11. Interview with Steve Elson, June 12, 2013.

12. Interview with Wayne McElrath, August 23, 2013.

13. Interview with Jayson Street, September 23, 2013.

14. Interview with Lt. Col. Brendan Mulvaney, May 1, 2014.

15. Interview with Charles Henderson, March 12, 2014.

16. Interview with Lt. Col. Daniel Geisenhof and a Marine Corps colonel, March 15, 2014.

17. Scott Eidelman, Christian Crandall, and Jennifer Pattershall, "The Existence Bias," *Journal of Personality and Social Psychology*, 97(5), 2009, pp. 765–775.

18. Interview with Rodney Faraon, May 27, 2014.

19. Interview with Marissa Michel, October 7, 2013.

20. Interview with Col. James Baker, January 14, 2014.

21. Interview with members of the CIA Red Cell, March 14, 2014.

22. Interview with Chris Nickerson, June 12, 2014.

23. University of Foreign Military and Cultural Studies, *Liberating Structures Handbook,* p. 27. The handbook lists forty-three red-teaming tactics, techniques, and procedures.

24. Interview with Raymond Parks, June 10, 2014.

25. Interview with Lt. Col. Bill Greenberg, March 10, 2014.

26. Interview with Ellyn Ogden, July 10, 2013.

27. Interview with Col. Mark Monroe, March 10, 2014.

28. Interview with Capt. James Waters, March 31, 2014.

29. Interview with Jeff Moss, September 24, 2013.

30. Interview with James Miller, March 27, 2014.

31. Interview with Robert Gates, June 24, 2014.

32. Nuclear Regulatory Commission, "Frequently Asked Questions About Force-on-Force Security Exercises at Nuclear Power Plants," updated March 25, 2013, accessed March 17, 2015 [www.nrc.gov/security/faq-force-on-force.html].

33. Interview with Jayson Street, September 23, 2013.

34. Interview with Catherine Pearce, June 3, 2014.

CHAPTER TWO

1. Karl Moore, "The New Chairman of the Joint Chiefs of Staff on 'Getting to the Truth'," *Forbes*, October 20, 2011.

2. Office of Management and Budget, *U.S. Fiscal Year 2016 Budget of the U.S. Government*, February 2, 2015, p. 134; Defense Manpower Data Center, "Department of Defense Active Duty Military Personnel by Rank/Grade," updated May 31, 2015, accessed June 23, 2015 [www.dmdc.osd.mil/appj/dwp/dwp_reports.jsp]; and Defense Manpower Data Center, "Department of Defense Selected Reserves by Rank/Grade," updated May 31, 2015, accessed June 23, 2015 [www.dmdc.osd.mil/appj/dwp/dwp_reports.jsp].

3. See the WGBH interview with RAND Corporation economist and Nobel Laureate Thomas Schelling for his colorful description of leading blue versus red nuclear war games during this period. WGBH, "Interview with Thomas Schelling," March 4, 1986.

4. George Dixon, "Pentagon Wages Weird Backward Inning Game," *Cape Girardeau Southeast Missourian*, dist. King Features Syndicate, May 31, 1963, p. 6.

5. Robert Davis, "Arms Control Simulation: The Search for an Acceptable Method," *Journal of Conflict Resolution*, 7(3), September 1, 1963, pp. 590–603.

6. Interview with James Miller, March 27, 2014.

7. Joint Chiefs of Staff, *Joint Publication 2–0: Joint Intelligence*, October 22, 2014, p. 1-28.

8. *Ibid*.

9. Department of Defense, *Department of Defense Base Structure Report FY2014 Baseline*, 2015, p. 6.

10. Spiegel staff, "Inside TAO: Documents Reveal Top NSA Hacking Unit," *Der Spiegel*, December 29, 2013.

11. Interview with Brendan Conlon, April 15, 2014.

12. Interview with an Army colonel, December 1, 2014.

13. Nellis Air Force Base, "414th Combat Training Squadron 'Red Flag'," updated July 6, 2014; and Interview with an Air Force colonel, November 24, 2014.

14. Mark Bowden, *Guests of the Ayatollah: The Iran Hostage Crisis: The First Battle in America's War with Militant Islam* (New York: Grove Press, 2007), pp. 452–461.

15. David C. Martin, "New Light on the Rescue Mission," *Newsweek*, June 30, 1980, p. 18.

16. Bowden, *Guests of the Ayatollah: The Iran Hostage Crisis: The First Battle in America's War with Militant Islam,* pp. 137 and 229.

17. Department of Defense, *Rescue Mission Report* (Washington, DC: Government Printing Office, August 23, 1980), p. 22.

18. Interview with an Army major general, November 19, 2014; and Stephen J. Gerras and Leonard Wong, *Changing Minds in the Army: Why It Is So Difficult and What to Do About It* (Carlisle Barracks, PA: U.S. Army War College Press, 2013), p. 9.

19. Interview with Lt. Col. Daniel Geisenhof, March 15, 2014.

20. Rumsfeld passed over eight active-duty four-star Army generals to bring

Schoomaker out of retirement. A ninth, Acting Army Chief of Staff Gen. John Keane, was offered the position, but declined it for family reasons. Schoomaker remains the only retired officer to become chief of staff in the Army's 238 years. Donald Rumsfeld, *Known and Unknown: A Memoir* (New York: Penguin, 2011), p. 653; Interview with Gen. Peter Schoomaker, February 4, 2014; Interview with Gen. John Keane, September 27, 2006; and Paul Wolfowitz, "Remarks as Delivered by Deputy Secretary of Defense Paul Wolfowitz," Eisenhower National Security Conference, Washington, DC, September 14, 2004.

21. Interview with Gen. Peter Schoomaker, February 4, 2014.

22. *Ibid*; and Hearing of the Senate Armed Services Committee, "Nominations Before the Senate Armed Services Committee," July 29, 2003.

23. *Ibid.*

24. Interview with Col. Steve Rotkoff, March 3, 2014.

25. Hearing of the Senate Armed Services Committee, Subcommittee on Strategic Forces, "Hearings on Fiscal Year 2005 Joint Military Intelligence Program (JMIP) and Army Tactical Intelligence and Related Activities (TIARA)," April 7, 2004.

26. Interview with Col. Gregory Fontenot, February 14, 2014.

27. University of Foreign Military and Cultural Studies (UFMCS), *Liberating Structures Handbook.*

28. UFMCS, *The Applied Critical Thinking Handbook 7.0*, January 2015, accessed March 17, 2015 [usacac.army.mil/sites/default/files/documents/ufmcs/The_Applied_Critical_Thinking_Handbook_v7.0.pdf].

29. The vast majority is from the US armed services, but now American officers also can take courses as an elective while they attend the Command and General Staff College located a short distance from UFMCS at Fort Leavenworth.

30. UFMCS uses the Net Promoter Score popularized by Fortune 500 companies and consultants to determine customer feedback and loyalty.

31. Interview with Col. Steve Rotkoff, December 4, 2014.

32. Interview with an Army official, April 2014.

33. Interview with Col. Steve Rotkoff, May 21, 2012; and Interview with Col. Mark Monroe, March 10, 2014.

34. Interview with a senior civilian Pentagon official, March 2014.

35. E-mail correspondence with a member of the J-7 red team, March 2014.

36. Interview with Col. Steve Rotkoff, March 3, 2014.

37. US Marine Corps, *35th Commandant of the Marine Corps Commandant's Planning Guidance*, 2010, p. 12.

38. Maj. Ronald Rega, *MEF and MEB Red Teams: Required Conditions and Placement Options*, thesis for master of military studies, US Marine Corps, 2012–2013, p. 17–18; When Napoleon and his general staff met to develop battle plans, Napoleon brought in a corporal to shine his boots, knowing that the corporal would listen to the briefing. Once the meeting concluded, Napoleon would consult the corporal, asking if he understood the plan. If the corporal responded "yes," Napoleon would command his staff to execute the plan, but if the corporal responded "no," then the plans were redrawn. See, Dale Eikmeier, "Design for Napoleon's Corporal," *Small Wars Journal*, September 27, 2010.

39. Rega, *MEF and MEB Red Teams: Required Conditions and Placement Options*, pp. 16–20.

40. Gidget Fuentes, "Amos Forms Front-Line Groups to Study Enemy," *Marine Corps Gazette*, December 21, 2010.

41. US Naval Institute Proceedings, "'We've Always Done Windows': Interview with Lt. Gen. James T. Conway," 129(11), November 2003, pp. 32–34.

42. Interview with a retired Marine colonel, March 2014.

43. Interview with Lt. Col. Brendan Mulvaney, May 1, 2014.

44. Interview with Col. Timothy Mundy, May 2014.

45. Interview with Lt. Gen. John Toolan, June 25, 2014.

46. Interview with a Marine colonel, November 20, 2014.

47. Interview with Lt. Col. Daniel Geisenhof and a Marine colonel, March 15, 2014.

48. Interviews with II MEF red teamers and staff, February–April 2014.

49. Interview with Maj. Jose Almazan, March 11, 2014.

50. E-mail correspondence with Brig. Gen. Dan Yoao and I MEF red teamers and staff, May 2014.

51. Interview with Lt. Gen. John Toolan, June 25, 2014.

52. Interviews with prior and current commandant red team members, and Marine officers, 2013 and 2014; and US Marine Corps, *US Marine Corps 36th Commandant's Planning Guidance*, January 23, 2015. Eventually, Amos's own commandant's red team was placed within the Strategic Initiatives Group (SIG), known as "The Commandant's Think Tank," but was physically located in Quantico, Virginia, at the Marine Corps Combat Development Command (MCCDC) until summer 2013, when it moved to the Office of the Director of the Marine Corps Staff, located within the Pentagon. Unlike at MCCDC, where it was buried and had almost no contact with the commandant to influence his decision-making, after moving to the Pentagon it has had a much greater ability to red team policy decisions, including on the consideration to place women in ground combat positions; and Interviews with prior and current commandant red team members, and Marine officers, 2013 and 2014. See also, US Marine Corps, "Strategic Initiatives Group (SIG): 'The Commandant's Think Tank'," accessed March 17, 2015 [www.hqmc.marines.mil/dmcs/Units /StrategicInitiativesgroup(SIG).aspx].

53. Interview with Lt. Col. Brian Ellis, November 25, 2014; and e-mail correspondence with Lt. Col. Brian Ellis, January 30, 2015.

54. Maj. Ron Rega spent three years as a Marine Corps red teamer, and completed a master's thesis on the effectiveness of red teaming at Marine Corps University. He wrote that red teaming "requires a decision by the senior leadership of the organization on where to place the red team within the organization, what areas the red team will focus on, and how the red team will interact with the rest of the organization." Rega, *MEF and MEB Red Teams: Required Conditions and Placement Options*, p. 43.

55. Melchor Antuñano, "Pilot Vision," Federal Aviation Administration, 2002, p. 3.

56. Interview with Lt. Col. William Rasgorshek, November 17, 2014.

57. P.L. 106–398, *Floyd D. Spence National Defense Authorization Act for Fiscal Year 2001*, sec. 213, "Fiscal Year 2002 Joint Field Experiment," October 30, 2000.

58. Roxana Tiron, "'Millennium Challenge' Will Test U.S. Military Jointness," *National Defense Magazine*, August 2001, p. 20; Lt. Col. H.R. McMaster, "Crack in the Foundation: Defense Transformation and the Underlying Assumption of Dominant Knowledge in Future War," US Army War College, November 2003; and Hearing of the Senate Armed Services Committee, Subcommittee on Emerging Threats and Capabilities, "Special Operations Military Capabilities, Operational Requirements, and Technology Acquisition in Review of the Defense Authorization Request for Fiscal Year 2003," March 12, 2002.

59. Department of Defense, "Media Availability with Defense Secretary Rumsfeld and Norwegian MoD," July 29, 2002.

60. Department of Defense, "General Kernan Briefs on Millennium Challenge 2002," July 18, 2002.

61. Interview with Gen. Buck Kernan, June 24, 2014.

62. For information on the Running Start plan, see, Bob Woodward, *Plan of Attack* (New York: Simon and Schuster, 2004), p. 97.

63. Joint Warfighting Center, "Commander's Handbook for an Effects-Based Approach to Joint Operations," February 24, 2006, p. viii.

64. Interview with Lt. Gen. Paul Van Riper, May 31, 2013.

65. Department of Defense, "General Kernan Briefs on Millennium Challenge 2002," July 18, 2002.

66. Thom Shanker, "Iran Encounter Grimly Echoes '02 War Game," *New York Times*, January 12, 2008, p. A1.

67. Interview with Lt. Gen. Paul Van Riper, May 23, 2014.

68. Interview with Gen. B. B. Bell, May 19, 2014.

69. Interview with Gen. Buck Kernan, June 24, 2014.

70. *Ibid.*

71. Interview with Lt. Gen. Paul Van Riper, May 31, 2013.

72. *Ibid.*

73. Interview with Lt. Gen. Paul Van Riper, May 23, 2014.

74. Sean D. Naylor, "Fixed War Games?" *Army Times*, August 26, 2002, p. 8; Van Riper later acknowledged, "I knew that e-mail would get into the media because the OPFOR guys were so ticked off." Interview with Lt. Gen. Paul Van Riper, May 23, 2014.

75. Department of Defense, "Gen. Kernan and Maj. Gen. Cash Discuss Millennium Challenge's Lessons Learned," September 17, 2002.

76. Naylor, "Fixed War Games?"

77. Department of Defense, "Pentagon Briefing," August 20, 2002.

78. US Joint Forces Command, "U.S. Joint Forces Command Millennium Challenge 2002: Experiment Report," undated.

79. *Ibid.*, p. F-11.

80. Department of Defense, *Defense Science Board Task Force on the Role and Status of DoD Red Teaming Activities*, September 2003, p. 18.

81. Sandra Erwin, "'Persistent' Intelligence Feeds Benefit Air Combat Planners," *National Defense Magazine*, October 2002, pp. 20–21.

82. Interview with Gen. B. B. Bell, May 19, 2014.

83. Interview with Gen. Buck Kernan, June 24, 2014.

84. Testimony of Maj. Gen. Eli Zeira, Agranat Commission, 1974.

85. Barbara Opall-Rome, "40 Years Later: Conflicted Accounts of Yom Kippur War," *Defense News*, October 6, 2013.

86. Testimony of Moshe Dayan, Agranat Commission, 1974.

87. Aryeh Shalev, *Israel's Intelligence Assessment Before the Yom Kippur War: Disentangling Deception and Distraction* (Portland, OR: Sussex Academic Press, 2010), p. viii.

88. Government of Israel, "Agranat Commission," 2008, accessed March 17, 2015 [www.knesset.gov.il/lexicon/eng/agranat_eng.htm].

89. Lt. Col. Shmuel, "The Imperative of Criticism," *Studies in Intelligence*, 24, 1985, p. 65. This was originally printed in *IDF Journal*, 2(3), May 1985.

90. It is at times also translated as "Research Unit" or "Internal Audit Unit," but is referred to by IDF officers and in internal documents as simply "control."

91. Zach Rosenzweig, "'The Devil's Advocate': The Functioning of the Oversight Department of [IDF] Military Intelligence," trans. Uri Sadot, Israel Defense Forces, April 10, 2013.

92. E-mail correspondence with a former Israeli military official, June 25, 2014; Yosef Kuperwasser, "Lessons from Israel's Intelligence Reforms," Saban Center for Middle East Policy, Analysis Paper no. 14, Brookings Institution, October 2007, p. 4; and Interview with a former CIA official, November 13, 2014. Mahleket Bakara alternative analyses have also been shared with their US intelligence counterparts, but primarily after the issue is no longer relevant.

93. Interview with Bruce Riedel, November 13, 2014.

94. United Kingdom Ministry of Defence, *Red Teaming Guide*, second ed., January 2013, p. 4–2.

95. Air Chief Marshal, Sir Jock Stirrup, Chief of Defence Staff, "RUSI Christmas Lecture," January 4, 2010.

96. Interview with Development, Concepts and Doctrine Centre red team members, April 20, 2015.

97. Interview with Brig. Tom Longland, November 25, 2014; and United Kingdom Ministry of Defence, *Red Teaming Guide*, pp. 1-4, 2-2.

98. Interview with Brig. Tom Longland, November 25, 2014; and interview with DCDC red team members, 2015.

99. United Kingdom Ministry of Defence, *Red Teaming Guide*, p. 2–2.

100. When establishing the unit at Norfolk, officials and staffers consciously rejected the terms "red team" and "red cell" in favor of "alternative analysis" in order to more clearly emphasize that "the capability provides and captures the importance of critical analysis over the adversarial mind-set implied by the name Red Team." See, North Atlantic Treaty Organisation, "Bi-Stratetic Commands Concept for Alternative Analsysis (AltA)," April 23, 2012, p. 5; and interview with NATO official, May 22, 2015.

101. Interview with Johannes "Hans" de Nijs, June 20, 2014.

102. Interview with Lt. Gen. Phil Jones, June 20, 2014.

103. *Ibid.*

104. Interview with Col. Kevin Benson, May 21, 2012.

105. E-mail correspondence with Col. Kevin Benson, July 15, 2014.

106. Defense Manpower Data Center, *Department of Defense Active Duty Military Personnel by Rank/Grade,* accessed July 17, 2014; and Congressional Budget Office, *Long-Term Implications of the 2013 Future Years Defense Program,* July 2012, p. 14.

107. Interview with Lt. Gen. John Toolan, June 25, 2014.

108. Malcolm Gladwell, "Paul Van Riper's Big Victory: Creating Structure for Spontaneity," in *Blink: The Power of Thinking Without Thinking* (New York: Little Brown and Company, 2005), pp. 99–146.

CHAPTER THREE

1. Robert Gates, "The Prediction of Soviet Intentions," *Studies in Intelligence,* 17(1), 1973, p. 46.

2. Office of the Director of National Intelligence, "DNI Releases Requested Budget Figure for FY 2016 Appropriations for the National Intelligence Program," February 2, 2015; and Department of Defense, "DoD Releases Military Intelligence Program Base Request for Fiscal Year 2016," February 2, 2015.

3. Richard Helms, *A Look over My Shoulder: A Life in the Central Intelligence Agency* (New York: Ballantine Books, 2003), p. 237.

4. Paul Pillar, *Terrorism and U.S. Foreign Policy* (Washington, DC: Brookings Institution Press, 2001), p. 114.

5. Most analytical products are supposed to be based upon formal requirements detailed in the National Intelligence Priorities Framework (NIPF), the mechanism by which the White House and the Office of the Director of National Intelligence—which oversees the other sixteen IC agencies—prioritizes intelligence collection and analysis tasks. Other analytical products are self-initiated by the analysts themselves with the approval of a supervisor, or are produced in an ad hoc manner in response to a pressing issue.

6. Interview with a senior intelligence community official, March 2014.

7. In March 2015, Director John Brennan announced a reorganization of the CIA. The final revamped structure had not been published as of June 2015. See, CIA, Unclassified Version of March 6, 2015, Message to the Workforce from CIA Director John Brennan, "Our Agency's Blueprint for the Future," March 6, 2015.

8. CIA, *The Performance of the Intelligence Community Before the Arab-Israeli War of October 1973: A Preliminary Post-Mortem Report,* December 1973, p. 22. In 1973, Director of Central Intelligence Richard Helms also mandated that the IC "develop regular systems to be implemented by the [National Intelligence Officers] to ensure that serious divergent points of view and conflicting elements of information not be submerged by managerial fiat or the mechanism of reinforcing consensus. . . . Such systems will also be charged with ensuring the establishment of means to provide the views of devils' advocates, adversary procedures, and the use of gaining techniques as appropriate." In practice, this recommendation was never implemented.

9. A January 2015 updated directive instructs: "Analysts must perform their functions with objectivity and with awareness of their own assumptions and reasoning. They must employ reasoning techniques and practical mechanisms that reveal and mitigate bias." This type of formal guidance is impossible for analysts to take into account when drafting analytical products day-to-day, according to several dozen analysts interviewed for this book. See, Office of the Director of National Intelligence, *Intelligence Community Directive 203*, updated January 2, 2015, p. 2.

10. Interview with Andrew Liepman, July 23, 2014.

11. Interview with Carmen Medina, June 2, 2014.

12. Interview with Gregory Treverton, January 6, 2014.

13. Interview with Gen. Michael Hayden, April 30, 2014.

14. Interview with a senior intelligence community official, April 2014.

15. Interview with Michael Morell, April 16, 2014.

16. Hearing of the House Permanent Select Committee on Intelligence, "Worldwide Threat Hearing," February 10, 2011.

17. Interviews with intelligence community analysts and officials, 2011–2014; and Paul Lehner, Avra Michelson, and Leonard Adelman, "Measuring the Forecast Accuracy of Intelligence Products," Mitre Corporation, December 2010.

18. CIA, "Estimate of Status of Atomic Warfare in the USSR," September 20, 1949, p. 1.

19. CIA, "Declassified National Intelligence Estimates on the Soviet Union and International Communism," updated October 5, 2001, accessed March 17, 2015.

20. Albert Wohlstetter, "Is There a Strategic Arms Race?" *Foreign Policy*, 15, 1974, pp. 3–20; and Anne Hessing Cahn, *Killing Détente: The Right Attacks the CIA* (University Park, PA: Pennsylvania State University Press, 1998), pp. 11–13.

21. CIA, NIE 11–3/8–74, *Soviet Forces for Intercontinental Conflict Through 1985*, November 14, 1974, pp. 10–11.

22. White House, Memorandum of Conversation, August 8, 1975.

23. Memorandum for Secretary of Defense, Deputy Secretary of State, and Director of Central Intelligence "Trial Modification to the NIE Process," undated.

24. Letter from the Director of Central Intelligence (Colby) to President Ford, November 21, 1975.

25. Letter from the Chairman of the President's Foreign Intelligence Advisory Board (Cherne) to the Director of Central Intelligence (Bush), June 8, 1976.

26. George A. Carver, Note for the Director [of Central Intelligence], May 26, 1976.

27. Cahn, *Killing Détente: The Right Attacks the CIA*, p. 139.

28. Interview with Robert Gates, June 24, 2014.

29. Cahn, *Killing Détente: The Right Attacks the CIA*, p. 153.

30. Richard Pipes, "Team B: The Reality Behind the Myth," *Commentary*, October 1986, pp. 25–40.

31. Interview with Maj. Gen. Jasper Welch, July 1, 2014. At the time, Welch was the Air Force's assistant chief of staff for studies and analysis, where he had been leading a study into why the Soviet expenditures on air defenses were far beyond what they required. When he received a call from one of his Air Force bosses asking if he wanted to serve on the Team B, he replied, "Sure, I will work on the Air

Defense panel." However, he was then instructed, "No, you will be on the [Strategic Objectives Panel]. You have to do it."

32. Cahn, *Killing Détente: The Right Attacks the CIA*, p. 159, citing interview with Adm. Daniel Murphy, November 9, 1989.

33. CIA, "Intelligence Community Experiment in Competitive Analysis: Soviet Strategic Objectives an Alternative View Report of Team B," National Archives, December 1976.

34. Melvin Goodman, "Chapter 6," in *National Insecurity: The Cost of American Militarism* (San Francisco, CA: City Lights Books, 2013).

35. Anne Hessing Cahn, who interviewed almost every participant in the Team B experiment for her masterful historical account, *Killing Détente: The Right Attacks the CIA*, recalled that all of its members were diametrically opposed to improved relations with the Soviet Union. Even speaking with them after the Cold War, she noted: "I could predict with one-hundred-percent accuracy their answer to most questions based upon their careers and ideological affiliation. They still hated the Soviet Union, and they distrusted the findings of the CIA." Interview with Anne Hessing Cahn, June 2, 2014.

36. CIA, "Intelligence Community Experiment in Competitive Analysis: Soviet Strategic Objectives an Alternate View Report of Team B," pp. 1 and 14.

37. Memorandum from the Director of Central Intelligence (Bush) to Recipients of National Intelligence Estimate 11-3/8-76, undated.

38. See, Murney Marde, "Carte to Inherit Intense Dispute on Soviet Intentions," *Washington Post,* January 2, 1977, p. A1. See also, Cahn, *Killing Détente: The Right Attacks the CIA*, p. 179; and *Ibid.*, p. 182, citing interview with Richard Pipes, August 15, 1990.

39. Senate Select Committee on Intelligence, Subcommittee on Collection, Production, and Quality, "The Nation's Intelligence Estimates A-B Team Episode Concerning Soviet Strategic Capability and Objectives," February 16, 1978.

40. Memorandum from the Director of Central Intelligence (Bush) to the Chairman of the President's Foreign Intelligence Advisory Board (Cherne), January 19, 1977.

41. Interview with Maj. Gen. Jasper Welch, July 1, 2014.

42. Cahn, *Killing Détente: The Right Attacks the CIA*, p. 160.

43. Interview with Robert Gates, June 24, 2014.

44. Office of Rep. Pete Hoekstra, "Hoekstra Calls for Independent Red Team on Iran Nuclear Issue," October 6, 2009. In fact, the 2007 NIE was red teamed because its key findings were so different from previous NIEs. This idea was refloated in April 2015 when Michael Mukasey, former US attorney general, and Kevin Carroll, former senior counsel to the House Committee on Homeland Security, called on "House and Senate leaders of both parties [to] ask former senior national-security officials to study raw intelligence-reporting on Iran, and direct the administration legislatively if necessary to give them the data needed to make an informed judgment. This 'Team B' should then report its findings periodically not only to the administration, but also to congressional leaders and the presidential nominees of both parties once they are chosen." See, Michael Mukasey and Kevin Carroll, "The CIA Needs an Iran 'Team B'," *Wall Street Journal*, April 14, 2015, p. A13.

45. Richard Clarke, *Against All Enemies: Inside America's War on Terror* (New York: Free Press, 2004), p. 184.

46. Interview with a former intelligence community official, May 2014.

47. National Commission on Terrorist Attacks upon the United States (herein 9/11 Comission), *The 9/11 Commission Report: The Attack from Planning to Aftermath*, 2004, p. 117.

48. *Ibid.*, p. 116.

49. Interview with Bruce Riedel, January 23, 2007.

50. Bill Clinton, *My Life* (New York: Knopf, 2004), p. 803.

51. Interview with John Lauder, director of the Nonproliferation Center at the time of Al Shifa, June 20, 2014.

52. Interview with Jami Miscik, June 9, 2014.

53. Interview with Mary McCarthy, May 15, 2014.

54. Interview with Phyllis Oakley, April 2014; and James Risen, "To Bomb Sudan Plant, or Not: A Year Later, Debates Rankle," *New York Times*, October 29, 1999, p. A1.

55. Interview with a former intelligence community official, May 2014; and Vernon Loeb, "U.S. Wasn't Sure Plant Had Nerve Gas Role; Before Sudan Strike, CIA Urged More Tests," *Washington Post,* August 21, 1999, p. A01.

56. Risen, "To Bomb Sudan Plant, or Not: A Year Later, Debates Rankle," p. A1.

57. Interview with Paul Pillar, deputy chief of central intelligence's Counterterrorist Center at the time of Al Shifa, September 2006; and Interviews with small group members, 2013–2014.

58. Interview with Gen. Anthony Zinni, February 2008.

59. Shelton recalled that, after the attack on Al Shifa, "the intel started to fade on us, and it turned out that this CIA intelligence had *not* really been collected at the pharmaceutical plant, but rather *three hundred yards away from it*. And now—by the way—the quarter teaspoon of soil sample turned out to have been collected *two years* earlier." See, Gen. Hugh Shelton with Ronald Levinson and Malcolm McConnell, *Without Hesitation: The Odyssey of an American Warrior* (New York: St. Martin's Press, 2010), p. 350.

60. Interview with a former White House official, May 2014.

61. Daniel Pearl, "New Doubts Surface over Claims That Plant Produced Nerve Gas," *Wall Street Journal*, August 28, 1998.

62. George Tenet, with Bill Harlow, *At the Center of the Storm: My Years at the CIA* (New York: HarperCollins, 2007), p. 117.

63. Statement of William S. Cohen to the National Commission on Terrorist Attacks Upon the United States, March 23, 2004, p. 14.

64. Interview with Jami Miscik, June 9, 2014.

65. Interview with Thomas Pickering, April 21, 2014.

66. The following section is based primarily upon interviews with current and former CIA and intelligence community staffers and officials, other government officials, and Tenet, with Harlow, *At the Center of the Storm*, pp. 194–195.

67. *Ibid.*, p. 185.

68. Interview with Gen. David Petraeus, February 19, 2014.

69. Interview with Carmen Medina, June 2, 2014.

70. Interview with Jami Miscik, May 21, 2012.

71. Interview with Paul Frandano, June 18, 2013.

She is famous for her role in the August 1969 hijacking of TWA Flight 840 and the Dawson's Field hijackings during Black September in Jordan in 1970. The quote is from an interview with Stephen Sloan, July 9, 2014.

7. *Ibid.;* ironically, the exact same office building from which federal and international law enforcement officials observed the simulated hostage-taking was where Zacarias Moussaoui, an Al Qaeda member intercepted by the FBI less than a month before 9/11 and later convicted for conspiracy to kill Americans, took simulated flight training classes a quarter-century later. Ihab Ali Nawawi, Osama bin Laden's personal pilot in the 1990s, also took lessons at the school.

8. US Department of State, Office of Combating Terrorism, *Terrorist Skyjackings: A Statistical Overview of Terrorist Skyjackings from January 1968 Through June 1982*, 1982.

9. Six-part series in *The Oklahoman*, July 28, 1974, September 30, 1974, October 2–4, 1974; six-part series in *The Oklahoman*, November 12–19, 1975; Stephen Sloan and Richard Kearney, "An Analysis of a Simulated Terrorist Incident," *The Police Chief*, June 1977, pp. 57–59; and Stephen Sloan, "Stimulating Terrorism: From Operational Techniques to Questions of Policy," *International Studies Notes*, 5(4), 1978.

10. Stephen Sloan, "Almost Present at the Creation: A Personal Perspective of a Continuing Journey," *The Journal of Conflict Studies*, 24(1), 2004.

11. Stephen Sloan and Robert Bunker, *Red Teams and Counterterrorism Training* (Norman, OK: University of Oklahoma Press, 2011), pp. 91–101.

12. Interview with a US Department of Homeland Security (DHS) official, March 12, 2014; and DHS, *U.S. Department of Homeland Security Annual Performance Report: Fiscal Years 2014–2016*, February 2, 2015, p. 119.

13. Interview with a DHS official, March 12, 2014.

14. Jason Miller, "DHS Teams Hunt for Weaknesses in Federal Cyber Networks," *Federal News Radio*, July 11, 2012.

15. Hearing of the Senate Committee on Commerce, Science, and Transportation, "Are Our Nation's Ports Secure? Examining the Transportation Worker Identification Credential Program," May 10, 2011.

16. Interview with Wayne McElrath, director of the Government Accountability Office's (GAO's) Office of Special Investigation, August 23, 2013; the standards for GAO and all government vulnerability probes can be found in the "yellow book." See GAO, "Government Auditing Standards," December 2011.

17. GAO, "Border Security: Summary of Covert Tests and Security Assessments for the Senate Committee on Finance, 2003–2007," May 2008, p. 3.

18. GAO, "Border Security: Additional Steps Needed to Ensure that Officers Are Fully Trained," December 2011, p. 4.

19. GAO, "Border Security: Summary of Covert Tests and Security Assessments for the Senate Committee on Finance, 2003–2007," May 2008, pp. 8–12.

20. GAO, "Combating Nuclear Smuggling: Risk-Informed Cover Assessments and Oversight of Corrective Actions Could Strengthen Capabilities at the Border," September 2014, pp. 14–15.

21. GAO, "Border Security: Additional Steps Needed to Ensure That Officers Are Fully Trained," December 2011 [www.gao.gov/products/GAO-12–269]. See, "Recommendations."

22. *Ibid.*, pp. 2 and 10.

23. Mark Holt and Anthony Andrews, "Nuclear Power Plant Security and Vulnerabilities," Congressional Research Service, January 3, 2014, p. 9.

24. Christine Cordner, "PG&E Offers More Details on Substation Attack, Tallies Up Recovery Cost at over $15M," SNL Federal Energy Regulatory Commission, June 25, 2014.

25. Richard Serrano and Evan Halper, "Sophisticated but Low-tech Power Grid Attack Baffles Authorities," *Los Angeles Times*, February 11, 2014, p. A1.

26. Pacific Gas and Electric, "PG&E Announces Request for Information on Metcalf Substation Attack," April 10, 2014.

27. David Baker, "Thieves Raid PG&E Substation Hit by Snipers in 2013," Sfgate.com, August 27, 2014.

28. Rebecca Smith, "Assault on California Power Station Raises Alarm on Potential for Terrorism," *Wall Street Journal*, February 5, 2014, p. A1.

29. Cordner, "PG&E Offers More Details on Substation Attack, Tallies Up Recovery Cost at over $15M."

30. Rebecca Smith, "Federal Government Is Urged to Prevent Grid Attacks," *Wall Street Journal*, July 6, 2014.

31. Interview with Steve Elson, June 12, 2013.

32. *Report of the President's Commission on Aviation Security and Terrorism*, May 15, 1990.

33. *Ibid.*, p. ii.

34. P.L. 104–64, *Federal Aviation Reauthorization Act of 1996*, sec. 312, "Enhanced Security Programs," October 9, 1996; and 9/11 Commission, Memorandum for the Record, Interview with Bruce Butterworth, former Director for Policy and Planning at the FAA, September 29, 2003, p. 5.

35. The associate administrator for Civil Aviation Security from 1993 to 2000 was Rear Adm. Cathal Flynn. When asked about his role and responsibility in overseeing the FAA red team, he puzzlingly replied: "We never used a Red Team in FAA Security." This is demonstrably false, but deciding not to remember the FAA Red Team might indicate what little impact it had within the CAS. See e-mail correspondence with Rear Adm. Cathal Flynn, May 20, 2014.

36. GAO, "Aviation Safety: Weaknesses in Inspection and Enforcement Limit FAA in Identifying and Responding to Risks," February 1998, pp. 7–8, 24, and 61–62.

37. Flynn told 9/11 Commission investigators that "red team testing was made 'easy' because it would help the FAA to obtain a civil penalty against the airline if the failure were obvious and glaring." Despite finding many obvious and glaring errors, there is no record of a red team finding ever resulting in such a civil penalty. 9/11 Commission, Memorandum for the Record, "Interview with Rear Admiral Cathal 'Irish' Flynn, USN (ret)," September 9, 2003.

38. Interviews with Steve Elson, June 12, 2013, and June 11, 2014.

39. US Department of Transportation (DOT), Office of Inspector General, *Semiannual Report to the Congress*, October 1, 1999–March 31, 2000, p. 17.

40. Letter from [Special Counsel] Elaine Kaplan to the President, "Re: OSC File No. DI-02–0207," March 18, 2003, p. 4.

41. For example, the FAA Administrator from 1993 to 1996 was David Hinson, cofounder of Midway Airlines. He was replaced from 1996 to 1997 by Linda Daschle, who previously was the chief lobbyist for the Air Transport Association, the airline industry's main lobby. She was replaced from 1997 to 2002 by Jane Garvey, who had been the director of Logan International Airport. See, Public Citizen, *Delay, Dilute and Discard: How the Aviation Industry and the FAA Have Stymied Aviation Security Recommendations*, October 2001; and Doug Ireland, "I'm Linda, Fly Me," *LA Weekly*, January 16, 2003.

42. Jim Morris, "Since Pan Am 103 a 'Façade of Security'," *U.S. News & World Report*, 130 (7), February 19, 2001, p. 28.

43. GAO, *Aviation Security: Long-Standing Problems Impair Airport Screeners' Performance*, June 2000, p. 7. In 1997, the FAA declared that the results of airport screeners' performances would henceforth be sensitive security information, and could therefore not be released.

44. Deborah Sherman, Investigative Report, Fox 25, May 6, 2001. The report was delivered along with a letter written by Sullivan that warned prophetically: "With the concept of jihad, do you think it would be difficult for a determined terrorist to get on a plane and destroy himself and all other passengers? . . . Think what the result would be of a coordinated attack that took down several domestic flights on the same day. The problem is that with our current screening system, this is more than possible. Given time, with current threats, it is almost likely." John Kerry's office sent the entire package that Dzakovic delivered to the DOT inspector general, where it was received by the same officials who had repeatedly heard these concerns from Dzakovic directly, but had decided not to investigate them.

45. *The 9/11 Commission Report: The Attack from Planning to Aftermath*, pp. 242–245.

46. The 9/11 Commission would not be formed for another thirteen months. After strongly opposing any meaningful investigation into the most lethal and costly terrorist attack in American history, President Bush reversed course in November 2002, and announced the forming of the Commission with Henry Kissinger as its chair.

47. Office of Special Counsel, "U.S. Office of Special Counsel Sends Report Confirming Gross Management of FAA's Red Team, Resulting in Substantial and Specific Danger to Public Safety," March 18, 2003.

48. Hearing of the House Committee on Homeland Security, Subcommittee on Transportation Security, "Examining TSA's Cadre of Criminal Investigators," January 28, 2014; Hearing of the House Homeland Security Committee Transportation Security Subcommittee, "Transportation Security Administration's Efforts to Advance Risk-Based Security," March 14, 2013; and Interview with Bogdan Dzakovic, June 11, 2013. These covert smuggling attempts were incorrectly reported by the media as "red team" tests. In fact, they were done by auditors without "any specialized background or training," including accountants. See, Hearing of the Senate Committee on Homeland Security and Governmental Affairs, "Transportation Security Administration Oversight," June 9, 2015. As a direct result of these well-publicized security shortcomings, the acting administrator for the TSA, Melvin Carraway, was reassigned within DHS.

49. "Press Release: Enhanced Security Measures at Certain Airports Overseas," US Department of Homeland Security, Transportation Security Administration, July 6, 2014.

50. Evan Booth, "Terminal Cornucopia," presentation at SkyDogCON 2013, Nashville, TN, October 26, 2013, accessed March 17, 2015 [www.youtube.com /watch?v=PiGK2rk5524].

51. Hearing of the Senate Committee on Appropriations and Senate Committee on the Budget, Subcommittee on Transportation, "Federal Aviation Administration: Challenges in Modernizing the Agency," February 3, 2000.

52. 9/11 Commission, Memorandum for the Record, "Interview with Bruce Butterworth, former Director for Policy and Planning at the FAA," September 29, 2003, p. 6.

53. Federation of American Scientists, *The Menace of MANPADS*, 2003.

54. Colin Powell, Comments to Asia-Pacific Economic Cooperation Forum, Bangkok, Thailand, October 18, 2003.

55. P. L. 108–458, *Intelligence Reform and Terrorism Prevention Act of 2004*, US Congress, December 17, 2004.

56. GAO, *Aviation Security: A National Strategy and Other Actions Would Strengthen TSA's Efforts to Secure Commercial Airport Perimeters and Access Controls*, September 2009, p. 21.

57. James Chow et al., *Protecting Commercial Aviation Against the Shoulder-Fired Missile Threat* (Santa Monica, CA: RAND Corporation, 2005), p. 15.

58. Paul May, "Going Gaga for Online Radio," *Guardian*, January 8, 2003, p. 5.

59. US Department of State, Bureau of Political-Military Affairs, "MANPADS: Combatting the Threat to Global Aviation from Man-Portable Air Defense Systems," July 27, 2011.

60. Office of the Director of National Intelligence, Press Briefing with Intelligence Officials, July 22, 2014.

61. Kirk Semple and Eric Schmitt, "Missiles of ISIS May Pose Peril for Aircrews in Iraq," *New York Times*, October 27, 2014, p. A1.

62. John Pistole, "TSA: Toward a Risk-Based Approach to Aviation Security," presentation at the Aspen Security Forum, Aspen, CO, July 23, 2014; and Rory Jones, Robert Wall, and Orr Hirschauge, "Attacks Spur Debate on Antimissile Systems for Passenger Jets," *Wall Street Journal*, July 24, 2014, p. A8.

63. Cathy Scott-Clark and Adrian Levy, *The Siege: 68 Hours Inside the Taj Hotel* (New York: Penguin Books, 2013); and Angela Rabasa et al., "The Lessons of Mumbai," Occasional Paper, RAND Corporation, January 2009.

64. NYPD Intelligence Division, "Mumbai Attack Analysis" (Law Enforcement Sensitive Information as of December 4, 2008).

65. Interviews with Commissioner Ray Kelly, January 2014; and Hearing of the Senate Committee on Homeland Security and Governmental Affairs, "Lessons from the Mumbai Terrorist Attacks," January 8, 2009.

66. Interview with Capt. James Waters and "Bob," March 31, 2014.

67. Interviews with Commissioner Ray Kelly, January 2014.

68. Interview with Capt. James Waters and "Bob," March 31, 2014.

69. *Star Trek II: The Wrath of Khan*, directed by Nicholas Meyer (Paramount Pictures, 1982).

70. Interview with Mitchell Silber, March 6, 2014.

71. Interviews with NYPD officials, January–March 2014.

72. In January 2015, this arrangement was formalized with the establishment of the Capital Strategic Response Group, which increased the number of officers dedicated specifically to responding to multiple gunman terrorist attacks, like those that had occurred against *Charlie Hebdo* magazine three weeks earlier. See, "Police Commissioner Bratton's Remarks at the 'State of the NYPD'," Police Foundation, January 29, 2015.

73. *Ibid.* As a result of the tabletop exercise, the NYPD also developed and implemented new highly secret methods for the pinpoint jamming of terrorists' cellphone communications in crisis situations.

74. *Ibid.*; Patrice O'Shaughnessy, "NYPD Learns from Mumbai Terrorist Attack that Killed 174," *New York Daily News*, February 15, 2009, p. 16.

75. Sean Gardiner, "NYPD Trains for New Type of Attack," *Wall Street Journal*, December 20, 2010, p. A21.

76. See, "Raymond Parks," LinkedIn, accessed March 17, 2015 [www.linkedin .com/pub/raymond-parks/6/566/a75].

77. Interviews with Raymond Parks, June 2014.

78. US Air Force, *Air Force System Safety Handbook*, Air Force Safety Agency, July 2000, p. 121.

79. iMPERVA, "Red Teaming, an Interview with Ray Parks of Sandia National Labs (SNL)," 2009.

80. Kevin Robinson-Avila, "Sandia Shows Off New Testing Complex," *Albuquerque Journal*, May 9, 2014; and Hearing of the House Armed Services Committee, "Nuclear Weapons Modernization Programs: Military, Technical, and Political Requirements for the B61 Life Extensions Program and Future Stockpile Strategy," October 29, 2013.

81. Interviews with Michael Skroch, June–July 2014.

82. Interview with Samuel Varnado, July 15, 2014.

83. Sandia National Laboratories, "Assessment Choices: When Choosing Sandia Makes Sense," undated.

84. In practice, once a statement of work had been agreed upon between the government sponsor and IDART, National Nuclear Security Administration always signed off on the red team engagement. Technically, the Sandia Corporation, a subsidiary of Lockheed Martin Corporation, is contracted by the NNSA to manage and operate Sandia National Laboratories, for which they earn about $27 million annually, which includes a small fee from each IDART engagement. Dan Mayfield, "New Lockheed Sandia Contract Finalized Today," *Albuquerque Business First*, April 30, 2014.

85. SCADA is used interchangeably with Industrial Control Systems (ICS). According to former National Security Agency (NSA) hacker Bob Stasio, who worked with IDART while at the NSA, IDART has a reputation for being especially effective at security assessments of critical infrastructure information systems. Interview with Stasio, June 30, 2014; on the growth of malicious SCADA attacks, see, Department

of Homeland Security (DHS), National Cybersecurity and Communications Integration Center, "Internet Accessible Control Systems At Risk," ICS-CERT Monitor, January–April 2014.

86. Interview with Samuel Varnado, July 15, 2014.

87. The program aired on April 24, 2003. Skroch noted that he wished he had said, "Duh! You think a national laboratory cannot impact an infrastructure? That's not the important question. What is important is understanding what kind of adversary can!" Interview with Michael Skroch, June-July 2014.

88. According to IDART members, what was particularly notable about Invicta was that it was owned by Victor Sheymov, who ran the Soviet Union's version of the NSA before he defected to the United States in 1980, and was staffed by former NSA hackers.

89. GAO, "Supply Chain Security: DHS Should Test and Evaluate Container Security Technologies Consistent with All Identified Operational Scenarios to Ensure the Technologies Will Function as Intended," September 2010, p. 3; and Mark Greaves, "Ultralog Survivable Logistics Information Systems," PowerPoint presentation, Defense Advanced Research Projects Agency, September 2002, slide 37.

90. Sandia National Laboratories, "Keep Telling Yourself: 'The Red Team Is My Friend . . . ',￼" 2000.

91. Interview with Dino Dai Zovi, July 18, 2014.

92. E-mail correspondence with Michael Skroch, July 17, 2014.

93. Sandia National Laboratories, "Red Teaming for Program Managers," accessed March 17, 2015 [www.idart.sandia.gov/methodology/RT4PM.html].

94. Interview with Michael Skroch, June 4, 2014.

95. Mark Mateski, who was with the Sandia unit from 2005 to 2008, observed that IDART specialized in developing a methodology that was process-oriented and easily understood by non-specialists. The drawback to this commodification was that it did not allow for creativity or stratagem in conducting vulnerability probes. Interview with Mark Mateski, July 25, 2014.

96. Interview with IDART members, May–July 2014.

97. Hearing of the House Committee on Oversight and Government Reform, "Addressing Concerns about the Integrity of the U.S. Department of Labor's Jobs Reporting," June 6, 2012.

98. Scott Maruoka, *CleanSweep Red Team Report*, Sandia Report SAND2011, Sandia Laboratories Information Design Assurance Red Team, August 2011, p. 9.

99. *Ibid.*, p. 11.

100. Denny Gulino, "US Labor Department Told 'Adversaries' Could Steal Data," *Market News International*, July 11, 2012.

101. Scott Maruoka, "CleanSweep Mitigation Measures Acceptance Testing," Sandia Laboratories Information Design Assurance Red Team, November 2012.

102. Department of Defense, *Joint Service Chemical and Biological Defense Program, FY00–02 Overview*, September 2001, p. 64.

103. Interview with Samuel Varnado, July 15, 2014.

CHAPTER FIVE

1. Dan Verton, "Companies Aim to Build Security Awareness," *Computerworld*, November 27, 2000, p. 24.

2. Of course, executives and employees involved in red-teaming exercises sign internal corporate nondisclosure agreements as well.

3. US Census Bureau, Center for Economic Studies, "Business Dynamics Statistics 1976–2012," updated 2012; and US Department of Labor Bureau of Labor Statistics, "Business Employment Dynamics: Establishment Age and Survival Data," updated November 19, 2014.

4. Business Wire, "Lex Machina Releases First-Ever Patent Litigation Damages Report," June 25, 2014.

5. H. Lee Murphy, "Saving More by Using Less: Efficiency Investments Can Pay Off over Time," *Crain's Chicago Business*, vol. 35, March 26, 2012, p. 23; and Sieben Energy Associates, "Strategic Consulting," accessed March 17, 2015 [www.siebenenergy.com /services/strategicconsulting.aspx].

6. BAE Systems, "Testing and Lab Services," 2014, accessed March 17, 2015 [www .baesystems.com/solutions-rai/cyber-security/cyber-security-solutions/penetration -testing].

7. John Gilbert, "Cyber Security 'A Must' for Telcos, Banking Institutions," *Malaysian Reserve*, April 21, 2014.

8. PR Newswire, "360 Advanced Warns About Insider Threats: Is Your Data Already Out There and You Don't Know It?" June 10, 2014.

9. Ram Shivakumar, "How to Tell Which Decisions Are Strategic," *California Management Review*, 56(3), 2014, pp. 78–97.

10. International Business Machines, *Chief Executive Office Study*, 2010, p. 54.

11. Henry Mintzberg, *The Rise and Fall of Strategic Planning: Reconceiving Roles for Planning, Plans, Planners* (New York: The Free Press, 1984); Kees van der Heijden, *Scenarios: The Art of Strategic Conversation*, second ed. (West Sussex, UK: John Wiley and Sons, 2005); and Thomas Chermack, *Scenario Planning in Organizations: How to Create, Use, and Assess Scenarios* (San Francisco, CA: Berrett-Kohler Publishers, 2011).

12. James March and Herbert Simon, *Organizations* (New York: John Wiley and Sons, 1958), p. 185. Gresham's Law is a monetary principle that explains what occurs when a new coin is given the same face value as an older coin that contains a greater amount of precious metal. The old coin will disappear from circulation as people begin to collect it because the value of the coin as a metal is now greater than its face currency value. See, "Gresham's law," Merriam Webster Dictionary, accessed March 17, 2015 [www.merriam-webster.com/dictionary/gresham's%20law].

13. William Tolbert, *The Power of Balance: Transforming Self, Society, and Scientific Inquiry* (London, UK: Sage, 1991).

14. Paul Carroll and Chunka Mui, *Billion Dollar Lessons: What You Can Learn from the Most Inexcusable Business Failures of the Last 25 Years* (New York: Penguin Putnam, 2009), p. 234.

15. Interview with Jami Miscik, June 9, 2014.

16. This assumes that employees have the space to think and identify problems. A 2014 poll of 7,000 employees in eleven countries found that just 56 percent of American workers said they had regular time for creative thinking, and just 52 percent feel their environment enables creative thinking. See, Jack Morton Worldwide, "Creativity: How Business Gets to Eureka!" June 2014.

17. Interview with Ethan Burris, June 20, 2014.

18. Darcy Steeg Morris, *Cornell National Social Survey 2009* (Ithaca, NY: Cornell University Survey Research Institute, 2009).

19. Ethan Burris, "The Risks and Rewards of Speaking Up: Managerial Reponses to Employee Voice," *Academy of Management Journal*, 55(4), 2012, pp. 851–875; Compounding this problem, managers who perceive themselves as less competent are more likely to avoid or minimize improvement ideas from employees, as they challenge the manager's already-threatened ego. See, Nathanael Fast, Ethan Burris, and Caroline Bartel, "Managing to Stay in the Dark: Managerial Self-efficacy, Ego Defensiveness, and the Aversion to Employee Voice," *Academy of Management Journal*, 57(4), August 2014, pp. 1013–1034.

20. James Detert, Ethan Burris, David Harrison, and Sean Martin, "Voice Flows to and Around Leaders: Understanding When Units Are Helped or Hurt by Employee Voice," *Administrative Science Quarterly*, 58(4), 2013, pp. 624–668.

21. Interview with Ethan Burris, June 20, 2014.

22. James Detert and Amy Edmondson, "Everyday Failures in Organizational Learning: Explaining the High Threshold for Speaking Up at Work," Working Paper, Harvard Business School, October 2006.

23. *Ibid.*, p. 3.

24. Carroll and Mui, *Billion Dollar Lessons*, pp. 277–291.

25. *Ibid.*, p. 3.

26. Renee Dye, Olivier Sibony, and Vincent Truong, "Flaws in Strategic Decision Making," McKinsey & Company, January 2009.

27. Though "business war game" is widely used to describe the activity, some consultants will use other terms if their clients are uncomfortable with the military connotation, such as "strategy review." Some executives confuse business war games with competitive-intelligence exercises. The latter gathers and analyzes granular information about other firms, while the former applies the available information to help a firm reach the best strategic decision. The linking of warfare and business strategies dates to the earliest days of game theory. See, John McDonald, *Strategy in Poker, Business, and War* (New York: W.W. Norton, 1950).

28. Interview with Ken Sawka, May 9, 2014.

29. For example, in 2013, among the world's 2,500 largest companies, 76 percent of all new CEOs were promoted from within. See, Strategy& and PricewaterhouseCoopers, *The 2013 Chief Executive Study: Women CEOs of the Last 10 Years*, April 2014, p. 3.

30. Sydney Finkelstein, *Why Smart Executives Fail: And What You Can Learn from Their Mistakes* (New York: Portfolio, 2003).

31. Interview with a financial-services sector senior vice president, June 28, 2014.

32. Interviews with Mark Chussil, June–July 2014.

33. *Ibid.*

34. *Ibid.*

35. Benjamin Gilad, *Business War Games: How Large, Small, and New Companies Can Vastly Improve Their Strategies and Outmaneuver the Competition* (Pompton Plains, NJ: Career Press, 2008).

36. Ben Gilad, war-gaming class, Fuld, Gilad, & Herring Academy of Competitive Intelligence, Cambridge, MA, June 16, 2014.

37. Interview with Ben Gilad, December 20, 2013.

38. Michael Porter, *Competitive Strategy: Techniques for Analyzing Industries and Competitors* (New York: Free Press, 1980); Demonstrating the inherent difficulty of beating the market through designing better strategies, in November 2012, Porter's own strategy consulting firm, the Monitor Group, filed for bankruptcy protection before they were bought out by Deloitte. See, "Monitor's End," *The Economist*, November 14, 2012 [www.economist.com/blogs/schumpeter/2012/11/consulting].

39. Ben Gilad, war-gaming class, June 16, 2014.

40. *Ibid.*

41. Interview with Ben Gilad, December 20, 2013.

42. IBM Institute for Business Value, *Capitalizing on Complexity: Insights from the Global Chief Executive Officer Study*, 2010.

43. Kapersky Lab, *IT Security Risks Survey 2014: A Business Approach to Managing Data Security Threats*, 2014, p. 18.

44. Ponemon Institute, *2014 Cost of Cyber Crime Study: United States*, sponsored by HP Enterprise Security, October 2014, p. 3.

45. *Ibid.;* and Verizon, *2015 Data Breach Investigations Report*, April 2015, p. 4.

46. Symantec, *Internet Security Threat Report*, vol. 20, April 2015, pp. 7, 14. In a 2013 survey of small business owners, 44 percent of respondents said that they were the victim of a cyber attack, with the average associated costs being $8,700. See, National Small Business Association, *2013 Small Business Technology Survey*, September 2013, p. 10.

47. Neiman Marcus Group, statement by Karen Katz, January 22, 2014.

48. Neiman Marcus Group, "Neiman Marcus Group LTD LLC Reports Second Quarter Results," February 28, 2014, p. 9.

49. Becky Yerak, "Schnucks Calculates Potential Breach Hit," *Chicago Tribune*, May 24, 2013, p. C1.

50. Target, "Target Reports Fourth Quarter and Full-Year 2013 Earnings," February 26, 2014; and Rachel Abrams, "Target Puts Data Breach Costs at $148 Million, and Forecasts Profit Drop," *New York Times*, August 5, 2014.

51. Market Research Media, "U.S. Federal Cybersecurity Market Forecast 2015–2020," May 4, 2014, accessed May 21, 2015 [www.marketresearchmedia.com/?p=206].

52. Gartner, "Gartner Says Worldwide Information Security Spending Will Grow Almost 8 Percent in 2014 as Organizations Become More Threat-Aware," August 22, 2014; and Gartner, "The Future of Global Information Security," 2013.

53. Dave Evans, *The Internet of Things: How the Next Evolution of the Internet Is Changing Everything*, Cisco, April 2011, p. 3; and "Home, Hacked Home," *The Economist*, July 12, 2014, p. SS14.

54. Daniel Halperin et al., "Pacemakers and Implantable Cardiac Defibrillators: Software Radio Attacks and Zero-Power Defenses," Proceedings of the 2008 IEEE Symposium on Security and Privacy, Oakland, CA, May 18–21, 2008; and Jay Radcliffe, "Fact and Fiction: Defending Medical Device," Black Hat 2013, July 31, 2013; It was not until June 2013 that the Federal Drug Administration (FDA) recommended vendors take voluntary steps "to prevent unauthorized access or modification to their medical devices." See, FDA, "Cybersecurity for Medical Devices and Hospital Networks: FDA Safety Communication," June 13, 2013.

55. Lillian Ablon, Martin Libicki, and Andrea Golay, Markets for Cybercrime Tools and Stolen Data, RAND Corporation, March 2014, pp. 13–14.

56. Intercrawler, "The Teenager Is the Author of BlackPOS/Kaptoxa Malware (Target), Several Other Breaches May Be Revealed Soon," January 17, 2014; Jeremy Kirk, "Two Coders Closely Tied to Target-Related Malware," computerworld.com, January 20, 2014; and Danny Yadron, Paul Ziobro, and Devlin Barrett, "Target Warned of Vulnerabilities Before Data Breach," Wall Street Journal, February 14, 2014.

57. It is commonly asserted that 80 percent of known cyber attacks can be prevented by adopting five best practices: inventory authorized and unauthorized devices, inventory authorized and unauthorized software, develop and manage secure configurations for all devices, conduct continuous (automated) vulnerability assessment and remediation, and actively manage and control the use of administrative privileges. See, Center for Internet Security, "Cyber Hygiene Campaign," accessed March 17, 2015 [www.cisecurity.org/about/CyberCampaign2014.cfm].

58. For more information, Pen Test Magazine has been a useful guide to emerging trends in the field since its founding in April 2011, as well as security conference presentations by hackers, which can often be found on YouTube soon after they are given.

59. Interviews with corporate and government cyber-security officials, 2012–2014; See also, James Kupsch and Barton Miller, "Manual vs. Automated Vulnerability Assessment: A Case Study," Proceedings of the First International Workshop on Managing Insider Security Threats (MIST) West, West Lafayette, IN, June 15–19, 2009; and Matthew Finifter and David Wagner, "Exploring the Relationship Between Web Application Development Tools and Security," Proceedings of the second USENIX Conference on Web Application Development, Portland, OR, June 15–16, 2011.

60. Women represent 11 percent of information security professionals. See, International Standard for Information Security (ISC) 2, Agents of Change: Women in the Information Security Profession, in partnership with Symantec, 2013; Catherine Pearce of the mobile security firm Neohapsis describes the community as "both liberal in its thinking, and sexist in its behavior. Conferences are also frankly dangerous. If you are a woman attending a conference, you have to be willing to punch someone in the face in public. Not all women want to do that." Interview with Catherine Pearce, June 3, 2014.

61. Interview with a cyber-security professional, July 7, 2014.

62. The International Council of E-commerce Consultants contends that the training it provides to security researchers "is the world's most advanced ethical

hacking course with 19 of the most current security domains any ethical hacker will ever want to know when they are planning to beef up the information security posture of their organization. . . . You walk out the door with hacking skills that are highly in demand, as well as the internationally recognized certified ethical hacker certification!"; International Council of E-Commerce Consultants, "Ethical Hacking and Countermeasures to Become a Certified Ethical Hacker," accessed May 4, 2015 [www.eccouncil.org/Certification/certified-ethical-hacker].

63. The purported hacker of the website called themselves "Eugene Bedford," which was the character of a reformed hacker in the 1995 movie, *Hackers*. See, Megan Geuss, "Security Certification Group EC-Council's Website Defaced with Snowden Passport," *ArsTechnica*, February 23, 2014.

64. "Hacking Conferences," Lanyrd, accessed March 17, 2015 [www.lanyrd.com/topics/hacking/]; and "Cybersecurity Conferences," Lanyrd, accessed March 17, 2015 [lanyrd.com/topics/cyber-security/].

65. Black Hat, "USA 2009 Prospectus," 2009; Paul Asadoorian, "Top 10 Things I Learned at Defcon 17," *Security Weekly*, August 4, 2009; and Richard Reilly, "Black Hat and Defcon See Record Attendance—Even Without the Government Spooks," *VentureBeat*, August 12, 2014.

66. Leyla Bilge and Tudor Dumitras, "Before We Knew It: An Empirical Study of Zero-Day Attacks in the Real World," Proceedings of the 2012 ACM conference on Computer and Communications Security, Raleigh, NC, October 16–18, 2012.

67. Stefan Frei, "The Known Unknowns: Empirical Analysis of Publicly Unknown Security Vulnerabilities," NSS Labs, December 2013; Barton Gellman and Ellen Nakashima, "U.S. Spy Agencies Mounted 231 Offensive Cyber-Operations in 2011, Documents Show," *Washington Post*, August 20, 2013; and Ablon, Libicki, and Golay, *Markets for Cybercrime Tools and Stolen Data*.

68. For an entertaining immersion into the world of DEF CON, see, "DEFCON: The Documentary (2013)," YouTube, accessed March 17, 2015 [www.youtube.com/watch?v=rVwaIe6CiHw].

69. Interview with Jeff Moss, September 24, 2013.

70. US Commodity Futures Trading Commission, "CTFC Staff Advisory No. 14–21: Division of Swap Dealer and Intermediary Oversight," February 26, 2014, accessed March 17, 2015 [www.cftc.gov/ucm/groups/public/@lrlettergeneral/documents/letter/14–21.pdf].

71. *U.S. Code of Federal Regulations 45*, "Public Welfare," section 164.308, "Administrative Safeguards," 2009; and Matthew Scholl et al., "An Introductory Resource Guide for Implementing the Health Insurance Portability and Accountability Act (HIPAA) Security Rule," National Institute of Standards and Technology, US Department of Commerce, October 2008.

72. The security procedures listed in the PCI standards are not required by federal law, and as of the summer of 2014 had been mandated in only three states: Minnesota, Nevada, and Washington.

73. Javier Panzar and Paresh Dave, "Spending on Cyberattack Insurance Soars as Hacks Become More Common," *Los Angeles Times*, February 10, 2015, p. C1.

74. Goldman Sachs also makes it a point to hire only smaller, boutique white-hat firms with highly specialized hacking skills, and to rotate security assessments among them so the same firm does not evaluate the same system repeatedly. Interview with Phil Venables, July 25, 2014.

75. Interviews with white-hat penetration testing firms, 2012–2014.

76. For example, a 2013 survey of 154 financial institutions in New York State found that while 85 percent used external white hats to conduct their penetration tests, only 13 percent commissioned them more than once a year—the minimum mandated by government regulations. See, New York State Department of Financial Services, *Report on Cyber Security in the Banking Sector*, May 2014, p. 5.

77. David Kennedy, keynote address at RVASEC, Richmond, Virginia, June 5, 2014. David Kennedy also rued, "I have folders of really cool and really sophisticated offensive tools, but I never get to use them during a pen test because I keep getting in the same way over and over for the past ten years."

78. Interview with Brendan Conlon, April 15, 2014.

79. For representative examples of more advanced breaches, see, Rob Havelt and Wendel Guglielmetti, "Earth vs. The Giant Spider: Amazingly True Stories of Real Penetration Tests," presentation at DEF CON 19, August 4–7, 2011; Deviant Ollam and Howard Payne, "Elevator Hacking: From the Pit to the Penthouse," presentation at DEF CON 22, August 7–10, 2014; or, see many other presentations given at Black Hat or DEF CON, most of which are freely available on YouTube.

80. Interview with Nicholas Percoco, July 28, 2014.

81. At times, executives at the targeted institution will ask the white-hat firm to sanitize its report in order, for example, to remove mentions of critical vulnerabilities that were uncovered in soon-to-be-released software systems.

82. Interview with Ira Winkler, July 23, 2014.

83. Bob Stasio has found that many industries would rather spend money on firewalls and intrusion-detection systems from well-known (and expensive) cyber-security firms—like FireEye and Symantec—than less expensive, but often more effective systems from less prominent firms. Interview with Bob Stasio, June 30, 2014; In April 2014, FireEye refused to participate in an NSS Labs test of breach-detection systems—one of the most widely trusted resources in the information-security field—citing their methodology as "flawed." FireEye claimed that NSS Labs' finding of 147 "missed" samples the year before meant that "nobody could take this approach seriously." See, Manish Gupta, "Real World vs Lab Testing: The FireEye Response to NSS Labs Breach Detection Systems Report," FireEye, April 2, 2014.

84. Interview with Dan Guido, July 7, 2014.

85. Nico Golde, Kevin Redon, and Ravishankar Borgaonkar, "Weaponizing Femtocells: The Effect of Rogue Devices on Mobile Telecommunication," Security in Telecommunications, Technische Universität Berlin, undated.

86. Between 2010 and 2013, Google paid out an average of $1,157 for each security vulnerability that was brought to its attention for its Chrome browser, while Mozilla paid an average of $3,000 for its Firefox. See, Matthew Finifter, Devdatta Akhawe, and David Wagner, "An Empirical Study of Vulnerability Rewards

Programs," paper presented at the USENIX Security Symposium, Washington, DC, August 14–16, 2013.

87. Interview with Nicholas Percoco, July 28, 2014. Percoco is a cofounder of the "I am the Cavalry" grassroots movement that is attempting to promote a more positive image of hacking, including its often under-appreciated and under-reported work on behalf of public safety and customer privacy.

88. Jared Allar, "Vulnerability Note VU#458007: Verizon Wireless Network Extender Multiple Vulnerabilities," CERT Vulnerability Notes Database, July 15, 2013.

89. Jim Finkle, "Researchers Hack Verizon Device, Turn It into Mobile Spy Station," Reuters, July 15, 2013. The iSEC Partners team had media-training sessions to practice and perfect the demonstrations and to keep their message simple; See also, Laura Sydell, "How Hackers Tapped into my Cellphone for Less Than $300," *National Public Radio*, July 15, 2013; and Erica Fink and Laurie Segall, "Femtocell Hack Reveals Mobile Phones' Calls, Texts and Photos," *CNN Money*, July 15, 2013.

90. The title of both their presentations, which are available on YouTube, was: "I Can Hear You Now: Traffic Interception" and "Remote Mobile Phone Cloning with a Compromised CDMA Femtocell."

91. For a comparable, publicly disclosed hack, see, Tobias Engel, "SS7: Locate, Track, Manipulate," presentation at the 31st Chaos Communication Congress of the Chaos Computer Club, Hamburg, Germany, December 28, 2014. Given the growth of hackers testing software, hardware, and operating systems, there have been other examples of multiple teams independently uncovering the same vulnerability.

92. The name of the government agency is not revealed here because the conversation scheduled with the senior official was on background. Furthermore, although the security at this agency happened to be particularly poor during my visit, it may not have been representative of its overall security posture, and the basic security flaws could likely have been replicated at similar facilities.

93. Gavin Watson, Andrew Mason, and Richard Ackroyd, *Social Engineering Penetration Testing: Executing Social Engineering Pen Tests, Assessments and Defense* (Waltham, MA: Syngress Publications, 2014).

94. E-mail correspondence with Dalton Fury, May 19, 2014. Though Fury provides an illustrative example of attempting to break in by subverting the expected characteristics of an enemy, it is worth noting that the field of physical penetration testing is even more male-dominated then the white-hat-hacking community.

95. *Ibid.*; and Tina Dupuy, "He Hunted Osama Bin Laden, He Breaks into Nuclear Power Plants," *Atlantic Online*, April 16, 2014.

96. Health Facilities Management and the American Society for Healthcare Engineering, "2012 Health Security Survey," June 2012; and Lee Ann Jarousse and Suzanna Hoppszallern, "2013 Hospital Vendor & Visitor Access Control Survey," Health Facilities Management and Hospitals & Health Networks, November 2013.

97. US Office of Personnel Management, "2014 Federal Employee Viewpoint Survey Results: Employees Influencing Change," 2014, p. 41.

98. Curt Anderson, "Feds Break Up Major Florida-based Drug Theft Ring," Associated Press, May 3, 2012; Although Eli Lilly and Company later filed a lawsuit

against Tyco Integrated Security claiming that Tyco had failed to safeguard the confidential findings of the vulnerability assessment, Tyco denied the allegations, claiming that there is no proof. See, Kelly Knaub, "Tyco Can't Ditch Suit over $60M Eli Lilly Warehouse Heist," Law360, March 4, 2014 [www.law360.com/articles/515169/tyco-can-t-ditch-suit-over-60m-eli-lilly-warehouse-heist].

99. Amy Pavuk, "Drug Thief Linked to Orlando Heist," *Orlando Sentinel*, August 9, 2013, p. A1. Eli Lilly and Co. later sued Tyco Integrated Security claiming that the thief must have gained access to the report.

100. Katie Dvorak, "33,000 Patient Records Stolen from California Radiology Facility," CBS5 KPIX, June 12, 2014.

101. Abby Sewell, "L.A. County Finds 3,500 More Patients Affected by Data Breach," *Los Angeles Times*, May 22, 2014, accessed March 17, 2015 [www.latimes.com/local/lanow/la-me-ln-county-data-breach-20140522-story.html].

102. Danielle Walker, "AvMed Breach Settlement Awards Plaintiffs Regardless of Suffered Fraud," *SC Magazine*, March 2014, accessed March 17, 2015 [www.scmagazine.com/avmed-breach-settlement-awards-plaintiffs-regardless-of-suffered-fraud/article/340140/].

103. Chris Boyette, "New Jersey Teen Sneaks to Top of 1 World Trade Center, Police Say," CNN, March 21, 2014.

104. Andrea Peyser, "WTC Wakeup Call for This Guy," *New York Post*, April 4, 2014, p. 11.

105. In addition, the new requirements explicitly state the need for correcting vulnerabilities and conducting repeat penetration testing to verify those corrections.

106. Pete Herzog, *OSSTMM 3: The Open Source Security Testing Methodology Manual*, Institute for Security and Open Methodologies, 2010, p. 1.

107. One example was the theft of $2.1 million from a Barclays bank by eight criminals, one of whom was an insider and posed as an IT engineer to attach a keyboard/video/mouse, which costs about twenty dollars, to a computer in a London branch so they could transfer money remotely. See, Haroon Siddique, "£1.3m Barclays Heist—Eight Held," *The Guardian*, September 21, 2013.

108. Verizon, *2011 Data Breach Investigations Report*, April 2011, p. 40; and Verizon, *2014 Data Breach Investigations Report*, April 2014, pp. 27–28.

109. Interview with Nicholas Percoco, July 28, 2014; and Interview with Charles Henderson, March 12, 2014.

110. TruTV, the episode first aired on December 25, 2007.

111. Interview with Chris Nickerson, June 12, 2014.

112. The book will be published by Elsevier B.V. and will be titled *Red Team Testing: Offensive Security Techniques for Network Defense*.

113. Chris Nickerson, "Hackers Are Like Curious Babies," presentation at TEDx FullertonStreet, June 10, 2014.

114. Interview with Chris Nickerson, June 12, 2014.

115. One of the most interesting subfields in the hacking community is "locksport"—the recreational or competitive hobby of lock picking. Unlike criminal lock picking, locksport promotes transparency and full disclosure of how mechanical, electronic, and biometric locks can be bypassed. It is truly remarkable, when

experienced firsthand, how relatively easy it is to defeat almost every lock that any thoughtful and diligent adversary would encounter in a supposedly secure facility. Search for "lock picking" videos on YouTube, especially those by the charming and obsessive Schuyler Towne, to learn how to pick locks.

116. Interview with Chris Nickerson, June 12, 2014.

117. *Ibid.*

118. Interview with Jayson Street, July 25, 2014.

119. Interview with Jayson Street, September 23, 2013.

120. Jayson Street, "Steal Everything, Kill Everyone, Cause Total Financial Ruin!" presentation at DEF CON 19, August 4–7 2011.

121. Interview with Jayson Street, September 23, 2013.

122. Interviews with Jayson Street, September 23, 2013 and July 25, 2014.

123. Steve Ragan, "Social Engineering: The Dangers of Positive Thinking," *CSOonline.com*, January 5, 2015.

124. Interviews with Jayson Street, September 23, 2013 and July 25, 2014.

125. Jayson Street, "How to Channel Your Inner Henry Rollins," presentation at DEF CON 20, July 26–29, 2012.

126. A 2014 survey of 1,600 IT security professionals found that while "more than ninety-six percent of organizations experienced a significant IT security incident in the past year . . . only thirty-three percent have confidence that their organizations would improve those security measures." See, Forescout, *IDG Survey: State of IT Cyber Defense Maturity*, July 2014.

127. Interview with Dino Dai Zovi, July 18, 2014.

128. Interview with Jayson Street, July 25, 2014.

CHAPTER SIX

1. Supreme Court of Tennessee, *The State of Tennessee v. John Thomas Scopes*, 1925.

2. World Health Assembly, "Global Eradication of Poliomyelitis by the Year 2000," WHA41.28, May 13, 1988.

3. Global Polio Eradication Initiative, *Budgetary Implications of the GPEI Strategic Plan and Financial Resource Requirements 2009–2013*, January 2009, p. 5; and "End Polio Now," Rotary International, accessed March 17, 2015 [www.endpolio .org/about-polio].

4. World Health Organization, "Poliomyelitis: Fact Sheet N144," April 2013; Global Polio Eradication Initiative, *Global Polio Eradication Progress 2000* (Geneva, Switzerland: World Health Organization, 2001); and Centers for Disease Control and Prevention, "CDC's Work to Eradicate Polio," updated September 2014.

5. Centers for Disease Control and Prevention, "Progress Toward Interruption of Wild Poliovirus Transmission–Worldwide, 2009," March 14, 2010.

6. Gregory Pirio and Judith Kaufmann, "Polio Eradication Is Just over the Horizon: The Challenges of Global Resource Mobilization," *Journal of Health Communication: International Perspectives* 15, supplement 1, 2010, pp. 66–83.

7. Interview with Gregory Pirio, July 18, 2013.

8. Interviews with Ellyn Ogden, April 25, 2012 and July 10, 2013.

9. Global Polio Eradication Initiative, *Polio Eradication and Endgame Strategic Plan 2013–2018*, 2013, p. 97.

10. Independent Monitoring Board of the Global Polio Eradication Initiative, *Eleventh Report*, May 2015, pp. 7, 10.

11. Barry Staw, "Is Group Creativity Really an Oxymoron? Some Thoughts on Bridging the Cohesion-Creativity Divide," in Elizabeth Mannix, Margaret Neal, and Jack Goncalo, eds. *Creativity in Groups, Research on Managing Groups and Teams*, vol. 12 (Bradford, UK: Emerald Publishing, 2009), pp. 311–323.

12. The website also features Mateski's invaluable Laws of Red Teaming, of which there are fifty. See, "The Laws of Red Teaming," *Red Team Journal*, accessed August 27, 2015 [www.redteamjournal.com/red-teaming-laws/]. He leads with Red Teaming Law #1: "The more powerful the stakeholders, the more at stake, the less interest in red teaming. *This law trumps all other laws*."

13. Interview with Mark Mateski, April 18, 2014.

14. Interviews with Mark Mateski, April 18, 2014 and July 25, 2014.

15. Interview with Chris Nickerson, June 12, 2014.

16. *World War Z*, directed by Marc Forster (Paramount Pictures, 2013).

17. *Babylonian Talmud*, "Tractate Sanhedrin: Come and Hear," Folio 17a. Princeton University professor Michael Walzer interprets this passage: "The absence of dissent means that there wasn't an adequate deliberation." See, Michael Walzer, "Is the Right Choice a Good Bargain?" *New York Review of Books*, 62(4), March 5, 2015.

18. Robert Kennedy, *Thirteen Days: A Memoir of the Cuban Missile Crisis* (New York: W.W. Norton & Company, 1969), p. 86.

19. In experimental settings, authentic dissenters stimulate more creative solutions than an individual assigned to a devil's advocate role. See, Charlan Nemeth, Keith Brown, and John Rogers, "Devil's Advocate Versus Authentic Dissent: Stimulating Quantity and Quality," *European Journal of Social Psychology*, 31, 2001, pp. 707–720.

20. Nicholas Hilling, *Procedure at the Roman Curia* (New York: Wagner, 1909), pp. 41–42.

21. *The Pentagon Papers*, Gravel Edition, vol. 4 (Boston, MA: Beacon Press, 1971), pp. 615–619.

22. George Ball, *The Past Has Another Pattern* (New York: W.W. Norton & Company, 1982), p. 384.

23. George Reedy, *The Twilight of the Presidency* (Cleveland, OH: World Publishing Company, 1970), p. 11.

24. James Thomson, "How Could Vietnam Happen? An Autopsy," *Atlantic Monthly*, 221(4), April 1968, pp. 47–53.

25. John Schlight, *The War in South Vietnam: The Years of the Offensive, 1965–1968* (Washington, DC: Department of the US Air Force, 1989).

26. Stefan Schulz-Hardt, Marc Jochims, and Dieter Frey, "Productive Conflict in Group Decision Making: Genuine and Contrived Dissent as Strategies to Counteract Biased Information Seeking," *Organizational Behavior and Human Decision Processes*, 88, 2002, pp. 563–586.

27. Michael Gordon, "The Iraq Red Team," *Foreign Policy*, September 24, 2012; Editorial Board, "The U.S. Is Not Ready for a Cyberwar," *Washington Post*, March

11, 2013, p. A14; Freedom of Information Act Request made by Ralph Hutchison to the US Department of Energy, Oak Ridge Environmental Peace Alliance, April 24, 2014, accessed March 17, 2015 [www.orepa.org/wp-content/uploads/2014/04/Red-Team-FOIA.pdf]; and Bill Gertz, "Military Report: Terms 'Jihad,' 'Islamist' Needed," *Washington Times*, October 20, 2008, p. A1.

28. Mark Perry, "Red Team: Centcom Thinks Outside the Box on Hamas and Hezbollah," *Foreign Policy*, June 30, 2010.

29. Bilal Saab, "What Do Red Teams Really Do?" *Foreign Policy*, September 3, 2010.

30. Interview with Gen. David Petraeus, February 19, 2014; and Interview with an Army colonel, January 2011.

31. Michael Gordon, "The Iraq Red Team." For more see, Michael Gordon and Gen. Bernard Trainor, *The Endgame: The Inside Story of the Struggle for Iraq, From George W. Bush to Barack Obama* (New York: Pantheon Books, 2012), pp. 95–97.

32. George Casey, "About that Red Team Report," *Foreign Policy*, September 27, 2012.

33. Interview with a former PACOM intelligence official, May 2014.

34. Lindsay Toler, "KSDK Investigation on School Safety in Kirkwood Reveals Journalists Are the Worst," *St. Louis Riverfront Times*, January 17, 2014, accessed March 17, 2015 [www.blogs.riverfronttimes.com/dailyrft/2014/01/ksdk_kirkwood_lockdown.php].

35. Jessica Bock, "KSDK Reporter Working on School Safety Story Prompted Kirkwood High Lockdown," *St. Louis Post-Dispatch*, January 17, 2014, p. A1.

36. KSDK, "News Channel 5 Report on School Safety," January 16, 2014, accessed March 17, 2015 [www.ksdk.com/story/news/local/2014/01/16/newschannel-5-statement-school-safety/4531859/].

37. *Ibid.*

38. NBC, "Rossen Reports: New Device Can Open Hotel Room Locks," *Today Show*, December 6, 2012; and Onity United Technologies, "Information for Onity HT and ADVANCE Customers," August 2012.

39. Interview with a Marine Corps colonel, May 2013; and Interview with an ISAF staff officer, November 2013.

40. Hearing of the House Foreign Affairs Committee, "U.S. Strategy in Afghanistan," December 2, 2009.

41. Bill Roggio and Lisa Lundquist, "Green-on-Blue Attacks in Afghanistan: The Data," *The Long War Journal*, August 23, 2012, data updated April 8, 2015.

42. Interview with an ISAF staff officer, November 2013.

43. M. G. Siegler, "The VP of Devil's Advocacy," *TechCrunch*, July 27, 2014.

44. David Fahrenthold, "Unrequired Reading," *Washington Post*, May 3, 2014, p. A1. On November 12, 2014, the House of Representatives unanimously voted in favor of the Government Reports Elimination Act (H.R. 4194), which would eliminate 321 reports from twenty-nine federal agencies.

45. US House of Representatives, *National Defense Authorization Act for Fiscal Year 2003 Conference Report*, November 12, 2002.

46. US Senate, *Intelligence Reform and Terrorism Prevention Act of 2004 Conference Report*, December 8, 2004.

47. US Senate, S. 2845, *National Intelligence Reform Act of 2004*, October 6, 2004.

48. P.L. 108–458, *Intelligence Reform and Terrorism Prevention Act of 2004*, December 17, 2004.

49. *The SAFE Port Act* (H.R. 4954) was passed into law on March 14, 2006. Seven others died in the Senate or House: the *Department of Homeland Security Authorization Act for Fiscal Year 2006* (H.R. 1817), *John Warner National Defense Authorization Act for Fiscal Year 2007* (S. 2766), *Chemical Facility Anti-Terrorism Act of 2006* (H.R. 5695), *Rail and Public Transportation Security Act of 2006* (H.R. 5714), *Department of Homeland Security Authorization Act for Fiscal Year 2007* (H.R. 5814), *Department of Homeland Security Authorization Act for Fiscal Year 2008* (H.R. 1684), and *Chemical Facility Anti-Terrorism Act of 2008* (H.R. 5577).

50. Office of Senator Angus King, "Senate Intelligence Committee Approves King and Rubio Amendment to Provide Independent Check on Targeting Decisions," November 6, 2013.

51. P.L. 113–126, *Intelligence Authorization Act for Fiscal Year 2014*, July 7, 2014. Reportedly, the language contained in the final version of the Act was similar to what King and Rubio had originally proposed. See, Office of Senator Marco Rubio, "Senate Intelligence Committee Approves Rubio & King Amendment to Provide Independent Check on Targeting Decisions," November 6, 2013. A competing bill would have declassified the alternative-analysis report after ten years, but that provision was removed from the legislation that became law.

52. Marco Rubio, "Senate Intelligence Committee Approves Rubio & King Amendment to Provide Independent Check Targeting Decision."

53. Interviews with Senate and House Intelligence Committee staffers, 2013 and 2014; moreover, seven of the eight US citizens believed to have been killed by US drone strikes were not knowingly targeted, so they would not have benefited from any additional review. See, Micah Zenko, "The United States Does Not Know Who It's Killing," *Foreign Policy*, April 23, 2015 [www.foreignpolicy.com/2015/04/23/the-united-states-does-not-know-who-its-killing-drone-strike-deaths-pakistan/].

54. For the proposal to permanently establish an independent strategic advisory board within the National Security Council (NSC), see David Gompert, Hans Binnendijk, and Bonny Lin, *Blinders, Blunders, and Wars: What America and China Can Learn*, RAND Corporation, 2014, pp. 203–208. This red team concept is intriguing, though as the authors acknowledge, a permanent board would most likely become institutionally captured by the NSC.

55. *Defense Science Board Task Force on the Role and Status of DoD Red Teaming Activities*, p. 1.

56. Susan Straus et al., *Innovative Leader Development: Evaluation of the U.S. Asymmetric Warfare Adaptive Leader Program*, RAND Corporation, 2014; and interview with a retired military officer, May 2015. One positive step toward improving the impact of red-teaming instruction was an effort by retired military officers in 2015 to draft a joint doctrine note specifically for red teaming. Joint doctrine notes provide non-authoritative, common fundamental guidance for how the armed services should develop and employ military concepts.

57. William Perry and John Abizaid, *Ensuring a Strong U.S. Defense for the Future: The National Defense Panel Review of the 2014 Quadrennial Defense Review*, United States Institute of Peace, July 31, 2014, p. 65.

58. All of the NDP members were defense industry lobbyists or corporate board members previously, at that time, or soon thereafter.

59. See, Perry and Abizaid, *Ensuring a Strong U.S. Defense for the Future*, appendix 6, pp. 69–72.

60. The suggestion comes from Jim Thomas, vice president and director of studies at the Center for Strategic and Budgetary Assessments, suggested during a February 26, 2013 hearing, "The Quadrennial Defense Review: Process, Policy, and Perspectives," of the House Armed Services Committee, Subcommittee on Oversight and Investigations.

61. Interview with Brig. Tom Longland, November 25, 2014.

62. A Bain & Company survey of management tools offers a warning for new tools, which could be applied to red teaming: "Hyperbole surrounding the trendiest of tools often leads to unrealistic expectations and disappointing results." See, Darrell Rigby, *Management Tools 2013: An Executive's Guide*, Bain & Company, 2013, p. 11.

63. Chris Thornton et al., "Automated Testing of Physical Security: Red Teaming Through Machine Learning," *Computational Intelligence*, published online February 27, 2014; Hussein Abbass, "Computational Red Teaming: Past, Present and Future," *IEEE Computational Intelligence Magazine*, 6(1), February 2011, pp. 30–42; and Philip Hingston, Mike Preuss, and Daniel Spierling, "RedTNet: A Network Model for Strategy Games," *Proceedings of the IEEE Congress on Evolutionary Computation*, CEC 2010, Barcelona, Spain, July 2010.

64. Eric Davisson and Ruben Alejandro, "Abuse of Blind Automation in Security Tools," presentation at DEF CON 22, August 8, 2014.

65. Interview with Samuel Visner, December 1, 2014.

66. Raphael Mudge, "Cortana: Rise of the Automated Red Team," presentation at DEF CON 20, August 28, 2012, accessed March 17, 2015 [www.youtube.com /watch?v=Eca1k-lgih4].

67. Philip Polstra, *Hacking and Penetration Testing with Low Power Devices* (Boston, MA: Syngress, 2012).

68. Gregg Schudel and Bardley Wood, "Adversary Work Factor as a Metric for Information Assurance," *Proceedings of the 2000 New Security Paradigm Workshop*, 2000, pp. 23–30.

69. Interview with a senior intelligence community official, April 2014.

70. Silas Allen, "University of Oklahoma Researchers Develop Video Game to Test for Biases," *Oklahoman*, October 14, 2013.

71. Interview with a senior intelligence community official, April 2014.

72. Interview with Nicholas Percoco, July 28, 2014.

73. Tom Head, eds., *Conversations with Carl Sagan* (Jackson, MS: University Press of Mississippi, 2006), p. 135.

INDEX

Rose Hogan

Micah Zenko is a senior fellow at
the Council on Foreign Relations.
He lives in New York.